NAK
EUROPE:

Searching for a Soul Mate in Paris, Amsterdam, Venice, Austria, Sweden, the Basque Country, the Canary Islands, Iceland, Hamburg, Gibraltar and a bunch more

by

Jon Breakfield

KW

Press

To John V M Rubin
And Chip, Dick and Tom, my skiing *amigos*

ACKNOWLEDGEMENTS

The following people deserve a special mention: Patti Bright, Paula Wynne, Günter Kranzinger, Alan Drew, Chuck Larson, Anne and Alec Luke, and Meko and Allende.

CHAPTER 1

This book might more accurately have been entitled *An Alarmingly Contagious Behind-the-Scenes Travel Narrative about a Young Man in the Hunt for that Special Someone in a Whole Bunch of European Destinations -- bursting with Irreverent Humour, Intoxicating Romance, Falstaffian Sidekicks, Offbeat Misadventure and, yes, even Sex.*

But that wouldn't fit on the front cover, would it?

Come with me to Europe as I take my quest for a soul mate *behind* the guidebook pages, and when I say behind the guidebook pages, I mean to say we won't be staying at the Ritz ordering room service, or waiting in a three-hour queue to see the Mona Lisa, or hopping onto an air-conditioned tour bus with the blue-rinse brigade. And we certainly won't be extracting every cultural, historical and leisure-pursuit titbit we need to know about Europe from a bloody guidebook, which tells us how romantic it is to picnic in the Bois de Boulogne during the day, but fails to mention that you and your date could get your arse royally kicked if you venture there at night.

Rather, dear traveller, we are going to dump the guidebook in the *pissoir*, strike out on our own and endeavour to find that special someone in the *real* Europe by hanging out with real live locals, living with locals, working with locals, drinking exotically vile concoctions with locals and consuming all sorts of suspect food we would never consider putting anywhere near our mouths back home (like rotten shark and ram's testicles).

In short, we will be hunting where the tourists don't hunt and doing what the tourists don't do, and we will have a damn good time along the way—in spite of the ram's testicles.

So now sit back and fasten your seat belt, we are about to go where no travel writer dare tread.

* * *

My Icelandair Boeing 757 pulled back from the blocks dead on time, and then I sat in a sweltering cabin with 236 dehydrated, hypoglycaemic co-passengers in a queue moving along the taxiway at the speed continents shift.

One hour and five enervating minutes later the captain's disembodied voice croaked over the intercom 'Cleared for takeoff' and we catapulted down the runway.

As the engines whined to an alarming pitch I observed with great interest the same passengers who had ignored the mandatory Safety Demo (in order to present an air of seasoned world-traveller), now gripping an armrest with one white-knuckled hand while holding a paperback in the other -- upside down.

The aircraft rocketed along for an unnervingly protracted there-can't-be-much-runway-left time, then finally reared like a great white stallion, fought gravity for that Yes. No. Yes. Yesss!!! moment and shuddered into the waning June twilight.

A collective release of tension rippled through the cabin as those rattled by flying were finally able to relax sphincterically and confirm -- yet again -- that a lumbering piece of machinery weighing 220,000 pounds could actually take off, remain airborne and not become a jagged piece of flotsam bobbing in the ocean.

And it was about now, as we climbed resolutely toward our cruising altitude that my mind drifted back to that memorable gap year I spent backpacking about Europe. I remember I was wide-eyed and naïve -- but well-researched. I dutifully visited all the obligatory tourist traps. I spent numbing hours in stifling museums gazing at the masters. I gawked in awe at the flying buttresses of the great cathedrals.

And I got religiously pissed in Old Town pubs.

All true learning experiences.

Perhaps it was the Alps, gondolas, piazzas, sidewalk cafés and quaint, well…everything, that first hooked me. Whatever it was, I've been back to Europe every chance I could revisiting a world I found more stimulating than the world I knew back home.

Then one day a friend of mine and I were sitting in Moeran's pub in Kenmare, County Kerry, Ireland (we'll call my friend John Rubin, as that's his name), when a catalyst of sorts occurred. Rubin had been extolling the health virtues of Guinness, when he suddenly stopped in mid-dissertation and said: 'How's your love life?'

'Nonexistent.'

'You're not getting any younger, mate.'

'Who's going to be attracted to a vagabond like me?'

'Someone who loves travel. Who loves Europe.' Rubin took a long draw on his Guinness, held his glass up to the light to view the rings. Then he made a fist and rapped my head with his knuckles. 'Hello, McFly! It's about time someone opened your eyes. You only visit those places in Europe that have a Marriott so you can use your frequent traveller points. Other than me, you never hang out with locals, or stay in one place more than a night or two, or even learn the language. Find the real Europe and you'll find Mademoiselle Right. Go for a year.'

'Can't afford to go for a year.'

'Why do you make life more complicated than it needs to be? Get dumb-arse jobs along the way.'

Gobsmacked, I stared at John Rubin for an eternity. He looked like a young Alfred Hitchcock, and he always had a knowing subtextual twinkle in his eye.

I quaffed my lager, then looked about the pub: A roaring fire crackled and popped in the fireplace, a black Labrador snoozed happily at the foot of the bar, five elderly men swilled pints and played a card game called 'Twenty-Five' over in a corner, 'Try A Little Tenderness' by the Commitments pounded out of dusty speakers: 'You got ... got got got to ... now now now ... got got got to ...'

And right then, sitting there with a local in a local's pub, it dawned on me. Rubin was right and his words had staggered me. I had been visiting the version of Europe that the myopic tourist visits. I had never looked behind the patina. I had never seen the *real* Europe. And I was never going to find an inamorata by being culturally short-sighted.

My gap year had created a monster: I had become an American who was enamoured with Europe and that fact alone had scared off all available female Americans.

Which perhaps is a good thing.

You see, once on a first date I mentioned that I wouldn't mind living in Europe one day, and the young lady got the look on her face that people get when they are told they need colonic irrigation. And then she said something that pretty much summed up the sentiments of all my first dates back home: 'Why do you want to go over there when we have everything better right here?'

And what about my job? To finance my habitual wanderlust, I was running an acting school in Hollywood, teaching English to foreigners and writing the odd TV script. Hollywood could certainly survive without me. And I could live without Hollywood (and all the beautiful people who looked down their noses at me because the car I was driving was twenty years old).

* * *

So now I'm sitting on an airplane, on my way back to Europe 'with vision' -- as Butch said to Sundance -- and this time around I'm going to take Rubin's advice and actually unpack, stay awhile, have a beer, have a life -- and find my soul mate.

* * *

We are being served the in-flight meal now and the hirsute female endomorph (wearing a beret) in the seat in front of me has her seat reclined so far back I can't see my entrée. Not that it matters. They ran out of my first choice -- the chicken. The flight attendant has apologised then slapped the beef in front of me. This particular morsel of meat, *Bouef Province de la Merde,* I'm guessing, has never seen a cow.

I've requested tea, but it hasn't arrived yet, which is okay as my creamer has just ejaculated all over the back of the trollop's beret and my collapsible umbrella which I have jammed in the seat pocket with the in-flight magazine and barf bag.

The dinner service is over before I get my tea, and the flight crew have quickly extinguished all the lights in the cabin so they can commence taking breaks.

I plug in my earphones and hear nothing but static. I try all the channels and fiddle with all the buttons, but the system appears to have gone walkabout. The passenger in the seat next to me is in the lavatory, so surreptitiously I plug into her audio and it works just fine. Then my neighbour returns from the lavatory so I quickly de-plug. She squeezes her derrière in front of me and I am only minor turbulence away from a lap dance.

I'm trying to sleep, but the cabin of the aircraft -- which was too hot when were stuck in that queue back on the taxiway -- is now too cold. I can never sleep on an airplane, but apparently everybody else can. We have been cruising for three hours and I have a front row seat at a concerto of snores and wheezes featuring the odd percussion section solo of rude bodily noises.

I'm about to drift off for the first time in my flying career -- my mouth is wide open and a rivulet of drool is happily making the decent down my chin -- but we encounter some shit-your-knickers turbulence. Eventually the turbulence abates and the seatbelt sign pings off and the bodily noises begin once again. Wired from the fear that the airplane would be broken apart and fall out of the sky, I stare bug-eyed into the black hole that is the temporal aerie of the economy traveller.

Now four hours have passed, so I rise and head for the lavatory and trip over a pair of stocking feet sticking out in the aisle. They are attached to a snoring lump under a stained burgundy blanket with a seatbelt extension wrapped around it.

I open the door to the lavatory and there is an elderly man of third-world ilk in there (and I mean that in the nicest way) who has failed to latch the door. I falter back and dive into the adjacent lavatory. The lavatory is your bog-standard bog: stinky and void of toilet paper but has an abundance of mouthwash. When I flush I watch the blue maelstrom swirl into the honey bucket with child-like wonder and am almost sucked out the aircraft.

The colour of the chemicals resembles the colour of the mouthwash. Coincidence?

I return to my aisle seat and have difficulty gaining access because Madame Hirsute now has her arms up over her head as if she's tied to a bed. In spite of the image, I can't imagine anyone actually wanting to do this to her. Except in a rodeo.

My neighbour, stage left, has unplugged her audio, so I make an attempt at entry with my plug, but can't do so without committing a felony.

A flight attendant silently passes wraith-like through the cabin offering water and juice to no one.

Up by the bulkhead, a baby lets go with a nightmarish wail.

I try *my* audio and now it's working. But only in Icelandic.

I consult my watch.

A black eternity passes in slow motion.

The aircraft drones on.

And on.

I consult my watch again.

It's only ten minutes later.

I pay a visit to one of the long, skinny aft lavatories and study the back of my head in the mirrors. I've never seen my hair look quite that flat in the back (and I have low standards for these sorts of things). I would say that it resembles a chimpanzee's bum, but that would be an insult to chimpanzees.

With jet-lag kicking in, I return to my seat, bent on catching a few winks. I settle into my seat, position the flat back of my hair on the headrest and the flight attendants flip on lights bright enough to make your eyeballs bleed.

It's time for the breakfast service.

Owl-eyed, I stare at La Maja Desnuda in the beret in front of me as she awakens with a start and makes a noise I have never heard before in my life -- except on the Animal Channel (that programme about the hyenas and the dic-dics?). The beast nearly breaks the seat as she rises to visit the facilities. She's taking a toothbrush and what I suspect is a shaving kit. And a book.

A shockingly cold breakfast, which even Bear Grylls would find of meagre portions, is slid prison-cell-like in front of me. It consists of a rubbery croissant, orange juice (that doesn't taste like orange juice) and water. I must say right up front that I don't usually drink a glass of orange juice and then chase it with a glass of water. Or vice versa. Ever. But what the heck. I butter my croissant with a miniature plastic knife and for some reason feel lonely. Desperately lonely. I wish I had someone to share my travels with. If I had someone to commiserate with, we could laugh. And I bet if there was someone asleep on my shoulder, I, too, could finally sleep.

We are on final approach to Iceland now (a country almost half the size of Great Britain, but with only 250,000 inhabitants) and I quickly realise that flying into Iceland is certainly not like flying in to Luton Airport.

When you fly into Iceland you fly over the largest glacier in Europe, the breathtaking Vatnajökull, where the ice in some places is over 3,000 feet deep. That's almost four times as high as the highest building at Canary Wharf.

Today we were attempting our final approach to the airport in Keflavík in the middle of a meteorological fiesta. As I peep out the window at angry clouds scudding by, I'm astonished to spy an Icelandic landscape way down below dotted with funnel-like cinder cones. More of a moonscape, I'm thinking, and I remember the astronauts trained here. A smile crosses my face, then that smile is wiped off as our aircraft suddenly drops out of the sky (for real this time) and plunges toward mother earth.

And it keeps on dropping. And dropping.

And passengers panic.

Wind shear! my mind screams.

The plane continues to plummet, then commences a slow rolling death dive. Down and down.

And down.

Overhead compartments spring open and spill their loads.

I chance a glance out the window and see the ground rushing up at us.

The aircraft is making that whistling sound we hear in movies when planes have been shot down and are streaking out of control toward a really bad day.

We are all hanging on for dear life as you would on a roller-coaster at its steepest stomach-dropping dive -- and some passengers vomit.

And I'm about to black out, but can muster just enough of a fear-driven inquiring mind to wonder: *What's keeping the cockpit crew from blacking out?* Being a certified pilot doesn't mean the blood will rush out of your brain in a more keep-your-wits-about-you, less shit-a-brick manner.

And then it's all over. As suddenly as it had plunged, the beleaguered aircraft swoops with frightening G-force and levels off -- all too close to those funnel-like cinder cones, might I add.

And somehow the wings stay on.

I glance up at one of the seasoned flight attendants and I see sincere fear. The sort of fear that comes from twenty-years' experience without anything quite like that little bowel-evacuating, life-pass-before-the-eyes interlude.

And then we are on the ground, still entombed in a long tube, mind you, but one which could plunge no further. And that brings comfort to us all (except the poor infant up by the bulkhead).

And everyone cheers and applauds.

* * *

The meteorological fiesta continues on my 45-minute bus ride from the airport to Iceland's capital Reykjavík as winds violently buffet the bus and rain stabs at us horizontally. Then the rain ceases and a blinding sun plays peek-a-boo. Just when I think it's going to turn out to be a nice day after all, I peer through the windshield and see rain drilling the horizon in front of a fast-moving black curtain of evil clouds. It is as if we were stuck in a carwash owned by Stephen King.

I remember reading that Iceland, with its creeping glaciers, active volcanoes and savage climate is one of the most inhospitable lands on the planet. Ask the locals and they will tell you: 'If you don't like the weather, wait five minutes, it'll get worse.'

The mercurial climate is influenced by a branch of the Gulf Stream that collides with absolutely perishing Arctic currents. I shudder to think what the climate would be like without the warming, caressing effects of the Gulf Stream. In summer -- if you catch the weather -- the temperatures can skyrocket up near a sweltering 69 degrees Fahrenheit during the day (imagine that!) and then plummet below freezing during the night. You could take a date in a sundress to the movies and then when you come out need skis.

* * *

The rain has ceased by the time I arrive at the bus station in downtown Reykjavík, so I decide to enjoy the day and walk over to the old harbour, hauling my paltry baggage allowance.

And what a grand city Reykjavík is!

Cosmopolitan. Modern. Vibrant. And set beside the sea with a sweep of coastline disappearing in the crystal-clear distance. It has a feel of being *the* place to be on the planet. And I'm glad I chose to come here first.

I carry on through the bustling centre of town and soon come to the old harbour. This is where I had secured accommodation. Through Icelandic classifieds on the Internet I had become acquainted with an Icelandic couple, and they had offered me cheap digs for the summer in exchange for English lessons.

Then the rain starts again, and it's a surprisingly cold rain, and everyone breaks out umbrellas. And this is when I realise I have left mine on the plane. By the time I present myself at the door of my new home, I'm soaking wet and shivering like one of those hideously hairless little dogs.

I knock on the door and wait. Nothing. I knock again. Still nothing. Have I come all this way and now have no place to stay? Visions of hard benches at bus stations (with sickos leering at me) and cold pews in churches (with sickos leering at me) are rifling through my brain when the door suddenly swings open, almost coming off its hinges. But there isn't a fresh-faced Icelandic family standing there as I had expected, rather two frisky fifty-something women. The ladies are short, fit, extremely blond, surprisingly tanned and dressed in colourful running suits.

'*Velkominn!* Welcome!' they laugh, and then they invite me inside.

Have you ever purchased a new puppy? Then taken it home and just sat there staring at it? That's what the two ladies are now doing. Inner amusement has reached their eyes and their mouths but it hasn't as yet surfaced as a smile.

Now they've pulled out a green bottle with a worrying black label and poured me a cold shot of delightfully vile schnapps called *Brennivín* (which tastes of caraway seed) and they are waiting for my reaction. My reaction would be to gag, but I don't want them to think me a piker.

'In Icelandic it is called *svarti dauði*. In your language it is called Black Death,' I'm finally told.

And this I don't doubt. The fiery nectar has seared its way down my throat and is presently boring a hole straight through to my feet.

The women get up and rush into the kitchen to make some coffee. They seem to do everything as if they are connected at the hip.

I have a little peep at my surroundings. The living room looks more like a library, there's a crackling fire in the fireplace and a photo of a gorgeous creature resting on top of an oak desk. I hear the banging of pans and smell fresh bread coming from the kitchen. And then the two ladies return with hot *flatbrauð*, 'flat bread' and *kaffi* which is clearly laced with some equally vile alcohol. Apparently, these two women are the world's greatest hosts or the Icelanders love their liquor. I'm thinking the latter.

'So why you choose Iceland?'

'The climate,' I say in an attempt to amuse.

Both women look at me long and hard. And then some.

'Not so very funny,' one says.

'Quite offended are we,' says the other.

'B-b-but …' say I, as I have a way with words.

Then the women explode with laughter. 'We got you!' they scream.

And I laugh. This is going to be a fun summer, I decide.

I shoot another glance over at that photo of the gorgeous creature on the oak desk, then tuck into the flat bread.

Finally, the ladies formally introduce themselves. I find their Icelandic names confusing since virtually no one in Iceland uses surnames. You see, Icelanders follow the patronymic custom of identifying themselves as the sons or daughters of their fathers. Here's how this works: Your father's name is, say, John. You are his daughter, so your name would be Johns*daughter*. Your brother's name would be Johns*son*. Get it?

The ladies tell me not to worry about remembering their names. Everyone in the family calls them simply the 'sister-aunts', and since I would be living in their house I could call them sister-aunts, as well. 'We have large family,' they clarify, 'and one of us is sister or aunt to everyone.'

I tilt my head to the side the way, well, your puppy does when it doesn't have a clue what you're talking about.

One sister-aunt rises to stoke the fire, then we share some crackling conversation and another Black Death. Now impervious to the cold I'm led up a rickety set of stairs to my room in a pinewood attic. The attic has old bunk beds, one lone window, no heating and is filled with spiders. But I can smell the fresh bread wafting up from below.

And apart from the debilitating effect the Black Death has had on my jet-lag, I couldn't be happier.

* * *

I don't know about you but when I go to Europe my life seems to be spent in a never-ending quest for a toilet. Let me explain. The sister-aunts lived in a cement-block house with a blue roof (many houses in Reykjavík have *blue* roofs). To get to the only available toilet, I had to go down that creaky, rickety set of stairs and through the bedroom the two sister-aunts shared. Are you getting the picture? This of course meant that not once during my stay did I visit that particular toilet out of office hours. If it was the middle of the night and the dreaded urge came upon me it didn't seem wise to tiptoe like a cartoon character down a moaning staircase, trip over a bearskin rug and tumble into bed with two women who hadn't had sex with a man since the end of the Cod Wars in 1976.

So I nitrogenated a large, leafy plant that shared my room.

One frigid night I knelt on the window ledge and tried to pee out the attic window, but a blast of arctic air whistled through my jammies and threw me off balance. Had I not grabbed hold of a certain large, leafy plant, I would have no doubt bobsledded down the blue roof to a thrilling but undeniably embarrassing demise.

Owing to the loo logistics, I became a regular at every public toilet in downtown Reykjavík (and most likely on a police list of lower scum). Let me tell you right now, public conveniences in the town are few and far between. There is one public restroom that deserves a mention though. It's on Bankastraeti near Laekjartorg Square and it smells faintly of pinewood attics.

* * *

Reykjavík is the world's most northernmost capital, and it's small, exceedingly charming and distinctly low-rise, in an end-of-the-world sort of way, and the best way to see it is on foot. So that's what I did. I spent numerous hours casing the litter-free streets, strolling from the bustling harbour over to picturesque Lake Tjörnin to watch the swans, then back to my favourite area, the surprisingly lively Old Town -- all the while seeking shelter from the unpredictable elements and hunting for public conveniences.

Over on Laugarvegi, at number 18, I unearthed a surprisingly large bookshop with English-language books and a cat that sat next to the till. The shop was called the 'Mál og menning'. I found a coffee-table picture book by the acclaimed Icelandic photographer Ragnar Axelsson and took it upstairs to the café on the third floor to gaze at the wonders of this great land (and enjoy a needed latte, and the chocolate cake the café is known for).

And, yes, I was careful not to get chocolate on the book. And, yes, I didn't bend it all out of shape. And, yes, I conveyed it back down the three flights and returned it to its proper home.

Icelanders love books and bookshops are shrines. Did you know that Icelanders write, print, buy and read more books per capita than any other nation in the world? In fact, 27 times more literature is published per capita in Iceland than in the States.

Indeed they love to improve their sense of culture.

With many dark winter months to fill with warm and agreeable indoor activity, lilliputian Reykjavík (pop. 118,000) offers galleries, museums, two theatre companies, numerous fringe theatres, an opera house (operas are sung in the original language with Icelandic subtitles), a symphony orchestra, six cinemas and a ballet company. How about that!

* * *

Reading books is a national pastime in Iceland (remember the sister-aunts living room?) but so is getting shit-faced (remember the sister-aunts living room?). I often went out on chilly Friday and Saturday evenings with the sister-aunts -- to do research, you understand—and noticed that when the hardworking Icelanders hit the streets, they do so with unbridled zest.

'You have to sell kidney to afford drink in pub, club or wine bar,' the sister-aunts informed me.

They went on to tell me that the crafty citizenry get seriously wasted at home on cheap booze, home-brewed brew and the local vodka known as *klarvin*. Then, when the clock strikes eleven, thousands of astonishingly palatic revellers pour into the streets, spill out of taxis and step from vehicles that have been driven up on kerbs to take part in the legendary scene of upstanding citizens stumbling drunkenly through downtown streets. This weekend ritual is called *runtur* and it's the Icelandic version of the pub crawl. The goal here is to hit as many bars, meet as many friends and destroy as many brain cells as is financially possible by the time drinking venues start to close down around 3 a.m. or 4 a.m. or 5 a.m. or even later.

In the wee hours, the city streets are bestrewn with so many prone, comatose bodies, downtown Reykjavík resembles a scene out of one of those hilariously bad disaster movies -- *Godzilla Shags Tokyo*, to name just one.

And I don't want to offend any Swedes here -- for they are the true professionals in the arena of public drunkenness -- but the Icelanders do display an unusual predilection for getting about as fall-down drunk in public as is clinically possible.

* * *

'Midsummer Day is coming and we have arranged a blond date for you,' sister-aunt #1 informed me one sunny morning over strong coffee (served with a small glass of water on the side).

'Do you mean *blind* date?'

Sister-aunt #1 looked across the table at sister-aunt #2 for assistance.

'Yes, yes, *blind* date,' sister-aunt #2 said, smiling.

'You told us you are not married and in hunt, so we took the Libertines ...' sister-aunt #1 went on.

'You took the *liberty*,' I coached.

Sister-aunt #1 sought succour from sister-aunt #2.

'Yes, yes. We took the *liberty* ...' Sister-aunt #2 concurred, then smiled.

And then the sister-aunts went on to tell me about the tradition of Midsummer. The holiday of Midsummer is observed on the 24th of June when it stays wondrously light until just after midnight. Then the sun just slightly dips below the horizon and you have two-hours-and-fifty-two minutes of shimmering *twilight* until the sun rises all over again.

This means you never have night -- even at night.

For sure it surprised me how late it stayed light, but what surprised me even more was when the sister-aunts let me in on the Midsummer tradition of going out in the middle of the night, getting naked and rolling around on the grass in the dew.

'Naked?' I said.

The sister-aunts arched their eyebrows and gave each other the look the doctor gives you when he's pulling on the rubber gloves.

'Naked,' sister-aunt #1 enthused.

'Yes, very, very naked,' sister-aunt #2 agreed, smiling. 'The Midsummer night's dew possesses magical healing powers that will cure 19 different health problems.'

I gave this some thought. Now, I may not be a qualified doctor but I bet I can name a few of these 19 health problems: how about alcohol poisoning, or frostbite of the willy, or tundra bum or chilled gazongas or icy twins?

* * *

On the evening of 24 June, I was dressed in my best togs, biting a nail and sitting in front of a roaring fire with the sister-aunts when there was a crushing knock on the door. I physically jumped as all sorts of images rose unbidden. My blind date was the hirsute endomorph from the plane? My blind date threw the hammer for the Icelandic women's national track team? My blind date's surname was Tors*daughter*?

I rose from my seat and steeled myself for the introduction. The door was opened and standing there was not the hirsute linebacker from the plane, but someone who could easily have been her doppelgänger. It goes without saying, but say it I must, the thought of rolling around naked in the dew quickly lost much of its appeal.

'It's just the hose skipper,' sister-aunt #1 said.

'Do you mean *housekeeper*?' I offered.

With her eyes, sister-aunt #1 sought closure from sister-aunt #2.

'Yes. Yes. *Housekeeper*,' clarified sister-aunt #2, smiling, and then she threw a log on the fire.

15

And right about then there was another knock at the door, but not a crushing blow this time. This was a winsome brush of femininity on aged wood. The door swung open and standing there was the young lady from the photo on the oak desk; the most lithe vision, with snow-white hair, glacier-blue eyes, tanned face and a smile that could melt ice. Global warming in the flesh.

And then everyone laughed.

I had been setup.

The sister-aunts disappeared into the kitchen to procure cheap alcohol and I just sat there smiling goofily at my date. Her name was Sula, she was wearing a mini-skirt and she really was the most gorgeous young lady I had ever set eyes upon.

'So does "Sula" mean anything?'

'It means "the sun".'

Sula was certainly brightening up my day.

The sister-aunts returned with four beers called Vikingsol.

'We have to get pissed at home or we won't be able to afford to go out,' Sula confirmed in flawless English, if not the Queen's. 'Let's drink an ocean of beer.' And then she winked at me. And it made my stomach jump.

The sister-aunts seemed bent on getting us alone, so after a few more beers, they shooed us out.

It was nearly eleven when we stepped outside yet the sun was still just over there in the western sky. Sula led me along the old harbour then up a sloping side street to a pub on Bergstaðastræti called the 'Kaffibarinn'. The Kaffibarinn had a London Underground sign bearing its name outside (part-owned by Blur's Damon Albarn) and an Amsterdam feel to it inside, and we sat at a table with a candle in the middle and we drank more Vikingsol. Sula told me the sister-aunts were some distant shadowy relation. And she said something else. She said the magic words: 'My passion is travelling.'

And I couldn't believe my good fortune.

'I just love Europe,' she said.

I asked her where in Europe she wished to go.

'Amsterdam, of course. I love the tulips and bicycles. And Austria, to ski. And Germany.'

'Germany?'

'Yes, Oktoberfest.' And then Sula ordered another round of Vikingsol. These Icelanders sure knew how to consume alcohol, I'm thinking, and I was beginning to feel decidedly outmatched.

Well, the night went on and on, and we talked about travel, languages, and hopes and dreams, and we ended up drinking that ocean of beer (much of it against my common sense) -- and too many Icelandic equivalents of Screaming Orgasms (all of it against my common sense) -- then, around three in the morning, it only took an unspoken twinkle in her eyes and we burst out of the pub and into the frigid night and ripped off all our clothes. And drunk beyond drunk or not, it was still a chilling, shrivelling, startling experience.

And the sun was already back up!

I shot a look around and the streets were just as busy as they had been at three that afternoon and I prayed, right then and there, that any aberrant behaviour on my part would not be captured by some deranged Nordic blackmailer and end up on YouTube.

Not that my mother looks at YouTube (other than to watch the *Chocolate Rain* guy and Susan Boyle).

And then we did indeed roll around in the Midsummer night's dew, and laughing and stimulated, we retrieved our clothes, dressed, and Sula led me to her flat in the Old Town where we took all our clothes back off again and she began to run her fingers over her body doing, I presume, it-stays-dark-for-an-awful-long-time-in-the-winter, indigenous Icelandic things. Things I had never seen before growing up in insular America, and then my head started to spin around and around like a pod of killer whales do when they're driving sardines into a feeding ball -- and I passed out.

I awoke late the next morning in my bed in my pinewood attic with a killer-whale headache and killer-whale breath, and the sister-aunts brought me lots of strong coffee, which made me really just a jittery drunk.

And I never saw Sula again. I asked the sister-aunts and I was told: 'She's travelling now.'

And I had had such hope for the two of us.

* * *

**Author's Note: At the completion of each chapter I will offer a little aside, of sorts, a titbit of information that we just couldn't go through life without. Here is your first instalment.

WHAT NOBODY WILL TELL YOU:

In Iceland, beer wasn't legalized until 1989. (So they're making up for it?)

First names of newborns that have not been used in Iceland before, have to be approved by the Icelandic Naming Committee. They are accepted or rejected based on whether or not they can be easily incorporated into the Icelandic language. First, they must contain only letters found in the Icelandic alphabet. Second, names must be able to be declined (that is, modified according to their grammatical case).

CHAPTER 2 - Icelandic facts and culinary delights

In spite of rolling around naked in the middle of the night, life expectancy in Iceland is one of the highest in the world.

According to *The World Factbook* -- from the CIA -- it's 81 years (that's just behind the world leader, Monaco, with an astonishing 89.68 years). In the USA it's lower -- 78.49 years (something to do with double-bacon-cheeseburger-combos and shit gun control). In the UK it's 80.17 years (which is damn good I would think, especially if one factors in the Kingston Bridge in Glasgow and Junction 21 on the M25). And let's pick another country, how about Italy, which is not bad -- 81.86 years (something to do with red wine...and *amore*).

Iceland may have a high life expectancy but don't pack up your bags and emigrate just yet. What they don't tell you in the Nordic fine print is that you could get absolutely Pompeii-ed by a volcano, slide unceremoniously on your arse into a bottomless ice-blue crevasse or possibly even die a horrible death by sampling the local cuisine. I'll get to this fun topic in a moment.

Things are indeed different in Iceland. Crime is virtually nonexistent, as is pollution. This means if you ever see a getaway car, thank goodness, it will at least have passed its MoT.

And tipping is not allowed. Now that's a refreshing concept!

* * *

The sister-aunts were keen swimmers (as are most Icelanders), so one warm morning they dragged me off to the expansive outdoor swimming pool at Laugardalur. The water was crystal clear, clean and warm, and smelled strongly of sulphur, just like the geothermally heated shower back home at the sister-aunts.

'We have about 120 swimming pools in Iceland,' sister-aunt #1 told me.

'And almost all are outdoors,' sister-aunt #2 said.

I found it interesting that the swimming pool offered bathing costumes for hire. Would you don a community cossie? Well, would you?

Anyway, we went to the pool early, to beat the crowds -- I presumed. We arrived just after 7 a.m. -- and the place was mobbed.

And everyone was wearing skimpy European bathing suits and there I was in my 'Book 'em, Danno baggies'.

At around 8 a.m. the pool emptied as if someone had yelled 'Shark!' or more likely 'Reasonably priced beer!' so while the sister-aunts finished their laps, I took advantage of the warm invigorating waters and went off to play on an empty flume.

When we were finished I asked the sister-aunts if they knew where I could buy a new bathing suit so I didn't stand out like a touron.

This morning swim became a routine, and for the rest of the summer we started the day by going swimming in the geothermally heated pools.

Even when it rained.

Or the temperature plunged.

* * *

As you now know, the sister-aunts had a wicked sense of humour and decided to further amuse themselves by guiding me through the captivating world of vividly provincial native cuisine. I had strict instructions to sample specific culinary specialties, and I wasn't allowed to ask in advance what I was ordering.

On one occasion -- which I will never forget -- we dressed up and went to an old-fashioned fish restaurant hidden away in a downtown residential area. The restaurant was called, get ready, 'þrír Frakkar Hjá Úlfari', you know, that little place on the corner? Here, we ordered a bottle of New Zealand Cabernet Blanc, then started with the *Hrár Hvalur að japönskum sið*, which I soon found out was 'Raw Whale Meat Prepared Japanese Style'. I took one bite. The meat was dark, sort of the texture of liver and had not a hint of fishiness to it. Then I remembered about whale hunting and Greenpeace, and I pushed my plate away.

For their entrée, the sister-aunts chose the *Pönnusteiktur saltfiskur með furuhnetum, rúsínum og eplum*, which of course you know as 'Pan-fried Fillet of Salted Cod with pine nuts, raisins, tomato and apple'.

The sister-aunts ordered for me the *Selshreyfar*, something I later found out to be seal flippers (which tasted sour and slimy and salty, pretty much what you would expect from an appendage). I had a lot of trouble with this, gnawing on a poor relative of Disney's André the seal, so I cut the meat into small pieces, secreted it in my napkin and slipped the napkin in my pocket.

On another occasion -- which I'm now trying to forget -- we dined in the glass atrium at Siggi Hall's. Siggi Hall is a famous TV chef/restaurateur and probably the closest thing Iceland has to Jamie Oliver.

The sister-aunts enjoyed Reindeer Kebab and I was told to wrap my lips around the *Hákarl.* 'Rotten Shark', to the rest of us. This is a delicacy, I was told. You know I couldn't wait to try it, as I had read it will make you vomit blood.

TIP O' DAY: It would behove you to eat the darker pieces, as the lighter pieces are much more pungent. And drink all the Black Death you can get your hands on as that's what one does, possibly as that's the only thing left on this great earth that is vile enough to help mask the toe-curling taste.

I only had one piece -- as one piece was enough -- you see, one second with putrefied shark in your mouth is a second you will not soon forget. The exquisitely presented Jaws bore the unmistakable stench of stale urine and tasted like a cross of dodgy fish and really bad French cheese.

'It's acquired taste,' the sister-aunts told me. The sister-aunts were masters of stating the obvious.

When I was finished with my one piece of rotten shark (and the sister-aunts were wetting themselves), sister-aunt #2, smiled and said: 'It may seem as if you are chewing on cadaver, but just wait, we have far worse things to eat in Iceland.'

'You've made great progress with your English this summer,' I said, then gagged.

(FYI: If you are taking notes, I just happen to have the recipe for Rotten Shark here in front of me: Take one large shark, gut and discard the innards, the cartilage and the toothy head. Wash the carcass in running water to get all the slime, gunk and blood-shit-crap off. Dig a very large hole in coarse gravel, preferably down by the seashore and as far as you can from the nearest inhabited house to ensure the stench doesn't offend anybody. Place shark in the deep hole. It's best to do this when the weather is fairly warm, but not hot -- not that it ever gets hot -- as that hastens the curing process. Cover with more gravel and place heavy rocks on top to press down. Leave for 6-7 weeks in summer, 8-12 weeks in winter. During this time, fluid -- uric acid -- will drain from shark and purification will set in. Gagging now. When shark is soft and reeks of ammonia, remove from gravel, cut flesh into large pieces, wash and hang in drying shed. Let hang until firm and fairly dry: 2-4 more months. Slice off tough brown crust. Cut off whitish flesh into small pieces and serve.)

On yet another occasion, at a wood-framed restaurant called 'Lækjarbrekka', I thought the sister-aunts were going to try to foist off the *Hangikjöt*, which you will be pleased to learn is 'Lamb Smoked Over Dried Sheep Dung', but I was wrong. Rather I was encouraged to try *Lundi*, but by then I knew what *Lundi* was. It was 'puffin'. And I couldn't do it. For those of you who may not know what a puffin looks like, imagine a charmingly awkward bird with big sad eyes. This adorable creature is sort of a cross between a penguin and a short-beaked toucan with a weight problem. How can a civilized individual eat a bird that mates for life, or *cuddles* the single egg it lays per year with a wing (instead of sitting on it), or sometimes burrows eight feet into the cliff so its lone hatchling has a dry and safe environment?

When baby puffins attempt their first flight, they do so at night when the moon is shining brightly. And sometimes because of cloud cover and the city lights they get disoriented, as one would, and fly into town instead of out to sea. To protect them, local children gently capture the lovable 'seabird clowns' as they are known and take them home for a good night's rest. Then the next morning the children take the refreshed baby puffins to the sea and set them happily on their way. So, you see, I certainly couldn't sample puffin, and I can't understand how any one else could either.

The sister-aunts were particularly pleased with themselves one evening when they took me to 'Perlan' (the pearl), a revolving restaurant that overlooks the city. My assignment was to sink my teeth into *Svið*. This turned out to be 'Singed Sheep's Head'. Here's how this exquisite dish works: A sheep's head is burned to rid it of the hair. The area around the eyes and inside the ears is cleaned, especially well (thank Christ for that). The head is sawn in half. The brain is removed, then half a head is boiled and served complete with the one lonely eye staring up at you.

'It is important to avoid eye contact,' sister-aunt #2 said, then smiled.

The sister-aunts never ate the food they recommended.

The last delectable delicacy that was to be foisted off on me before graduation was the ever popular *Súrsaðir Hrútspungar* (which is pronounced *Súrsaðir Hrútspungar*, by the way). We had made reservations and were walking to the restaurant, which was quite a distance, when the sister-aunts suddenly realised we were late.

'We will lose our table!' sister-aunt #1 yelled.

'I can prevent that!' sister-aunt #2 hollered, then she let go with a seriously impressive whistle and bellowed: 'Taxi!!!' And then smiled.

We were conveyed to an upmarket restaurant on the ground floor of a certain hotel, which shall remain unnamed to avoid giving the buggers any press.

The sister-aunts decided they wanted to speak only English, to practice, and interestingly enough, this was the only establishment where we ran into a rude local.

'May I take your order,' a starchily clad waiter sniffed.

The sister-aunts ordered first. 'I would like to try the Mountain and Bay,' sister-aunt #1 said. 'What is that exactly?'

'It's lobster tail and lamb.'

The Icelandic equivalent of Surf and Turf, I'm thinking.

'And a glass of white wine. The Pinot Grigio.'

Then it was sister-aunt #2's turn. 'And I would like Minke Whale for starters, the Salted Cod for my entrée and a glass of white wine. The Chenin Blanc. And sparkling water. And coffee later. After dessert,' sister-aunt #2 said, revelling in her English.

'Are you quite sure?' said the waiter in a condescending tone.

'Quite sure am I,' she said, beaming.

Then it was my turn, but I was on assignment and had been instructed to try to pronounce the Icelandic name of my entrée. 'I'll have the *Súrsaðir Hrútspungar.*'

Long beat.

Then the waiter said, 'Do you have any idea at all what you've just ordered?'

'Not a bleeding clue.'

'Pickled Ram's Testicles,' the waiter said haughtily. He hoped the naked truth would cause me to decline -- or possibly heave the cheap alcohol I'd consumed with the sister-aunts before we'd left home.

'Super,' I said. 'Do you recommend the red or the white with your testicles?'

The waiter just glared back at me (making eye contact) and bored holes in my eyeballs, not unlike the Black Death bored a hole all the way to my feet, then he huffed off.

Sister-aunt #1 gave me a nod and: 'High marks for that one!' And sister-aunt #2 just smiled approvingly as, well, your sister-aunt would.

Just in case you're wondering what ram's testicles taste like, they weren't that bad. Don't get me wrong, they weren't good by any means, but they weren't bad as testicles go. They were pickled in whey and that helped a great deal -- except for the image, of course.

We had to endure excruciating arrogance from the waiter over the *eight* courses of the meal, so the sister-aunts were not so enamoured with this lout by the time the bill was presented. 'Watch this,' they said.

And they left a tip.

When the pain-in-the-tuchas waiter returned and saw the tip, he snarled at us, 'It's an insult to leave a tip!'

And on that sister-aunt #1 said in radiant Icelandic, 'We are knowing that.'

And sister-aunt #2 said, smiling, 'Completely familiar with the custom.'

And we rose in unison, like meerkats, and walked out of the restaurant, heads held high.

As the summer rolled on, the days became shorter—and night became night again. By the end of August, Reykjavík was already closing down venues and rolling up sidewalks. Gales were blowing in off the Atlantic. Time had come for me to move on to my next port of call, Amsterdam, but I didn't want to go.

Iceland is that glorious of a country.

The sister-aunts kissed me madly about the face, commended me for doing all the foolish things they had asked, thanked me for helping them with their English and marvelled at how the plant in the attic had flourished during my stay.

And I asked after Sula one last time.

'Still travelling,' I was told.

Oh.

So with the ever-nagging question Ping-Ponging in my head: 'Why is Iceland vastly green and Greenland absolutely bestrewn with ice?' I took leave of staggeringly beautiful Iceland.

* * *

WHAT NOBODY WILL TELL YOU:

Guidebooks will tell you that Iceland is named 'Iceland' on account of a 9th-century Norwegian Viking with bad planning. Seems a certain Hrafna-Flóki ('Ravens' Flóki to his close friends because he navigated with, ah, ravens) went on a working holiday to the mercurial island with a boatload of livestock, but very little fodder. By the end of winter all his cattle were soundly dead, having long starved to death. Upon leaving the meteorologically volatile land, Ravens Flóki saw icebergs in the fjord and understandably upset by his recent misfortune yelled something to the effect of: 'I'm never coming back here to this hellhole. This shit-hole. This *ice*-land!' And there you have it, a rough translation.

Anyway, this is what the guidebooks say. But what the engaging, lovely folk of Iceland say is really quite something different altogether. In fact, ol' Flóki was so taken with the grand and eminent scenery he named the enchanted land 'Iceland' to dupe other settlers and explorers from wanting to visit. Clever lad, our Flóki, even though he did navigate with ravens.

Since you are dying to know: Greenland was so named by none other than Erik the Red (makes perfect sense, doesn't it?) In 985 Erik the Red named Greenland hoping the beguiling appellation would attract settlers. As of this printing, few have fallen for the marketing ploy.

CHAPTER 3 - Amsterdam: the red-light district is my backyard

'Wanna be in a porno movie?'

I spun around. Standing in a splash of sunshine on the houseboat next to mine was a swooningly gorgeous siren with misbehaving hair.

'What did you say?'

'I said, "Wanna be in a porno movie?"'

'That's what I thought you said.'

'I'm Natascha. I'm your neighbour.'

I was back in Amsterdam, a town where old buildings lean at odd angles, morals are thrillingly twisted and a sex change can be procured on the National Health.

* * *

If you don't already know it, let me be the first to tell you, finding accommodation in Amsterdam is about as difficult to find as a tourist who hasn't come to the Netherlands to smoke ganja. This is especially true between Easter and the end of summer. If you plan to visit Amsterdam during this period, book well ahead, say, the minute you finish this chapter.

Or do what I did.

Go in the off season. And, please, in the spirit of adventure, do try to be creative. This translates: Just because you dumped the guidebook in the *pissoir*, don't try to find a *pension*, hotel, or B&B by utilizing one of the room-finding services. And don't seek a room from one of the irksomely cheery hotel touts or 'runners'. They, like dog shit, are everywhere in Amsterdam. Sure, you will end up with a place to lay your head, but where's the adventure here, eh? Try to secure a room on your own. Don't be a sheep. Endeavour to rise above mutton. Live a little for once in your life.

Take a risk.

It's Amsterdam!

I just love gambolling about a city in the hunt for a room for the night. I take my time. I pop into cosy cafés for a latte. I loiter in front of pastry shops. I stop and have a cold beer. There's no hurry. Something will turn up. The hunt is half the fun.

There's a thrillingly forbidding area in the centre of Amsterdam called Frederiksplein (not far from the Heineken Brewery). Here at number 15, I unearthed a welcoming, albeit curiously odiferous, little establishment called the Hemp Hotel.

I entered and was greeted by a young woman who resembled the chanteuse Adele -- on a bad day, which would be most days. Amsterdam Adele, who wore a tampon on a cut finger and spoke flawless English (unlike, well, Adele), felt it her obligation to show me a few of the rooms on offer.

'The rooms are themed,' Amsterdam Adele told me, opening the door to the first. 'This is our Tibetan room.'

I peered in. There was no mistaking it, it was all about Tibet in there. And then we moved on down the hall.

'And this is the Indian room. And the Afghanistani room. And the Caribbean room.'

I noticed that the rooms had exotically carved furniture and dramatic murals and moody colours.

'See that futon there?' Amsterdam Adele said. 'It's made of hemp.'

'Hemp?'

10

'Yes, much of our furniture is made of hemp.'

A picture was starting to develop and I wasn't so sure about the final print.

Then Amsterdam Adele showed me the bar downstairs.

'This we call the Hemple Temple Nightbar. If you don't feel like venturing out, this is a great place to chill.'

She said 'chill', but her subtext read: 'Getting fucked up'. And I think my mouth fell open just a bit.

'The bar is open until 4 a.m. and we have delightful hemp snacks and eleven delicious varieties of hemp beer.'

'Thus the "hemp" hotel,' I surmised.

'Nothing gets by you, does it?' Amsterdam Adele said, not with a twinkle in her eye, rather that glow that a roll-your-own ciggie makes in the dark.

Well, need I go on? This joint was not my calling and the weather was behaving today, just, so I didn't book the medicinally laid-back Hemp Hotel, but chose to carry on wandering through a jumble of narrow, tree-lined streets, past gabled houses four storeys high but only one room wide and along the spider web of canals that is the signature of Amsterdam.

Wait until I tell you about the next place I came across. It was called the Black Tulip Hotel. Sounds innocent enough, doesn't it? That's what I thought.

The Black Tulip is at Geldersekade 16 and, I should warn you right off, if you don't want to be privy to a host of kinky stuff, look away now.

The Black Tulip is not your standard hotel and will never be a 'named accommodation' from First Choice. In fact, I doubt there is anything quite like it in this great wonderful world of ours and certainly not in Newton Mearns, Chorley or even Hay-on-Wye. On the outside you may see a wholesomely quaint 16th-century canal house, but on the inside you see a torture chamber.

A frightfully butch desk clerk -- wearing black leather chaps, black combat boots and no shirt -- greeted me. The fellow was all muscles and bulges and chest hair.

Clearly this was not the place for me, but I was at a loss for words, so I just blurted out: 'You don't happen to have a room, do you?'

'Actually we do,' dungeon master said. 'We've just had a cancellation. Someone died. On the rack.'

I shot him a look.

'Just joking,' he said, bursting into a surprisingly cheerful smile.

Butch was exceedingly likeable, but much to my horror, he then went on to tell me that the rooms featured an eclectic array of sex equipment such as metal cages, stocks and the odd *multifunctional* love chair. Need I go on?

'We also have S&M facilities, bondage hooks and fist-fuck chairs,' he said with genuine pride.

'F-f-f-f ...' I said.

I was scanning the area for escape routes when I heard a noise behind me. I spun around -- subconsciously covering my fundament with both hands -- and watched gobsmacked as two macho-macho members of the Village People descended the stairs singing 'Y-M-C-A!' They, too, were dressed in black leather and with their chiselled torsos and multiple bulges seemed to have stepped out of that trendy, fetish magazine *Whip Me, Slap Me, Make Me Squeal* (perhaps inspired by the movie *Deliverance?*).

'So, the room,' whip master said. 'Will you be taking it?'

I was at a loss for words, so I thought: *What would Bill Bryson do in a situation like this?* Then, it came to me. I turned back to the dick master: 'So let me get this straight, excuse the choice of words, you offer a multifunctional love chair, a St. Andrew's Cross and bondage hooks and stocks?'

'Correct.'

'And you have fist-f-f-f- chairs?'

'Exactly.'

'What about a trouser press?'

'Sorry.'

(Pssst: If you are into a little bondage as a holiday diversion, but didn't feel it appropriate to pack the black leather combat boots and rope in front of your mum back home in Scunthorpe, not to worry, the Black Tulip has the combat boots and various lengths of rope on sale in the gift shop -- right next to the mouthwash.)

Here's something else. Guess who supplies much of the equipment and paraphernalia at the Black Tulip? Why none other than Fetters of London -- in case you want to add that to your Blackberry.)

So, is this better than using a room-finding service, or what? Nobody said you have to actually stay at these places, but we are all the better for knowing they exist. And, besides, wouldn't it be fun to book in a couple of your seriously uptight co-workers from the office without them knowing?

As the day wore on, the weather deteriorated dramatically. The North Sea is just right there and it wreaks meteorological havoc all year round. Rain was now scudding off shop windows and somehow I ended up on P.C. Hoofstraat with its elegant and fashionable boutiques. To escape the shoppers who frequent elegant and fashionable boutiques, I hung a right and soon met Museumplein and hordes and hordes of tourists spilling out of the Rijksmuseum (they wanted to be able to tell their friends they had seen The Night Watch). Where were all these people from? If Amsterdam was awash with tourists on a shit-weather, rainy, off-season day, you can imagine what sort of a crush of humanity it would be like in the height of summer.

Miraculously the rain ceased and a slash of gold pierced restive skies right out of a Rembrandt painting. And isn't Amsterdam gorgeous on the rare occasion when the sun turns the town golden and the canals to emerald and the wind has blown all the litter to Belgium?

I carried on and soon came to the Café Americain. I decided to dive in, fortify myself and regroup. And it was here that something fortuitous happened. You see, if I hadn't come in, then I wouldn't have spotted the little bulletin board back by the bar. And if I hadn't spotted the bulletin board, then I wouldn't have heard the cry for help. Some fellow by the name of Rob had a room for rent: 'Nightly, Weekly, Monthly'.

This could be my ticket to adventure (or serious trouble), I thought, so I rang this Rob. When Rob heard my accent, he said: 'The room is yours. With you I can practice my speaking of English.'

'Don't you want to meet me first?' I said.

'What for? You carry a concealed weapon?'

I assured him that despite being American, I didn't.

'Stay a day or a week or as long as you want. Hope you don't mind living on a houseboat. It's damp, but I have a cat.'

Living on a houseboat in Amsterdam is an experience not to be missed. And it's an even greater joy if you share it with a capricious local by the name of Rob. You see, Rob, who bore a scary resemblance to Hugh Grant's flatmate in *Notting Hill*, was a lively delight (he had that poster of a kitten doing chin-ups in his bedroom), a loyal friend and an Amsterdammer. If there was ever anything I needed to know, whether it be the good, the bad or the kinky, Rob seemed to know it.

We were sitting out on the deck of the houseboat one sunny morning drinking *koffie verkeerd*. I was scouring an English language newspaper. Rob was looking for a job in the local *Via Via* ('I'm in between careers,' he had told me) and playing with his patently overweight cat, 'Sumo Cat'.

'Here's a possibility,' Rob said. 'But it says you have to be able to multi-task.'

'Men are incapable of multi-tasking, Rob. Only women can multi-task.'

'Does reading a book in the bog count?'

'Probably not in the context of that job, Rob.'

I went back to my newspaper. 'Hey, check this out. They have an advertisement for prostitutes right here under Help Wanted.'

The ad was for a flourishing company called Amsterdam Call Girls. Here were the qualifications: 'If you are 18+, very attractive, sophisticated, interesting, fun to be with and have the right attitude, why not give us a call? A second language is an asset.' Sounded like an ad for British Airways.

Rob looked over the top of his paper. 'Ever pay to get it?'

'Eh?'

Rob was a master of accents and having spent the night in a Dallas hoosegow once upon a time responded with a credible Texas drawl: 'Ever pay to get it, partner?'

'Does dinner count?'

'No.'

'Then, no. You?'

'Does an evening of alcohol and drug abuse count?'

'No.'

'Then, me neither.'

We turned back to our papers.

A moment passed. Rob's head peeped above his paper. 'Whaddaya lookin' for?'

'A bicycle.'

'You don't want to do that?'

'Why not?'

Now Rob was Dame Edna: 'I'll show you why not, darling!' And on that, he threw down his paper, leapt ashore, jumped on his bike and pedalled off along the canal. As Rob rode away I could see the back of his dark-blue T-shirt. Big white letters stood out: DEA. 'Drug Enforcement Agency', I presumed, but no, small letters underneath clarified: 'Drink Every Afternoon'.

Within fifteen minutes he was back, guiding a second bicycle with a free hand.

Rob extended a flamboyant stage gesture. 'This is your welcome-to-Amsterdam present,' he beamed. 'Everyone in Holland has a bike. Even the Queen.'

'You didn't have to do that,' I said.

'Didn't do anything. Pinched it.'

'Pinched it! What's the poor person going to do when he finds his bicycle missing?'

'Pinch someone else's. It's a tradition in Amsterdam. Look. It even has a bell.'

(FYI: Once upon a time, the fearless Amsterdam city council came up with a sure-fire idea to combat bicycle theft: Twenty-thousand white bicycles were positioned in the town centre and anyone who wanted to borrow one could simply climb on and pedal away. In theory this was brilliant, but in reality crap. You see, within a short period of time there wasn't a white bicycle to be found anywhere in greater Amsterdam. They had all been nicked. Note: Amsterdam boasts 400,000 bicycles of which 180,000 are stolen annually -- or 180,001 if you count mine.)

* * *

If you read anything ever written about Amsterdam, one word will shine more brightly than others. This illuminative word will lurk in the first page or two and then when you are least expecting leap out at you to describe Amsterdam's citizens, laws and attitudes.

Can you guess what it is?

You are so clever.

The word is 'tolerant'.

And what pray tell instilled such unwavering tolerance in the kindly folk of Amsterdam? Was it the commingling of the 145 nationalities who sought various freedoms in Amsterdam over the years, was it the reclamation of land from an unforgiving sea (it takes a special breed to live *below* sea level) or was it brought about by residing in one of the world's most densely populated countries? Check out these figures: China has an average population density of 342 lacking-in-human-rights folk per square mile. The UK boasts 632 sick-of-Posh-and-Becks citizens per square mile. India checks in with 789 multi-dialected, IT-out-sourced Vinadloo zealots per square mile. And the Netherlands, aka Sardine City, has a whopping population density of 1,010 spliffing souls per square mile. How could you be anything other than tolerant?

* * *

Rob was uncannily intuitive and startled me one day with: 'There's something you're not telling me, Jon-Boy. You got a secret. I can feel it. Spill.'

16

When I told Rob that my quest in life was to meet someone to share languages and adventure and travelling with, I thought he was going to laugh, but he didn't. Rather, he responded by saying: 'There's someone here for everyone! Even you. Guess we'll have to do the rounds -- all of them.'

That evening was foggy and moody and we pedalled along the handsome Singel Canal and over to 'De Rokerij', not far from Centraal Station. I was about to experience my first coffee shop. I wasn't going to partake, mind you, and I was sure I would never find my type of person here, but Rob insisted on going.

'Remember, nothing in Amsterdam is as it seems,' Rob instructed, as we stepped through De Rokerij's front door and entered a murky world of African murals, pounding, ear-bleeding tribal music and low, squishy seats. I couldn't believe it, it was as foggy inside as it was outside. We sliced our way through a fug of purple haze and took a seat in a corner. I think it was a corner. The coffee shop was decidedly mellow. In fact, I was surprised to see that some of the patrons were so laid back they were horizontal.

Rob ordered juices, then decided to enlighten me to the vagaries of the coffee shop scene.

'A coffee shop is not really a coffee shop -- more of a cannabis general store,' Rob began reverently. 'You go to a coffee shop if you want to build a doobie as big as the Hindenburg, lose yourself in a deep sofa and struggle to form small sentences.'

'So where do you go if you want a traditional café environment. A café?'

'No, a café is not a café but really a tearoom. You'll never find a café environment in a café. In a tearoom you can sip a latte and read the newspaper. No alcohol. No cannabis. Usually.'

Rob took a sip of his juice, looked up at a bumper sticker stuck to the wall that read ESCHEW OBFUSCATION, gave me a what-the-fuck? look, then sidled up to the bar to snag a 'menu' from a tall, willowy woman with orange hair and a silver stud in her tongue. The young damsel was squeezed into a tube dress with wide black-and-white horizontal stripes. She looked like a Belisha beacon and clearly could not have found employment in any other establishment in the world other than a coffee shop in Amsterdam.

When she wasn't looking, Rob pointed at her and shook his head 'Yes?'

I shook my head 'No.'

Rob made his way back to our table. 'Sorry, Jon-Boy, don't know unless I ask.'

Then he carried on with his lecture. 'In a coffee shop you are allowed to buy small amounts of marijuana and hash, like Dutch-grown *nederwiet*, for example...' Rob leaned closer, did the Magnum, P.I. thing with his eyebrows, 'which will kick your arse all the way to the Parvati Valley and back, my good friend.'

Rob studied the menu for a moment, then tacked over and ordered some Skunk from a man isolated in a little hutch near the front door. When Rob returned, he went on to tell me that you may spliff up in the coffee shop, but you may *not* sell it on the street. This is considered bad form. Coffee shops are not allowed to openly advertise the sale of cannabis, but they are allowed to have 'menus' tucked away behind the bar. A good menu will list the cream of the crop, so to speak, and may well tell you which country or hidden valley your pleasure comes from.

Then Rob completed his speech with: 'Remember, Jon-Boy, all rules and regulations in Amsterdam are there to be bent, twisted, broken and thoroughly abused, so don't be surprised if you find a tearoom or coffee shop that doesn't fit this generalised pattern. Again, nothing is as it seems.' Rob lit up. I decided to stick with my juice.

* * *

Rob took me on a tour of the red-light district. After all, it was just there in our backyard.

'A lot of heavy breathing goes on in Amsterdam,' Rob said, 'so if you have come for sex then your choices are unlimited.'

18

I stopped walking. Looked around. There were so many people milling about you could barely move. I saw open drug deals going on and overheard some guy proclaim: 'I'm going for a blow-job and a Big Mac').

Then I turned my attention back on Rob. 'Rob-Boy,' I said, 'I didn't come to Amsterdam for sex. I just don't want to be sitting in a rattan chair with a shawl wrapped around my shoulders and all alone when I'm eighty. What about you?'

'Of course I want to find someone, someday, but I know I won't find someone if I'm looking.'

'A watched pot never boils.'

'What the hell's that supposed to mean?'

'It means the same. My mother used to always tell me that.'

Rob and I watched just a bit bugged-eyed as a young couple guided a pushchair through the masses. They were strolling in the heart of the red-light district, 'window shopping', as you would on Buchanan Street or Oxford Street. Then we witnessed entire families (the same demographics as Disney World) moving from window to window, pointing, gawking, blushing. *Cheap* entertainment (unlike Disney World).

'Got a great idea,' Rob said. 'I've always wanted to engage one of the "ladies of the windows" in conversation. In order to converse with me she will have to open her door. If she opens her door perhaps I could sneak a peep over her shoulder and see what it looks like back in there.'

'This is important to you?'

'Very. Want to come along?'

'No.'

'Haven't you always been curious about the naughty atelier of love?'

'Atelier of love! Where do you get this stuff from?'

'Okay, I'll go on my own.'

'Y'know, you have the potential to be a nice, normal person.'

'Not my calling. You coming?'

'I'm coming. You're my friend. Just be discreet.'

Rob put an offended look on his face. 'I am the picture of discretion.'

Determined to experience the full dissolute flavour of the quarter, Rob and I waited until after midnight to begin our foray. At the bewitching hour the area became a Sargasso Sea of randy, pallatic, whacked-out, voyeuristic humanity (sort of Ascot without the fancy dress).

'Okay,' Rob said. 'Let's go!'

Then Rob stopped so quickly, I almost ran into him: 'Watch out for pickpockets.'

As we approached the inner core of the district, the little red or pink lights in the ladies' windows gave the quarter its eponymous hue. And wasn't business booming (no downswing of the economy here).

Rob spotted one young lady, who bore an uncanny resemblance to a young Goldie Hawn. Goldie seemed innocuous enough and Rob felt she might be 'worthy of an interview and a peep.' Before he could muster the necessary courage to tap on her window, a fellow with hell-bent intent beat him to it and the curtain was quickly drawn.

For research purposes we decided to tarry and time the evil deed. Within 15 minutes an exceedingly spent and shaken debauchee staggered out. A few minutes later the curtain reopened and Goldie reappeared. Interestingly enough, Goldie didn't look any worse for wear, possibly as if she had just stepped in the back for a skinny latte and a blow-dry.

'A real pro,' Rob noted.

Goldie assumed her position in the window and Rob forced his way through the shifty crowd. By the time he got there, though, someone had beaten him yet again.

Rob and I waited patiently and this time the act of deep love took little time. A world record possibly. Debauchee number two emerged and, now bandy-legged, wobbled off into the shadows.

I looked at Rob. 'What the hell's going on in there?'

'I'm getting seriously curious,' Rob said, and pushed me forward.

But now a queue had formed. Goldie apparently had something uniquely special to offer that the others didn't. We computed the number of waiting Johns and multiplied times 15 minutes, max. It was going to be a profitable night for Goldie and, research-wise, an unrequited one for Rob, so we plunged into the crowd and down a narrow side street only a few metres wide (Rob led, I draughted along).

'Do you even know what colouring you'd like?'

'It's not important, Rob.'

'Can't hurt to get an idea, though. C'mon.'

We nosed around for awhile and here's what we saw: We saw golden Scandinavian women, dark Eastern European women, ebony African women and almond-eyed Asian women. Women from all four corners of the earth (and one 'possibly from elsewhere' as Rob noted). We actually stopped and talked to one vulnerable young lady from Sarajevo who reeked of an overdose of Georgio Beverly Hills and looked too innocent to have chosen such a career. I asked her why she had turned to prostitution. I just knew she was going to say 'Better to be a prostitute in Amsterdam than poor back home in Sarajevo,' but she didn't, rather: 'My mother was in the trade.'

Rob then asked her how many times a night she had to perform.

'Ten to 20,' she said. 'Depending on ...'

'Depending on what?' Rob said, trying to peer over her shoulder.

'Depending on ...' But she didn't get to finish her sentence. Some older English bloke, who was a ringer for Lord Snowdon, had tried to photograph the girl next door (who was anything but the girl next door) and all hell broke loose.

(FYI: It is not cricket to photograph any of these ladies. They don't like it. Many of these damsels lead a double life and, if I may state the obvious, they aren't all that keen to have parents or boyfriends or teachers find out about any alternative pursuits.)

Anyway, some knuckle-draggers emerged out of nowhere and tried to relieve Lord Snowdon of his Nikon. When His

Lowliness, in his alcohol-induced dotage, continued to try to photograph the young lass, the Nikon was unceremoniously tossed into the canal along with His Shutterbugness still attached to it.

Justice.

We looked back at the pretty, young thing from Sarajevo. She now had cold steel in those Bosnian Serb eyes. It was clear our little interview was history, so Rob and I split stage right.

'Did that help?' Rob asked.

'It only frightened me.'

Parched from our peregrinations, and needing to calm our overloaded synapses, Rob and I popped in for a beer at a heaving establishment by the name of Durty Nelly's at Warmoesstraat 115. It turned out to be an Irish pub and it's right in the heart of the red-light district. A good watering hole if you are the sort of person who finds it necessary to drink in an English-speaking environment while abroad.

The place was smoky and boisterously merry. The music was awful. English football was playing on a large screen (Scunthorpe vs Exeter City). Rob ordered a Grolsch for each of us, then enlightened me to Amsterdam's idea of higher education.

'Did you know that if you want to continue your studies in Amsterdam there's a place called the Prostitution Information Centre? You can enrol in classes in "How To Become A Prostitute" and they have Beginning and Advanced levels.'

Rob and I tried to conjure up an image of what the first class would entail. We concurred that the professor would walk in wearing a purple suit and a floppy hat and would give the new students the course's syllabus: Night One: 'Ablutions', Night Two: 'The Scope of Kama Sutra', Night Three: 'The Fake Orgasm'.

We had a couple more beers then Rob told me that besides courses in STD 101, Amsterdam also has unlimited extracurricular opportunities for expanding one's sexual horizons by attending one of the many Sex Shows. There's the nutritional 'Banana Show', the handy 'Vibrator Shooting Show' (risky to sit in the front row, Rob cautioned), and the wish-you-were-here 'Postcard Writing Show' (guess how the pen is held...guess again).

'By the way,' Rob added, now using a French accent. 'If you intend to see any of these shows, be sure you are suitably intoxicated before you go.' On this, Rob's face suddenly went blank, as if he had just been shot.

'What?' I said.

'Should've taken a pee two beers ago,' Rob hissed, and did the Ministry of Silly Walks to the toilet.

I looked around the bar. The football match was now over (Exeter City 2 Scunthorpe 1) and suddenly the place resembled the *Mary Celeste*. Where was everybody? I consulted my watch. It was getting late, as much as that can be said for the red-light district. When Rob returned, we finished our beers then went back out into the flow of over-sexed humanity.

But the atmosphere had changed. The quarter was thick with drunks and stale smells and slowly winding down. Now we saw girls in the windows with TVs flickering and radios blaring. Some were redoing make-up, others painting toenails and, get ready, one girl was knitting! Conjure up that image: Frederick's of Hollywood diaphanous lingerie, garish make-up, knit a row, purl a row.

Then struggle with this image: A dark-haired woman (or a 'dark, hairy woman' as Rob described her) -- and not attractive by anybody's standards -- was plucking the hairs from around her panty line with tweezers. Rob said he was never going to be able to have sex again, ever.

Now it was really late, so we decided to head for home. We turned right, then left, then sidled down a narrow alley. Then scooted along a canal. And guess what? We turned a corner and, yes, strange but true, right there in front of us was Goldie. She was sitting in her window. And she was alone.

'Go!' I said, pushing Rob forward as teenagers do to each other at a teen dance. 'Go before she starts knitting or plucking.'

So he went. And he gave her a dopey smile. And she gave him a come-hither look with her knees. It was now or never.

Even though Rob was the one doing the research, I was so nervous, I wondered how anybody with real intent could ever get it up. But then I guess those with real intent have no trouble—and that's why no one remains for long. You get yourself so wound up, like a coiled spring, the only thing the young lady has to do is bat her eyes and utter 'Oooh ... the Dow Jones is up' in a breathy manner and, well, you get the picture—just like Tom Hanks in *Forrest Gump*.

Rob levitated the last few feet to Goldie's window and she already had her door open. I knew he wasn't going to partake of her charms, you understand, as even Rob has standards, but he was definitely making his move.

I slipped up close behind Rob and now I was curious what it looked like back in there. How big was it? Did it reek of dissolution? Was there a mini-bar?

Anyway, I could now easily see that Goldie was young, for sure under twenty, and blond, possibly even a true blond (one can only surmise until one pays). She was chatty and sensual and asked Rob how he wanted it. This way. That way. Any which way and loose. Rob kept looking over her shoulder and for some reason she kept backing up.

Then they both stepped across the threshold.

I took a few baby steps forward, and from the glow of her red light I could see inside. I saw the bed where the evil acts are done, a little bidet in a corner (where the evil acts are washed), and then she closed the door.

Anyway, to make a long boring story, a short boring story, I heard the most unearthly out-of-this-world scream, a scream that would even impress the Harpies and Rob came exploding out the door and almost bulled me over.

'Who was screaming?' I asked.

'I was screaming,' Rob shouted. 'Run! Run like hell, Jon-Boy!'

And run we did indeed.

Scarpered really, all the way back to Durty Nelly's and burst in through the front door. Rob literally ran up to the bartender and ordered two shots of Dutch schnapps.

The shots arrived.

'Thanks, Rob,' I said, but Rob threw both shots down and ordered two more. Only after his fourth shot did Rob settle down and tell me what had transpired.

'After she closed the door, someone from behind goosed me -- I mean *goosed* me -- and when I scraped myself off the ceiling I saw a mirror image of young Goldie. Goldie had a twin sister. And they were doing a tag team. I was so shocked I jumped back from Goldie's twin and I guess I inadvertently activated the panic button.'

Rob ordered two more shots. They arrived. He threw one down. Slid the other across the transom to me, 'For your nerves.' Then: 'Guess it shows that even these girls have standards because they tossed me the hell out.'

* * *

A month or so into my stay, Rob and I were sitting out on the deck of the houseboat with Sumo Cat. We were sipping a local beer called Oranjeboom (Sumo Cat, too). Rob was discoursing on why fringe royals should be eradicated. I was watching a young father playing football on the street that ran alongside the canal. The father had his two-year-old son on his shoulders and was kicking the ball around with a friend. The little boy was greatly enjoying this new game, as was his dad. It was a warm scene.

'Hey!' I yelled over. 'Who's having more fun?'

The father gave me a big smile. 'That's a good question!'

The Dutch. They are friendly. They have a wicked sense of humour (other than Goldie and her sister). And they love their families.

About now, a canal boat slipped by.

'See that one there,' Rob pointed. 'At night they have a "smoke cruise" for those who want to see Amsterdam through furry eyes. Cool, eh?'

'I'm getting conflicting signals, Rob,' I said. 'Will the real Amsterdam please stand up. Is it bicycles, canals and tulips? Or is it sex, drugs and bacchanalian excesses?'

'It's all of the above. Plus some.'

I gave this some thought. Then I cast my mind back to that evening and Rob's narrow escape with Goldie. If Rob could get himself into trouble, so could I. I was going to have to really watch my step. Amsterdam, I was learning, was a never-ending minefield of sin.

Then a mine exploded.

'Y'know, Amsterdam is where you can do all the things you wouldn't be caught dead doing back home,' a female voice interjected. 'Nobody will ever find out.'

I spun around. It was Natascha on the neighbouring houseboat. She was sitting on a deck chair doing the Sharon Stone *Basic Instinct* thing with her legs.

'So, the skin-flute movie, you in? You've never given me an answer.'

* * *

WHAT NOBODY WILL TELL YOU:

After meticulously cleaning Rembrandt's most famous work, *The Night Watch*, historians were shocked to find that the centuries' old masterpiece -- was actually a *daytime* scene.

CHAPTER 4 - Amsterdam: the smutty denouement

I studied Natascha for a moment. Natascha was a fledgling filmmaker and fully fledged flirt. She was like a bad book, tough to read. And it didn't help that she was going through her minimalist period and felt it part of her persona to wear as precious little as humanly possible.

'I could use a job,' I said, pretending to avert my eyes. 'But maybe not that kind of a job.'

'You're in Amsterdam, you clown. You only live once.'

'Precisely my point. My mother would kill me.'

'Your mother doesn't have to know. Listen, everyone who comes to Amsterdam ends up doing something he or she wouldn't be caught dead doing back home.'

'But...but...I don't speak Dutch.'

'Don't need to. It's in English. It's called *All American Girls in Amsterdam.*'

'Thanks, but no thanks.'

'Wuss.'

'Eh?'

'You're a wuss.'

'I am not a wuss. I'm usually game for anything, but perhaps not game for everything that goes on in Amsterdam.'

'And that's why you should do it.'

I looked over at Rob. Rob suddenly found something interesting about his sandals. I looked back at Natascha, and she hit me with this: 'You come to Amsterdam. You tell Rob you want to get behind the guidebook pages ...'

I shot a glance at Rob. Now he was leaning over the side of the houseboat as people do when they're about to be sick. I turned my attention back to Natascha.

'Yes. Yes. Yes. I *do* want to get behind the guidebook pages, but ...'

'But what?'

'But what if I did it and then someone I know saw me in it?'

'First of all you won't have to do anything disgusting, they've got third-rate actors hung like horses who'll do that. And second of all you'll be lost in a crowd scene and nobody'll recognise you.'

'But there's always a chance *somebody'll* recognise me.'

Natascha uncrossed her legs then crossed them the other way.

'None of these films makes it big, so nobody'll ever see it anyway.'

I looked over at Rob. Rob was now in league with Natascha. 'I think you should do it, Jon. You did say that you wanted to see what the tourists normally don't see. You can't say stuff like that and then not follow it through.'

'Okay. Okay. Okay. I'll do it. God help me.' I looked at Natascha. 'But I'll only do it on one condition.'

'Name it.'

'I'll do it, if Rob does it.'

We looked over at Rob and his mouth was as wide as the carp that live down in the Amstel. 'I can't do a movie like that,' Rob protested. 'I can't act.'

'You don't have to act,' I said. 'You're going to be an extra. You just have to stand there and look dopey. Just be you.'

28

Rob gave me a 'Ha-Ha-funny look', but still wasn't convinced. 'But what if somebody I know sees me in it?'

'If someone does,' I said, glancing at Natascha, 'then you go right up to him and ask him just what in the hell he's doing watching that kind of film in one of those sleazy raincoat movie houses.' Suddenly, I was an expert.

Then I fortified my case with the same balderdash that Natascha had fed me. 'Rob, *none* of these movies ever makes it big.'

Rob lit a cigarette with a shaky hand, sucked the fag halfway down to the filter and then looked up at us with sad bloodhound eyes. 'All right, I'm in.'

Well, here's what happened: Part of the movie was to be filmed in a late-medieval warehouse near the Amstel and the other part near the Singel in a squat hotel. Charming surroundings. Perfect for a career change.

Rob and I were told to wear business suits (Rob understood *birthday* suits). Since we were going to be extras, we were informed that our parts would be filmed first and then later on all the hard-core saucy scenes would be filmed and edited in. This way we wouldn't have to stand around and be party to all the smutty X-rated stuff. Hello!

Then, inexplicably, Rob got cold feet. 'What if my mother sees me in it?'

'Has your mother gone to the movies in the last century?' I asked.

'No.'

'Does she own a DVD player?'

'No.'

'Does your mother hang out in dirty bookshops?'

Rob had to give this one some thought. 'Not that I know of.'

'Then your mother will not see this picture.'

Rob tried to be calmed by these assurances but couldn't muster the necessary leap of faith. 'But what if somehow someone finds out? I don't have a great reputation, but I have to uphold the little I have.'

'Peruse my lips, Rob. Nobody'll ever hear of this movie.'

We started filming late Saturday night at the hotel. The hotel was chilly and reeked of sex and hash and smelled oddly of ether. The feeling around the set was somewhere between beguilingly erotic and mega-sleazy.

I procured a copy of the script and read it. It didn't have a beginning or a middle or an ending -- thus no story -- but no one seemed concerned by this oversight.

'Jon, can you do a French accent?' came a distant voice. It was Max, the director. With his pencil-thin moustache, Max appeared to have sprung from the same gene pool as John Waters. 'Natascha said you used to hang in France.'

'But of course,' I said, sounding a bit too much like Peter Sellers.

'Good. I'm going to give you a bigger part. I want you to play the French waiter.'

'Wait,' I said. 'Why don't you give the part to Rob. He's a master of accents.'

Max turned to Rob. 'Is this true, Rob?'

'But of course,' Rob said, sounding even more like Peter Sellers than I.

'Okay, the part is yours, Rob. But you won't be an extra anymore. You'll have to stand there while all the sucky-lippy stuff is going on. Hope you don't mind.'

'Anything for show business,' Rob said. Then he turned toward me and mouthed: 'Yessss!'

Max moved off to check his lighting or something, and I turned to Natascha. 'That guy's name can't be Max,' I said. 'There's no way he looks like a Max.'

'You're right. His name isn't Max,' Natascha said. 'He doesn't want anybody to know his real name.'

'Why not?' Rob asked, as we followed two scantily-clad candidates for breast reduction float off to wardrobe.

'He's afraid someone might find out he's doin' a porno film. Doesn't want to sully his reputation.'

Rob looked at Natascha for a long beat as his brain fought with the consequences, then he suddenly screamed like that boy in *Home Alone*.

'Not to worry, Rob,' I said. 'How much trouble can you get into in a restaurant?'

Well, it was many months later and I was working as a ski instructor in the Austrian Alps when the phone rang late one evening. A tiny, distant voice crackled through the night: 'It's a … Jon! I'm going to … you! It's a goddamn …!'

'Rob? Is that you? I can't make out what you're saying.'

Rob was breathing heavily, like a man struggling to keep from slipping below the surface of life. 'I'm going to kill you!' Pant. Pant. 'That movie we did. It's playing here in Amsterdam, and it's a hit. Enormous.' Pant. Pant. 'Boffo! SRO! They softened it and it's gone right through the roof. They're saying it might be one of the biggest ever! Bigger than *Emmanuelle*.'

'Are you sure?'

'Of course I'm sure! The whole town is talking about it.' And then near tears: 'There's a couple doing it on the table in the restaurant, Jon-Boy, and there I am as big as Dallas asking: "*Excusez-moi*, would like the lobster bisque!"'

* * *

WHAT NOBODY WILL TELL YOU:

Amsterdam is known worldwide for its vast array of porn outlets. But here's one for you: There are many more outlets for hard-core porn in the USA (approaching 20,000, and that's not counting the Internet). To get an idea on how big a number that is, there are presently 14,000 McDonald's restaurants.

Which statistic do you find more appalling?

CHAPTER 5 - Luxembourg: Time to regroup

I profess a certain fondness for countries where it's cheaper to buy a glass of beer than a cup of coffee.

The Grand Duchy of Luxembourg is one of those countries.

Did you know that if you can't find the time for a protracted trip to Europe, all you have to do is visit Luxembourg? That's right. You see, Luxembourg is 'Europe in Miniature'. It has romantic castles, a fetching wine country, a quaint cosmopolitan city, deep river valleys and a multi-lingual populace. On any given day you could well hear French, German, Dutch, Portuguese and Italian.

And these were the languages I was hearing as I basked in a warm patch of late-afternoon sunlight along the Place d'Armes, in Luxembourg City, quaffing a reasonably priced Funck beer and planning my next move. It didn't take me long to make up my mind. All I had to do was look around. The clouds resembled an Italian Renaissance painting and the trees were ablaze with burnt oranges, crimson reds and seared yellows. In another week the colours would be past their peak, so I decided to just spend the night in Luxembourg and then take the train down through France, Switzerland, Liechtenstein and over to

Kitzbühel, in the Austrian Alps. I wanted to be settled for the winter and since Austria was a 'ski nation' and Kitzbühel was an international ski resort, this indeed seemed a sensible place to hole up for the snowy months.

Plus, I needed to find a job.

I took another sip of my Funck and watched with absorbed interest as a young, blonde backpacker -- nose dipping in and out of her guidebook -- emerged from behind the square's bandstand. She was fresh-faced and wide-eyed and had legs up to here, and she was eagerly taking in all the out-of-her-price-range sights, sounds and smells. She wore a hat that said 'Bad Hair Day'. A small flag sewn on the back of her rucksack proclaimed she was from Canada, but in reality it screamed out 'I am not American!'

The lone traveller crossed the square, stopped in front of a nearby *patisserie* and stared longingly at the seductive treasures within. Miss Bad Hair Day rubbed her arms to warm herself, slipped off her backpack, foraged inside, extracted a sweater and wriggled into it. I desperately wanted to treat her to a Luxembourg *quetsch* tart or *knippercher* (local chocolate) and then invite her back to my hotel for steaming coffee and decaffeinated sex. But I didn't. I just sipped some more of my Funck (see I could have said 'invite her back to my room for a good Funck' but then you'd understandably groan), and with the buzz of the brew enveloping me in a stupid cocoon, I cast my mind back to when I first stumbled into Luxembourg.

And you are welcome to come along.

Bring a friend, even.

As now, it was autumn (my gap year), and I remember wandering about the town ostensibly in the hunt for a low-end-of-the-spectrum pension but in reality goggle-eyed by the glorious sights. You see, Luxembourg could have been created by Walt Disney. It's not large, but it is breathtakingly gorgeous and intriguingly complex.

The town rests on an upper level and a lower level and is cut by two stunning rivers, the Alzette and the Pétrusse. This makes any sort of passage from one part of town to another something between a joyous amble and a mountaineering expedition.

After casing the town, I found a potential pension in the narrowest building I had ever seen -- but the anorexic establishment was way too dear for my meagre means. Then I found a real dive, which gave me great hope, but it was even more dear. I searched suspect back alleys and once again clambered up and down formidable hills, but couldn't find anything within my 'Europe-on-a-Gap-Year' budget. But it didn't really matter. I had blind confidence that some place would eventually turn up, and this is when it first dawned on me that 'Hey! The hunt was half the fun.'

Eventually I unearthed an umlaut-infested pension in a charming section of town that I would never have considered venturing into if I hadn't ended up hopelessly lost. I booked a room for the night, but had only dollars, so I scampered back down the street to one of Luxembourg's 240 banks and tried to decipher international currency exchange. Not being so very au fait with currency exchange, I cashed five-hundred dollars' worth of traveller's cheques into Luxembourg francs, received a lousy rate, paid a ransom instead of a commission and hurried back to the pension.

The proprietress of the pension, a flirtatious forty-something ex-slut, explained the rules of the house to me in Lëtzebuergesch (a language that *nobody* understands). She bent over, displaying scary cleavage, and peeled note after note off my outstretched hand. After I paid off the hotel's mortgage, the proprietress handed me a key that was attached to something I only describe as a wood phallus. I stared down at the remaining mound of money in my hand. It was funny-looking, colourful currency -- currency that even Belgium wouldn't accept.

I was excited to see where I would be spending the night, so I dragged my bag up four creaking flights and entered a stuffy room with a saggy bed. There was no shower and no toilet, just a chipped sink hanging off the wall and a curious oval porcelain fixture over in a corner. What was more important than the crapper?

I opened my window to blast the room with fresh air and enjoyed a view of Luxembourg City's turreted rooftops and the Pétrusse valley far below. Then I unpacked my backpack, arranged my belongings on top of the bed and set out to find the nearest loo before I turned myself loose on unsuspecting Luxembourg.

The closest toilet to my room (searching for toilets even back then) was down a flight, around a corner and at the end of a long ill-lit hall that smelled faintly of bad French perfume. It was here I encountered my first commode with a platform. *Quelle révélation!* Why do Europeans insist on putting turds on display?

It was still light out, so I went downstairs, hung my phallus on a hook behind the front desk and headed out.

But wait! What about my backpack? If my key was sitting right there behind the reception, then any old smackhead could grab the key and nick my backpack. Why leave keys to locked rooms right out in the open? I ran back inside, threw my stuff in my backpack, slung it on and was soon happily on my way.

I visited the splendid Cathédrale Notre-Dame and wondered why I had always thought it was in Paris. Then I went to the Musée National d'Histoire et d'Art to gaze upon the modern art of the local painters and muse upon the unusual collection of weapons. The museum was aswarm with German tourists who didn't know how to queue. When the Germans moved off to another hall to queue-jump, I fled out the front door and over to the Magasin Anglais.

The Magasin Anglais, at Allée Scheffer 13, is a good little bookshop with English language books, only problem is you have to be able to read French to know that they sell English language books.

I nosed around the bookshop and eventually purchased a thin guidebook on Luxembourg. It was called *Luxembourg By Night*, or something like that, and it had lots of coloured pictures (which is why I bought it). Then, I melted back into the streets and did some more sightseeing until a certain *je-ne-sais-quoi* sensation appeared in my throat.

I dived into the first oasis that materialized. It was an astonishingly miniature pub called Die Kleine Bar, and if you sat at the bar, you also sat at the front door. The bar was exceedingly European in decor and I liked that. Up until this trip my closest European experience had been limited to the purchase of Toblerone.

Luxembourg is famous for a modest array of mediocre beers, but I didn't know that at the time, so it was with sincere enthusiasm that I plunged into a creamy stein of semi-orgasmic *gezwickelte* (unfiltered) beer. I toasted adventure by testing beer after beer, some double dark, some Pilsner, some God knows what. I didn't know and I didn't care. Finally, I settled into a blonde ale and basked in the thrill of being in Europe -- and the stupor from beer that was much stronger than the brew I knew back home. And then you know what? Hours later, when I swung around on my barstool and fell face-first out into the crisp autumnal air, it had magically become evening, and it was dark and misty, and Luxembourg with its twinkly lights looked enchanting and romantic -- and startlingly different. And I didn't have the foggiest idea where the hell my pension was.

Okay, so I'm more than just a little embarrassed to say I never found my pension. I searched for hours, abseiling steep hills and passing cosy restaurants where everybody was sitting in a relaxed fashion enjoying a hearty meal and grog. Finally, I gave up the hunt and took refuge in a public toilet (no remarks, please), riding the porcelain bus, keeping watch through a little hole that someone had been kind enough to bore and that looked out onto the urinals. To pass the lonely hours, I read *Luxembourg By Night*.

But that was all back then.

I watched the Canadian backpacker until she disappeared behind the only building in Luxembourg City that wasn't a bank, then I finished my lonely Funck and scoured the town for a few hours and eventually unearthed a fetching bistro down a quaint alley.

Luxembourg cuisine, it is said, is where 'Gallic quality collides with Teutonic quantity'. I sat down at my table, bibbed my napkin into my collar and began to study a menu loaded with exotic regional specialties. The menu was in four languages: French, German, English and the nasty Lëtzebuergesch. I wrote down some of the Lëtzebuergesch entrées for you and their English translations, such as they are. Are you ready? It went something like this: *Huesenziwi* or 'Jugged Hare', which is a whole hare, cut into pieces, marinated and cooked with red wine and juniper berries in a tall *jug* that stands in a pan of water; *Wëllschwainsragout*, or the 'Wild-Boar Casserole', sautéed with onions and garlic; *Réiréck* or 'Haunch of Venison', deer bum; and of course, the somewhat forgettable *Fierkelsjhelli*, 'Suckling Pig in Aspic'.

I had the boar, by the way, and if I must say so, it was exquisite as 'wild meat' always has a unique, richer flavour and is leaner.

The next morning I was on the way to the train station when I spotted a woman in a shop window. She was sitting at her computer and a cat was playing with the mouse. I smiled and the woman smiled back. What a grand city Luxembourg is. It's decidedly civilized. It's refreshingly clean. It has the highest per capita income in Europe. When locals choose their evening attire, they err on the side of *très* chic (restaurants err on the side of *très cher*). On Mondays, many shops and department stores don't open until two in the afternoon. (Good on the Luxembourgers. Let the hardworking folk enjoy a lie-in after a busy weekend of counting their money.)

Here's something else for you and I'll buy you a Funck if you can follow me: The people of Luxembourg speak French, German and the impenetrable Lëtzebuergesch. Lëtzebuergesch is a Mosel-Frankish low-German dialect (with a little French thrown in to give it some class) and it's their national language and mother tongue. French and German are administrative languages. All three languages are official languages, but Lëtzebuergesch -- the mother tongue, or 'the language learned at the mother's knee' -- has only been an official language since 1984. Stop and think about all this for a moment, it's going to get worse. A lot worse.

Newspapers are normally printed in French and German -- but some articles (and classifieds) do appear in Lëtzebuergesch. In criminal cases, the questioning of the accused, the victims and the witnesses, is done in Lëtzebuergesch. Lawyers plead in French. The ruling is handed down and published in French.

Jokes about attorneys are in Lëtzebuergesch.

Civil cases are carried out between judges and lawyers, in the absence of the affected parties, in French. If there is to be questioning of the parties -- it is performed in Lëtzebuergesch. If the party does not speak Lëtzebuergesch, the judges will not hesitate to use French or German. And last, but far from least, lawyers, even if they are foreign, are required to understand Lëtzebuergesch.

* * *

WHAT NOBODY WILL TELL YOU:

There are no adequate facilities for the Luxembourg army to train in their own country, so guess where they train? ... Sandhurst, England, where the famed Royal Military Academy is located.

CHAPTER 6 - Austria: I find work as a ski instructor up in the Alps

In preparation for my gap year visit to Austria, I camped out at my local bookshop. I sat on the floor (so the cashiers couldn't see me) and read with deep interest guidebook after guidebook. By the time I was rudely frogmarched to the front door and thrown the hell out, I had conjured up dazzling images of the *Altstadt* and *Goldenes Dachl* in Innsbruck, the Fortress *Hohensalzburg* and the Mozart-commercialized *Getreidegasse* in Salzburg, and St Stephen's cathedral and the Prater with its famous *Riesenrad* (Ferris wheel) in Vienna. These are just a few of the great wonders of these great cities. And these are the cities many people go to see first. Since I hadn't developed a mind of my own yet, this is where I went as well.

The guidebooks had assured me how warm and friendly the Austrians were, but the Austrians certainly weren't warm and friendly at the cafés in and around the Graben quarter in Vienna -- only the Turks were. The Viennese were dreary and moody and obsessed with conveying the impression that they were somehow superior to everyone else on the planet. What's worse, they were bad at geography (they believe the rest of Europe revolves around Vienna).

The Salzburgers were not nearly as cold as the Viennese, as nobody can be that icy, but those I encountered in the restaurants and cafés along the *Getreidegasse* were frosty nevertheless and wanted a good slapping. Moreover, they suffered from a bedevilling inferiority complex, a result of what comes from always ending up on the arse-end of the cultural comparison with Vienna.

Then there was Innsbruck, Austria's fourth largest city and even here the locals in the *Kneipes* (pubs) of the Altstadt didn't extend many smiles. Besides the traditional big city character flaws the Innsbruckers suffered from another curious affliction. It's called *Engstirnig*, or being 'ineffably narrow minded'. This malady is rampant in Tyrol and it is said (and this no doubt is a well-founded clinical diagnosis) brought on by 'growing up in the narrow alpine valleys'.

In a country with a population of eight million (and almost as many sheep), surely there had to be friendly natives somewhere. With this in mind, I left the teeming museums, the metropolitan mentality and the chill of the city behind, and took the train up into the wondrously sunny Alps.

And it was up here that I discovered a fairytale village called Kitzbühel.

If you tried to imagine what a quintessential storybook village up in the Alps would be like you may well summon images such as a cobblestoned pedestrian zone, oompah bands on the corner, pastry shops at every turn, buxom Fräuleins bending over a lot and serving golden steins of beer, little old men hobbling around in Lederhosen (coveting buxom Fräuleins serving golden steins of beer) and a humongous bell clanging away in the church steeple. This is exactly what I found.

This is Kitzbühel.

Most of us who have already heard of Kitzbühel were first introduced by watching *Ski Sunday* in the UK or the *Wide World of Sports* in the States. We sat with toes curling in front of our

TVs as the best downhill ski racers in the world risked life, limb and illegal winnings as they positively screamed down free-fall drops, catapulted off precipitous cliffs and smart-missiled through dark, moody woods. It was Jean-Claude Killy who dubbed Kitzbühel's Hahnenkamm Downhill the 'most dangerous in the world'. And Jean-Claude is a man who knows what he's talking about.

* * *

A light rain was falling as the train ground to a halt in Kitzbühel. The arrival caught me off guard because what little attention span I possess was focused on a neighbouring pasture where a grunting bull (with a fashionable nose ring) was trying to put an amorous move on the south end of a northbound cow.

I grabbed my backpack and bolted only to be reminded that my backpack was still chained to the leg of my seat. I had read in a guidebook that this would deter crime (as crime has increased since the Wall came down). It almost deterred me from arriving at my chosen destination. I must have looked just a bit like one of those calves that gets royally jerked when it's lassoed in a rodeo. And what did the other passengers think when they saw me scoot from the compartment, only to be unceremoniously yanked back in?

Panicking now, I leapt off the train just before it juddered off. Trains in Austria do not stop for so very long. There are rigid schedules to be met. Teutonic reputations to uphold.

I looked around at all the chalets with geraniums and impatiens spilling over the front of their balconies. I took a deep pull of the piney mountain air into my lungs. I glanced up as clouds scudded across the face of the Hahnenkamm mountain. It was great to be back.

My plan was to weave myself into the fabric of local life by procuring a job and a roof over my head for the winter. If I could find employment with real live locals and get behind the guidebook pages, who knew what could happen.

The *Fremdenverkehrsbureau* (this is the tourist office, but the literal translation is 'strangers traffic office') in Kitzbühel is located right next to the *Kino* (cinema) and upon arrival this is the first place you want to avoid. If you endeavour to secure accommodation here, cherubic Heidi-types will enter your particulars into a computer (number of nights, price range, single-bed or double, bath or shower, toilet three flights down and out the back door), then print out a list of ten or 20 possibilities. You must then schlep your worldly goods up and down miniature versions of the Matterhorn, as you search, oft in vain, to find the appropriate chalet.

Anyway, forget this, do what I did -- go to the 'Londoner'.

The Londoner (just around the corner from the tourist office and across from McDonald's) is a lively ex-pat pub run by wacky Brits and rat-assed Aussies, and they do the Tom Cruise *Cocktail* thing behind the bar. Here you can sip a Stiegel beer, listen to Tyrolean Rap (the honest truth) and watch as the bartenders juggle bottles, break all the glasses and drink themselves into an oblivious state just this side of embalmed.

Since it's required to make a fashion statement in ski resorts, the Londoner staff wear T-shirts and sweatshirts that read: WHY SKI? I'M GOING DOWNHILL FAST ENOUGH ANYWAY.

Are you getting the picture here?

By the time you have finished your first beer, you will have numerous leads pointing you in the direction of a reasonably priced B&B. You will also have made friends for life. Makes sense doesn't it? The staff in the Londoner have had to endure what you are about to slog through, so use the Londoner as your room-finding service. They will understand your needs much better than Heidi. And Heidi won't offer you free schnapps.

Anyway, two pints later I was unpacking my bags in the centrally located Haus Johanna (and wondering why there were small, dried-up pieces of seal flipper in a napkin in the right pocket of my sports jacket).

* * *

Kitzbühel is an easy place to find a job -- if you can take all the verbal abuse. What! Hang on a second. Thought we were in a fairytale village. So did I. Here's the naked truth: Until the snow falls, you pound on a lot of doors and have a lot of doors literally slammed in your face. That's how non-Austrians in search of glamorous-menial work are treated in Kitzbühel. Cows with foot-and-mouth are treated with more respect than are the swarming hordes of Brits, Aussies, Kiwis, Canadians and the odd American. But once the snow flies, it suddenly dawns on the procrastinating Austrians that their little *pension* or mountain restaurant or hotel isn't going to run so well, or long, without seasonal chalet girls/guys. You see, up until those first fluffy flurries no one will hire you for the winter season lest there is no winter season.

(FYI: Snow is like gold dust to the Kitzbühelers. Snow means skiing and the ski industry is big money. This white gold has made the locals rich, but it has also given them amnesia. They no longer can remember that there used to be farms where there are now ski pistes. And they have forgotten that they once shovelled manure for a living.)

Flurries did fall from the heavens one night and I awoke to 'mouse-knee-deep snow' as the Austrians like to call it -- and I was offered a job at the Kitzbüheler Horn Ski School. I acquired this skill-demanding position, not because I knew how to ski and not because I spoke German (at that point I could only say *Grüss Gott* and *Leck mich am Arsch*), but because I spoke English.

'We need you to speak English,' Wasti Zwicknagl, the owner of the ski school, told me. 'Kitz is predominantly a British destination.'

I didn't offer the fact that Great Britain and America were two countries 'separated by a common language'.

Now get ready for this, Wasti's wife knew *everybody* in town, and she found me accommodation in the staff quarters of the eerily un-grand Grand Hotel -- once the haunt of that vile cur Hermann Wilhelm Göring, commander of the *Luftwaffe* and founder of the Gestapo. The Grand Hotel resembled in frightening detail that hotel in the movie *The Shining*.

I had a free day before I had to embark on a week's training course to become an Austrian qualified ski instructor, so I borrowed Wasti's mountain bike and took a little tour. I pedalled up the high street, through the arch of the *Jochbergertor* and into the pedestrian area or *Fussgängerzone*. I paused here and gazed off through the centre of Kitzbühel at the Wilder Kaiser mountain range in the background. The peaks were draped in snow and drenched in sun.

Austria is an astonishingly lovely country and Kitzbühel is heart-lurchingly picturesque, especially on autumnal days when the sun is shining brightly and the tops of the mountain peaks are *angezuckert* ('sprinkled with powered sugar').

Kitzbühel is impressively clean and tidy. Littering is almost nonexistent, unlike, say, the UK where littering is a national pastime. When it comes to their shops, restaurants, toilets and windows—everything except their teeth and armpits -- you could say that the Austrians are obsessed with cleanliness.

Just to my left was the Hotel zur Tenne. This is where some scenes from Robert Redford's *Downhill Racer* were filmed. This is also where I saw a man sweeping the street with a witch's broom and an elderly *Putzfrau* down on the pavement in front of the hotel's main entrance on her hands and knees scrubbing the sidewalk with soap and water. That's obsessive. And maybe this is why no one litters in Kitzbühel. Would you litter on a sidewalk after your grandma got down on her hands and knees and scrubbed it? I think not.

In order to fortify myself before venturing up the valley, I patronised the Pirchl bakery. And it was here I spied a young Swedish tour guide with blazing blue eyes and a deeply tanned face. The young lass was purchasing a hot *Leberkäsesemmel* and a carton of *Milch*. I slipped in behind her and saw her company's name on the back of her yellow and blue ski jacket: 'Ving Alpin'. I looked at my watch. Eight-thirty. Did she come in here everyday and purchase her breakfast?

I heard the woman behind the till say: '*Danke*, Ingeborg.' Then the woman turned to me: '*Haben Sie einen Wunsch?*'

'*Leberkäsesemmel und Milch,*' I said, watching Ingeborg scoot out the door.

For those of you who are connoisseurs of suspect breakfast choices, may I just mention that *Leberkäsesemmel* literally means 'liver-cheese sandwich', and as disgusting as it sounds, they really are quite tasty -- if you can get past the name.

I hopped back on my bike and pedalled slowly toward the neighbouring village of Aurach, and stayed off the main highway by following a path that runs along the foothills and the gorgeously forbidding mountains off to your right.

About an hour out of Kitzbühel I was passing an old farmhouse when the sun suddenly dropped out of the sky and set behind the Hahnenkamm. Let me clue you in to something, when you are up in the Alps and an autumnal sun suddenly drops out of the sky -- make tracks! It gets cold fast.

I decided to turn around and go back. Now, catch this: The path I was riding on was narrow and to turn around I had to pedal about three feet into the farmer's field (there were no fences). Within seconds the farmer and his jackbooted teenage son exploded out of a nearby barn. They were carrying pitchforks and gave chase, spewing a torrent of foul-mouthed abuse. Instead of checking cow teats for blisters, they must have been lying in wait for some poor unsuspecting *Ausländer* (foreigner) like me to set foot on their precious dung-covered property. I was horrified by such treatment and particularly by the teenage lad. I'm sure he would have inflicted bodily harm if I hadn't turned up the turbo.

When I was finally out of harm's way (I am laudably swift on a bicycle when someone is trying to stick a pitchfork up my arse) and had caught my breath, I gave this sporty little interlude some thought. It was obvious the farmer and his ill-bred seed could ascertain from the way I was dressed that I was not from the valley. And they could also establish that I was not a threat to their field. Or even their sheep. Yet, I was some foreign interloper and clearly fair game. Now, this conjures up a plethora of questions: Were they starved for a little blood sport? How would this family have responded during, say, *Kristallnacht*? Probably would have jumped right into the maltreatment, wouldn't you say? What sort of heinous mentality reacts this way? How would they react if there was suddenly a war and a big neighbouring country like, say, Germany did the *Anschluss* thing? How would they respond if, say, a *KZ* (concentration camp) was suddenly built next to their little village as it had been built at not so distant Mauthausen? Would they plead ignorance regarding its presence as Austrians who lived near concentration camps did back then?

(FYI: There were more concentration camps in Austria than any other region in the Third Reich.)

* * *

All prospective ski instructors had to endure a humiliating week-long course, where our once-thought-to-be-perfectly-acceptable ski styles were ripped apart and remoulded into that of the great Austrian ski instructor. From early morning to late afternoon we were skied all over the mountain, and then for three hours in the evening we had lectures in German, given by some grumpy old ski instructor who couldn't give a flying shit if we understood his back-of-the-mountain dialect or not. Try understanding back-of-beyond Tyrolian dialect sometime when you have only just learnt the *Hochdeutsch* equivalent.

At the end of the week we were tested on the icy mountain and then in the icy classroom. Wasti and his wife had spent the week pounding dialect into my head, so I was able to pass the written German test (which was given orally!), but when it came to the *Test am Schnee*, I flunked the snowplough. Yes, you heard right, I flunked the snowplough.

Thanks to my inability to perform the most basic ski technique known to man, I had to repeat the week-long course. And thank you very much for asking and shouting it out loud so everyone could hear, yes, I eventually passed the friggin' snowplough.

Arbeit macht frei.

I was thrilled to be an Austrian Qualified Ski Instructor, so I jumped with unbridled enthusiasm at my first chance to teach. Perhaps I would meet the woman of my dreams as I led her across the snowy sun-drenched Alps?

But, alas, my first student was a four-year-old boy from

Luxembourg who only spoke Lëtzebuergesch.

* * *

I remember it was just before Christmas when one of my co-ski instructors came running up to me with a panicked look on his face.

'He's back! He's back!'

'Who's back?'

'The Saudi Arabian prince who gave one of our ski instructors a thousand dollar tip last season. He's back!' Then: 'Make damn sure you don't get him. He's a bleedin' nightmare!'

That evening, we had our first *Versammlung* of the season at the ski school. There were about 50 ski instructors at the meeting, and for some reason everyone was keeping a low profile instead of being their usual raucous, arrogant selves. I know this as I was sitting in the front row and I could see everyone cowering behind me.

'As you are all aware,' Wasti the ski school director began, 'the prince is back...'

Groans.

'And as he is one of our most important guests, we want to provide him with five-star service...'

More groans.

Wasti had scorching subtext going, sort of trying to believe himself what he was saying. '*Jawohl*, the prince is back and this time he wants a private instructor for his number one son. And another private instructor for his number two son. And yet another private instructor for his number three son. He also wants a private instructor for number one daughter and number two daughter. And he will take a private instructor for himself. Now just so you know, this is not cheap. Three hundred euros a day. Per person. For two weeks. Plus lavish tip. It adds up.'

Wails.

'So I'm asking for volunteers. Who will step forward? Do we have any *Profis* (professionals) out there?' Wasti said this in that blind-hope tone the police negotiator uses when trying to talk the guy off the ledge.

I looked around. It was as if someone had tossed a grenade in the ski school. Everyone had taken cover.

'*Und so.* I will have to assign. Andy Zössmayer, you take number one son. Andy Pendl, number two son. Georg, number three. Hildegarde, you take the youngest daughter. And Balasch, you take the oldest daughter.'

I heard squeaks and scratches as ski instructors tried to dig themselves deeper into corners.

'That leaves just the prince. Who speaks English as a first language here? We need someone who has English as a native tongue.'

I heard rustling and movement behind me. All my Austrian colleagues were sitting upright and visible. They all had smiles on their faces. And they were all smiling at me.

'Jon! Our English-speaking instructor!'

* * *

It had snowed a few inches of fresh powder during the night and the sun made the slopes appear to be composed of millions of diamonds the next morning. The Alps are enchanting when the slopes are bejewelled like this, and I figured that perhaps this wasn't going to be as bad as everyone had made out. Two hours in the morning and two hours in the afternoon. Four hours of glorious sunshine. How bad could it be?

But when I arrived at the beginners' area, I couldn't believe what I saw before me: Besides the prince and the five kids, there was a travelling harem bedecked in expensive fur, three nannies to look after the brats and four bodyguards to look after the entire sheikdom.

The women had Minoltas. The nannies had spare mittens. The bodyguards had .357 Magnums. I am *not* making this up.

So now, envisage this menagerie hovering around the baby lift with six ski instructors frantically trying to do their best to teach skiing in this heavily armed, heavily class-conscious atmosphere. And it's not so easy, because every time the primogenital son fell over, a flurry of nannies and bodyguards sprang into action and picked the spoiled little shit up off the snow. (Can you imagine being so rich you have servants to pick your arse up off the snow when you fall down skiing?)

The morning started out *wunderbar,* but deteriorated quickly to *Scheisse* with the prince and his eldest son being verbally abusive and arrogant. 'Out of my way! Don't you know who I am!' They thought they owned the mountain and they kept cutting the queue. It drove us crazy and we wanted them all dead. At the end of the day, Andy Zössmayer, who was in charge of number one son, came to me: 'What mean "sook deek"?'

'You mean "suck dick"?'

'*Jawohl,* "sook deek".'

I told Andy and I thought his eyeballs were going to explode. 'Boy say all afternoon to me. Boy only twelve. Thousand dollar tip! *Nicht!*'

After a nightmarish week tempered only by the thought of various forms of homicide, Wasti came to me and said: 'We got big group of British women. I take you off prince.'

The prince was an example of one type of individual who came to our ski school, but we also had more down-to-earth types -- and that type was well represented by my group of British *Weiberleut,* in fact, one young lady in particular from that group. And her name was Jane. Jane was from Kidderminster (not known as one of Britain's garden spots, Jane told me that locals say they are 'going to the Kidderminster' when they are going to the loo). Now, it is important to note here, that while the prince skied in only the most chic Italian fashions, Jane skied in a borrowed, package-holiday outfit with painted-on pants (embarrassingly, one other woman in my class had the same outfit).

Jane was a commendably well-built young woman -- all orchestra and balcony -- and she was a complete beginner.

I loved teaching the beginning classes. Beginners were fun. Doctor, attorney, rock star, fringe royal, big-six publisher, literary agent who requests full MS then doesn't get back to you, it didn't matter, beginning skiing is an equalizer of egos. Beginners are thrilled if they can just stand up. And if they can slide down a gentle slope and stop without running into a tree -

- they become Rocky Balboa at the end of the movie.

There were twelve in my group and Jane was the slowest to learn, but I didn't mind, I liked Jane. Where my other eleven students were already going up the baby lift on their own and coming down the nursery slope, Jane was still fighting gravity. After much effort, I finally succeeded in teaching Jane to sidestep up a little mini-hill next to the baby lift. There, like a drowning swimmer, she would grasp onto me, turn around and slowly ski down all fifteen feet (with her bum sticking provocatively out), attempting to stop in something resembling an unorthodox snowplough. And I know snowploughs!

I was pleased with her progress. 'Jane you're doing great!' I encouraged her. 'Just keep the hands forward, quit looking down at your skis and point the ski poles backwards instead of forwards like a water diviner. You'll be just fine. Now all you need is time on skis.'

'Okay, Jon, I'll try,' she would respond with a big smile.

'Good -- I'll go over to the baby lift now and help the others. You just keep sliding gently down, then sidestep slowly back up. Slide gently down, sidestep slowly back up. I'll be right back, okay?'

'Okay, I think I can just manage that.'

It was always like this with beginners. If you had twelve in your class, it was the same as trying to babysit twelve puppies. Everyone was always hurtling off in a different direction.

I left Jane at the top of the mini-hill and glided over to the baby lift. While I waited in the queue, I watched another ski instructor with his group. His name was Chip and he was from a competing ski school, the Red Devils. Chip was about to take a group of advanced skiers into the deep powder for the ski of their lives, and he had all his people lined up like soldiers in one neat row, elaborating on the finer points of where to buy a beer in the village.

I hopped on the lift and was admiring Chips's oratory, when I heard the woeful moan. It sounded like a wolf in heat, 'WHOOOOOOA!' Only it wasn't a wolf in heat, it was Jane, and she was slipping backwards, out of control, right at Chip's soldiers.

I watched in sincere horror as she flew down the hill and shot backwards right across the tops of the skis of Chip's first seven advanced students giving them a pedicure and then, as if that wasn't embarrassing enough, took out the last five skiers, like a well-built bowling ball.

Chip, whose sense of humour rivalled anybody's, just calmly bent over Jane, who was lying in a heap at his feet, and announced in his best English so the whole mountain could hear: 'YOU MUST BE IN JON'S GROUP!'

About an hour later I felt much better about everything because Jane felt much better about everything. She had progressed swimmingly and had finally graduated to the baby lift. Cheers and shouts of glee!

So now I'm being pulled slowly up the drag lift. Jane is twenty feet in front of me, holding on for dear life. I'm cooing gentle words to her to keep her calm on her first ascent. I knew if I could just get her to the top of the baby hill with no problems, her confidence would soar and she would be able to manage the baby lift all on her own. T-bars, rope-tows and baby lifts always scare the bejesus out of the beginning skier.

Jane followed my instructions explicitly and had almost reached her goal, when I heard the wolf in heat again. 'WHOOOOOOA!' I couldn't believe my eyes. Jane hadn't waited till she reached the top of the lift where it was flat to get off, rather she decided to disembark one foot too soon. She wasn't over the hump, so she started to slide backwards down the mountain, picking up speed, bent over, bum sticking out -- straight at me!

Her speed increased and 'WHOOOOOA!!!' Jane's backside crashed into my front side and all I could do was grab her to keep her from going farther down the mountain and taking out all the other skiers on the lift behind me. So there I was straddling Jane from behind like that bull with the fashionable nose ring had mounted the south end of the northbound cow, and all the while we were still being dragged up the mountain by the drag lift. I didn't think things could get any worse, but because I was leaning over so much the ski-lift caught under my rucksack and jerked ... jerked ... jerked me up the mountain, while I inadvertently humped ... humped ... humped Jane from behind.

Somehow we made it to the top and I was able to dismount and get Jane back standing on her own. I shot a look down the hill praying nobody had witnessed this sexually aberrant performance.

But Chip and his soldiers were back. And they were applauding us, and then Chip yelled up to Jane: 'Did the earth move for you?'

Whoever said teaching skiing was glamorous?

I had Jane compose herself for a moment -- while I composed myself for a moment -- then I gave her, her next assignment.

'Okay, Jane, here's what I want you to do. Just stay in snowplough and go straight ahead, slowly. We won't worry about turns until we have our brakes sorted out, okay?'

Jane flashed me a nervous smile and then started cautiously, and in control -- sort of. She seemed to be struggling with some powerful inner force. Her face contorted as she attempted the snowplough and her arms seemed to have a mind of their own, trying to do what her skis wouldn't. But Jane was slowly succeeding. There was hope. My nightmares were finally over.

I gave a couple pointers to my other students as they came up the baby lift and snowploughed down the nursery slope. One by one they were doing laps now. Taking the lift up. Skiing down. Taking the lift up. Skiing down.

And here came Jane up the lift and she did it all on her own this time. She had no problems and she was beaming, exhilarated by the sport of skiing. She was hooked.

'Can I go down again, Jon? Can I give it another try?'

'Of course, Jane. Go for it. I'm really proud of you. You've really got the hang of it now.'

Jane snowploughed down the mountain like molasses, still fighting an inner battle with gravity. I watched her go, then looked around at the scenery. Ah, at last, this is what it was all about, to be up in the Alps with the sun sparkling off the snow. To look as far as you could and see nothing but snowcapped peaks. And to be finally successful with someone like Jane. I wasn't taking the advanced skiers down the backside of the mountain in the deep powder like Chip was, but I was immensely proud of myself. Yes, this is what life was all about and nothing could wrench me from my reverie.

'WHOOOOOA!' the wolf bitch moaned. My God no! Jane was schussing out of control straight down the mountain like a world-class downhill racer. I prayed that everybody would get out of her way, and they did -- all but one.

And that one ... was the insufferable prince.

And he couldn't do anything about it because he had his face stuck in his expensive, top-of-the-line, state-of-the-art camcorder as he videoed brat number one cutting the queue.

'WHOOOOOA!'

If anything, Jane seemed to be going faster and like a smart-bomb she took unintentional dead aim at the backside and ostrich spread legs of the prince himself. And I guess Jane really couldn't be faulted, for at the precise moment of impact she did something that comes natural to all of us -- she covered her face with her hands. Only problem was she still had her ski poles in her hands (tips pointed unfortunately forward) and like the best Samurai warrior she sent her dual rapiers slashing into the frightfully expensive, achingly private part of the prince's bespoke ten-thousand dollar Emilio Pucci ski suit.

'WHOOOOOA!' the wail came from the prince this time, then there was a flurry of snow and all I saw was a cartoon-esque kaleidoscope of multicoloured arms and legs and video equipment.

Horror stricken, I raced to the side of my fallen student. Lying to the right of Jane was the camcorder, still running. Lying to her left was the prince, barely running. I kicked off my skis and knelt by my student.

'Jane! Jane! Are you okay?'

'Yes, I am, but I'm not so sure he is,' she said, trying to keep from laughing.

53

'Why's that?'

'I got the pillock good,' Jane went on. 'Got him right in the gonies.'

* * *

After teaching skiing for the day, I would often take one last run down the mountain to the family-run Hagstein restaurant and partake of a late-afternoon *Tiroler Gröstl* (bubble & squeak Tyrolean-style) or *Kaiserschmarrn* (shredded pancakes with raisins topped with various fruit compote and powdered sugar) or *Bauernomlette* ('farmer's omlette' made with sliced potatoes, bacon and onions) or *Germknodel* (bowling-ball-sized dumpling with plum jam and smothered in powdered sugar, vanilla sauce or melted butter), then I would ski right to the front of the ski school, store my skis and boots and head into the centre of the village. Here I would pop into the Londoner to meet Chip for a pint of Stiegl or slip over to café Langer for a *Kännchen* (small pot) of coffee and a wicked slice of *Sachertorte*).

And some days I would forgo the foodfest and simply stroll about the town and observe the end-of-the-day skiers as they slid off the mountain and partook of the pagan rituals of après-ski. And it was during these après-ski hours when I became aware of something I hadn't noticed before -- Austrians are world-class poseurs.

And no one, I mean no one, does it better -- except possibly the Germans. Now, bear with me for a moment while I set the stage for the history of the ski-resort pose in Kitzbühel: The Kitzbühelers dislike the Viennese because the Viennese are 'pompous fuckwits'. The Viennese dislike the agrarian Kitzbühelers because they 'lack culture' and eat like grazing animals in public (I can bear witness to this). The Kitzbühelers dislike the *Weisswurst*-gobbling Munichers because the Munichers think Kitzbühel is a suburb of Munich and their personal playground. The Munichers dislike the Kitzbühelers for the simple fact that they are Kitzbühelers -- and the Munichers aren't and never will be. Now here's the thing. The Kitzbühelers endure the Munichers and the Viennese because they want their euros, but that doesn't mean they have to be polite or cordial while they take it. The Kitzbühelers really don't like anybody, especially each other, but that's another story. So can you possibly guess what occurs when all these diametrically wanking forces get together?

They pose.

They pose and try to impress the very people they despise. Now stop and think. Does it make sense to have to impress somebody you regard with disdain? That neighbour from hell? That prick at the office? That slut at the fitness centre?

There's a bestially snooty little restaurant just across the street from the Londoner. And this is one of the places the beautiful people go to pose and assert an arrogant suzerainty over anyone who walks by. The restaurant is called the Stamperl and it used to be a glorious little haunt until the Viennese and the Munichers got a hold of it. If you pass by on a sunny afternoon, just after skiing, all the crème de la crap are there holding sway at the 'snow bar' out front, supping Veuve Clique champagne and vodka *Feiges*, drunk to the gills, and looking down their noses at everyone and anyone who happens by. But they are wasting a lot of their wannabe-blue-blood energy, you see, for most of the people who pass by just happen to have emerged from the neighbouring restaurant: McDonald's. And the McDonald's clientele in Kitzbühel traditionally consist of drugged-out, fucked-up, copping-an-attitude snowboarders. Alas, the arrogance of the poseurs is clearly lost on the rebellious couldn't-give-a-rodent's-arse subculture.

In a last-ditch attempt to really stick it to the Kitzbühelers, the Viennese and Munichers began parading around town gaudily bedizened in expensive fur coats and leading tongue-lolling Afghan dogs. Would it surprise you that the dogs and the fur coats matched? This self-absorbed parade went on for most of the winter but then stopped abruptly. Can you guess what happened? Word got out that the big furry coats and slavering hairy beasts -- were rented.

* * *

Skiing in Kitzbühel can be a wonderfully pleasant pastime as these Alps are the 'lower Alps' and wintry conditions are rarely severe. Even in January, I've skied in streaming sunshine on spring conditions. Yes, skiing in Austria can be great fun -- when you don't have to queue.

Standing in a ski-lift queue in Austria (or any queue for that matter) is a nasty and perilous business. You see, Austrians are anything but au fait with queuing etiquette. I have been bulldozed in ski-lift queues, rudely jostled in the check-out queue at the market and virtually hockey-checked while in pursuit of a lonely stamp at the post office.

At Christmas, when the glow of goodwill should have been oozing from every man, woman, child and beast of burden, a baby-seal-skinned-adorned Viennese woman and her blubbery porcine daughter actually laid hands on me in the Billa Supermarket and wrestled their way in front of me. To protect my interests, and to discourage them from ever attempting something so foolish in the future, I ran my shopping trolley over the back of their Achilles tendons, repeatedly, until they repaired to their original aft positions.

On another occasion, I was up on the Pengelstein standing in the world's longest ski-lift queue, which was really more of a ski-outfit fashion show (snazzy ski suits usually demonstrate that you have loads of money, but little taste). I had been waiting patiently, growing older, soaking up the sun and was almost to the front when two Austrians skipped right in front of me. I asked them, politely, in German, if they would consider getting to the back of the goddamn fucking queue. When the older Austrian heard my accent and noticed that I was mildly aggressive, he responded with: 'You must be American. You Americans think everywhere is still the Wild West.'

At first I was stunned, but then I was overjoyed, for that's when I remembered a phrase that Wasti, the director of the ski school, had taught me for just such an occasion: *Was für ein Nazi Ton?* ('What's with the Nazi tone?')

And this doesn't go down so very well in Austria.

The two interlopers glared fiercely at me and began to move

off. Then the younger of the two stopped and motioned for his mate to get back in the queue.

Bastards.

Inspired by my former student, Jane, I considered emasculating both of them with the point of my ski stick but chose to bide my time instead. You see, this is when I realised that these two inconsiderate sods looked frighteningly familiar. They were the farmer and his dick-breath seed who had chased me with the pitchforks at the start of the ski season. Now, being the happiest person on the face of the earth, I waited until the two were just about to board the chair-lift. Then I struck like a viper. I grabbed the father's expensive Bogner ski hat, and the little prick's coveted Snoopy aviator hat with the ear flaps and asked the skiers behind me if they would be so kind as to pass the hats back—way back. This was the first time I ever saw Austrians and Germans and Britons unite, by design. One by one, each skier obliged and gladly took the hats and passed them to the back of the queue -- estimated wait, one hour.

Well, I've said a lot of not so nice things about the Austrians, and perhaps a little bit about the Germans ('It's always tempting,' an Austrian friend once said to me) and I don't want you to get the wrong impression, although it is all true.

So maybe Kitzbühel is not Shangri-La, but it's still a place worth seeing -- just watch out for those queues (and the pitchforks).

* * *

WHAT NOBODY WILL TELL YOU:

The Austrians don't claim Hitler, who was born in Austria, but greedily claim Freud, who wasn't born in present-day Austria, rather in Freiberg, Moravia, which is now part of the Czech Republic.

* * *

A going joke in Austria: 'What is the difference between God and an Austrian ski instructor? Answer: God doesn't think he's an Austrian ski instructor.'

* * *

When things started to go into the toilet for Adolph Hitler back at the Bunker, Hermann Wilhelm Göring cabled Hitler and said something to the effect of: 'Listen, if you're in the hunt for a replacement, then I'm your guy!' Hitler refused and, to demonstrate his sincere sentiments, had a communiqué sent out to find and kill Göring. Not one for violence when he was on the receiving end of it, Göring fled across the border into Austria and surrendered to the advancing Americans and actually said these words: 'War is like a football match. We fight hard during the game, but when it is all over, winner or loser, we are still friends. *Ja?*'

CHAPTER 7 - The Austrian Alps: Death in the bakery, I share a bottle of schnapps with a corpse

There was an expression I heard bandied about during the winter. It went something like this: 'Austria would be a great place, if it weren't for the Austrians.'

After my last chapter this may almost seem true, but to be fair to the locals of Kitzbühel, I did meet some wonderful people who were generous and gracious and hardworking -- and filled with *joie de vivre*. Wasti and his wife, Isabelle, from the ski school remain close friends, but there was another fellow I met, and I want to recount a little story about him. His name was Pepi.

I lived just around the corner from the bakery Pepi's parents owned (that's the same bakery where Ingeborg bought her breakfast). When the garrulous Pepi -- envisage a young Gerard Depardieu -- found out someone from the English-speaking world was popping by at exactly the same time every morning hoping to bump into a certain Swedish tour guide, he made it a point to introduce himself.

Pepi loved to try out his unusual strain of English on me ('I'll set fire to the car' instead of 'I'll fire up the car'), and he

59

was sincerely mesmerized by the English language, its peculiarities and so many exceptions to the rules. He wondered how some words could be pronounced the same but spelled differently and yet how others could be spelled the same but be pronounced differently. (While we're at it, just for fun, name one from each category. You have one minute).

My newfound friend brought an interesting element of personality to life. He might have been a baker by trade but Pepi was really more of an Evel Knievel trapped inside a baker's body. When it came to sports, the more dangerous the sport the more it seemed to his liking. Pepi was one of the first to hang-glide in Kitzbühel and I would often see him riding the old red gondola to the top of the Hahnenkamm. When Pepi reached the top, he carried his hang-glider over his shoulder a hundred metres or so to where he and a ski instructor named Albin had built a death-defying wooden runway that stuck out over a free-fall cliff. Here on the top of the mountain Pepi would unfurl his hang-glider, assemble it, then stick a finger into the air to check the wind and simply run off the wooden ramp into space. With hang-gliding in its infancy in Kitzbühel, there were many hilarious moments and many serious mishaps.

But Pepi revelled in the borderline life-threatening, and I always felt that deep down he would have been happier risking his life in some romantic manner in some far-flung corner of the world than preparing marzipan.

Over the course of the winter, Pepi and I shared many a good laugh together and we remained close until his death hang-gliding off that same wooden ramp on his beloved Hahnenkamm.

When I think of Pepi now, I think back on how many of my scaringly thrilling adventures and many of my eye-opening experiences were directly related to Pepi Pirchl -- baker.

I remember one time started innocently enough. It was well into the ski season, a howling snowstorm had blanketed the village with nearly a metre of fresh snow and Pepi invited me down into the *Keller* at two in the morning to see where they did all the baking. Pepi was proud of what he did and delighted in giving me a grand tour of the *Backstube*.

'This,' Pepi said as he swung open the door that led into the bakery, 'is where we create.'

Before me I saw blazing ovens and whirring mixers and humming grinders. And everything was white. All the equipment was white, all the walls were white, even the faces of all the bakers were white. As the bakers ran around in their white shorts and white T-shirts and white clogs, they resembled kabuki dancers caught in their underwear. It might have been freezing and ferocious outside, but with all the baking, it was warm and tropical in the bakery.

'Impressive, eh?' Pepi said proudly.

It was great fun to watch the bakers as they scurried about in an almost choreographed fashion -- and at a remarkable pace. Like the swallows at Capistrano they swooped around, diving in and out of ovens, somehow just missing one another, bantering back and forth, slaying each other with their jokes.

I was marvelling at how efficient the entire setup was when the door to the cellar blew open, a blizzard whistled in and two skiers completely encrusted in ice and snow slid down the stairs. I looked at my watch. It was almost three in the morning. Why were they just returning from skiing now?

One of the bakers wrestled the door shut, as Pepi, always the clown, draped a towel over his arm like a first-class waiter: 'Will it be a table for two tonight, gentlemen?'

'Three, actually,' said one of the skiers, icicles hanging from his beard, and on that he reopened the cellar door and, as the storm fought with icy fingers to come inside, reached out and dragged a wooden sled down into the bakery. Strapped on top was a blue-faced frozen corpse.

All the bakers gasped, as did I, but Pepi didn't. Still in the guise of the first-class waiter, he simply bowed and graciously beckoned them all in: 'Table for three, it is.'

Pepi installed the party in a corner by the door and went to fetch his two frozen friends some sustenance.

Suddenly, here I was sitting in a bakery way up in the Alps in the middle of the night eating *Krapfen* (jelly doughnuts to die for) and drinking caustic Slivovitz schnapps with a bunch of crazy bakers, two frozen mountain men and a stiff.

'The hell's going on?' I whispered to Pepi when there was a lull in the excitement.

'That skier,' Pepi said pointing to the corpse. 'He died in avalanche yesterday afternoon up on backside of Steinbergkogel, and these two guys are part of mountain rescue team. They didn't find body until couple hours ago. It take so long to get down mountain with body.'

'They were up there in this weather, tonight?'

'They hardy folk, these types. They go up in screaming storm, during darkest hour, in most dangerous avalanche conditions to try to save someone. They wonderful husbands and fathers but they have rough side. They hard. They have to be to look death in face in middle of raging storm.'

Pepi poured another round of schnapps for his frozen friends, and I took a closer look at the mountain men. They were tough lads, indeed, I decided. To chill their schnapps glasses, they had placed them on top of the prone, frozen corpse.

'Why'd they bring the body down here?'

'They were on way to morgue when they smelled fresh doughnuts. They often stop in,' Pepi went on matter-of-factly, 'but this is first time they bring guest.'

Pepi poured another schnapps. Then another. Then, yet another. And soon before I knew it, a few hours had passed and the hearty mountain men were warm, happy and paralytic. I knew they had warmed up because now they were sitting and drinking in their underwear. Like I said, it was hot in the bakery.

And it was about now that it happened.

Without any warning, the corpse thawed, let loose with a roaring god-awful belch—and sat bolt upright. And let me tell you, none of us was afraid to admit it (even Pepi), when that corpse bellowed and sprang up like he was spring loaded -- we shit ourselves.

All of us that is except those two rugged mountain men.

One yelled 'Chill out!' while the other, without even missing a beat, jammed a jelly doughnut in the corpse's mouth.

A jelly doughnut to die for.

* * *

As the ski season came to an end and the snow began to melt, I realised I had mixed feelings about Kitzbühel. For sure the village is drop-dead gorgeous, and I'd made some dear friends. And come to think of it, I'd really only been made to feel unwelcome in the post office, *Hallenbad* (swimming hall), Billa Supermarket, Spar Supermarket, Tourist Office, Drop-In nightclub, Hotel Tenne (at breakfast), doctor's office (hit a tree skiing), chemists (throaties), *Meldeamt* (where foreigners must register), train station (ticket to Stockholm), two banks, the travel agency, and all pubs that weren't run by Brits.

So how can anyone possibly say that 'Austria would be a great place if it weren't for the Austrians'?

* * *

WHAT NOBODY WILL TELL YOU:

A general rule is, if you are caught in an avalanche and aren't crushed by tons of snow and ice, or wrapped around a tree as you are unmercifully sucked down the mountain, you will survive only 30 minutes before you suffocate in your pitch-black, claustrophobic netherworld.

CHAPTER 8 - Stockholm: I shower with the coed volleyball team

Stockholm is a long way from everywhere.

Kitzbühel to Stockholm is thirty hours by train, if there aren't any 'bovine incursions' on the tracks (that was the English used to explain the dead cow ... and the screeching stop ... and the spilled coffee). That's a long trip. And the journey seems even longer due to the time warp. You see, when I said *aufwiedersehen* to Kitzbühel, it was spring, but when I said *Hej! Hej!* to Stockholm, it had magically become winter again. There was black ice on the streets, the trees were ghostly barren and the wind whistled snow in my hair. In contrast to Austria's effulgent and verdant spring, Stockholm was still romantically dark and wondrously foreboding in a haunting *Doctor Zhivago* sort of way.

I spent my first week living in a damp and chilly *botel* (boat/hotel) watching ferryboats dodge ice floes. And here's a tip: If you are considering staying in one of these rocking, shuddering, freeze-your-heinie-off establishments, be forewarned, many have foolishly restrictive curfews that will not allow you to order that second pint. This of course mattered not to me since the price of alcohol is so spectacularly high in Stockholm I couldn't afford to go out of an evening anyway.

After a week of spending the night in the foetal position, my life's quest became warmer surroundings, so I contacted Ingeborg's tour company, Ving Alpin, to see if she was in town for the summer. She wouldn't have a clue who I was, but perhaps owing to the Kitzbühel connection, she would at least be kind enough to give me a tip on how I could upgrade my living situation.

Surprisingly, Ving Alpin gladly gave out her phone number and address. Ingeborg resided in a section of Stockholm called Södermalm. Södermalm is sort of Stockholm's answer to Soho. Perhaps that's why they gave out the address.

Anyway, I phoned Inge*bonk/boink* (due to sexual tension on my part, bizarre strains of her name began to arise unbidden) and she said she did indeed remember me: 'The ski instructor who lived in the bakery!' Then she shocked me with: 'You can stay here. I only have one bedroom, though. Hope you don't mind ...'

'Don't mind!' I said, as all sorts of fantasies began to arise.

'That's right. Don't mind sleeping on the couch.'

From Ingebore's flat it was easy to walk up to the *Gamla Stan* (Old Town) and then across one of the many bridges and over to the city centre. If you do this, or really just walk for any distance in Stockholm at all, two things become crystal clear: Stockholm is an exceedingly handsome city, and there is a hell of a lot of water.

Something else you notice right away in Stockholm is that a glass of beer is not cheaper than a cup of coffee. According to Inge*barista*, in Sweden it's cheaper to buy a politician than a beer.

I had always attributed Sweden's high rate of suicide to the price of a beer, but I've done a little research from dubious sources of late and have come to find that in fact Austria's rate of suicide is even higher than Sweden's (taking your own life is apparently more attractive than being led one day by the likes of one of the emerging, far-right political parties sympathetic of Nazis and contemptuous of Jews); Finland is significantly higher than even Austria and would seem on the verge of being over the top if it weren't for good old Hungary, who's suicide rate is more than double Sweden's. It's a wonder the country has anyone left, ready and able, to emigrate.

There are a lot of credible theories out there why Sweden's suicide rate is still way too high: inherent depression, drug abuse and the fact its national football team can't ever seem to get to the quarterfinals, but I'm going to stick with my gut instinct about the larcenous price of a beer.

Remember how in Iceland everyone drank tankards of cheap alcohol at home so they could get righteously pissed without having to fork out the big bucks in the pubs and clubs? Well, forget about employing that penny-saving technique here in Sweden. Even the equivalent of your local Threshers is financially daunting. You see, the liquor stores in Sweden are government owned and operated. These frightening little venues are called *System Bolaget* and they appear to be architecturally inspired by the Bank of Sweden (with banking hours). It's unquestionably cheaper to purchase alcohol here than at a bar, pub or club, but still no great deal. Here's how this works: You stand in a long queue holding a week's wages in your sweaty, trembling little hand until you reach the front where an officious barracuda awaits you at the till. You point up at one lonely can of Carlsberg on display on a rack behind the barracuda, hand over your week's wages, go home, chug your beer and then contemplate suicide.

There ares an abundance of clubs and discos in Stockholm where there is an age requirement to get in. What's the big deal? The big deal is the age restriction can be anywhere from 18 to 30 depending on the clientele they wish to serve (or not serve) - - that's the big deal. Stop and think about that. You've been drinking (legally) since you were 18 or 21 and you go on holiday with your wife of ten years and you leave the seven kids in the botel to watch ice floes. It's your second honeymoon with wifey (gran wouldn't take the kids), and you go up to the bouncer of some hot little 'in' club, and he refuses you entry because you are too young! This may not be a strong enough motivation for suicide, but most certainly for homicide.

Swedes are obsessed with holding open doors. They just love to do it. And they do it with panache and patience. Have you ever been somewhere in this wonderful world of ours where you were carrying a splitting bag of groceries or a large pet or a 12-pack of Bud, and someone walked through the door in front of you and let it slam smack in your face? Well, take heart, *that* won't happen in Stockholm. The Swedes have made an art out of holding the door for you. Some countries just seem to be more civilized than others. Some people more polite. Once, a young lady was about to enter 'NK', a frightfully posh department store, and like all Swedes turned to see if anybody might be coming out of the nearby green and leafy *Kungsträdgåden* (King's Garden) or on final approach at Arlanda Airport and just possibly needed the door held open. Well, my bus was just careening around the corner and she must have recognised the glint of hope in my eye. She waited patiently holding that door until the #46 stopped down at the corner of Hamngatan and Norrmalmstorg, 20 schoolchildren spilled out, a little old lady (carrying a large pet) hobbled off, then I de-bussed and sprinted down the street and through the door. '*Tack så mycket!*' I said, out of breath.

'*Varsågod,*' she beamed, and scurried off to purchase sexy underwear and scout for another door she could hold open for someone.

Stockholm is lovely like that.

* * *

One typically bleak summer's day, I was leaning into a gale force wind trying to make my way across the Strömbron bridge to the *Gamla Stan* when I was stopped dead in my Pumas by the sight of a fisherman hauling a humongous flopping salmon out of the harbour. I had a close look at the fish and was taken aback -- this was Super Fish, a bursting-with-vitality (or at least had been) top-quality creature. There were no lesions on its back and no bubble-like tumours growing out the side of its head. I was so impressed with the state of the salmon, I abandoned the espresso I'd planned on taking at Cassi's in *Gamla Stan* and turned around and hurried to the *Kulturhuset* (Culture House) where they have a library. (You can also check your e-mail at the cyber-café down in the cellar. I had no mail). This is the essence of what I learned: In the 1970s Stockholm went on an ambitious, hell-bent campaign to clean up the city's waterways that course and flow through and around the 14 islands upon which the great city rests. And guess what? Despite government involvement the results were environmentally spectacular! You can now bathe nearly in front of city hall (without fear of contracting E-coli or eczema), or if you would prefer to angle, you can fish right off the downtown bridges. Thrashing specimens the size of Saabs are routinely pulled from the waters in the heart of downtown *and* you can even eat the fish. Now, if the Stockholmers could only put an end to the layers of litter that swirl with tornadic fury through the wonderful shopping districts making downtown Stockholm resemble London.

* * *

Fishing, swimming, skiing -- sports of any kind -- Swedes are fanatical. And they are remarkably athletic and fit. This I know up close and personal as Ingebounce invited me to a friendly volleyball game that had been arranged by her co-workers at Ving Alpin. The teams were made up of well-muscled stallions, curvaceous young crumpet -- and me. And if no one has ever told you, may I be the first, Swedes are known for their extreme good looks. This statement will make more sense in a moment. Anyway, I explained to Ingebotch that I thought I might not fit in. She assured me in an oddly insightful way: 'Oh, but you will. Swedes are friendly to foreigners -- they just aren't friendly to each other.'

We met at a gym somewhere, I don't know the location as I was taken there blindfolded (and already suffering from Stockholm Syndrome). The game was fought valiantly and I'll never forget it. Not because of the sterling play on both sides but because of what transpired afterwards. I threw in the towel early on account of a dicky leg and headed for the steamy showers. Halfway through lathering up, Ingebare walked in -- stark-buck naked. Well, you can imagine my joy. I thought our platonic relationship had suddenly taken a dramatic turn for the worst, when in jiggled the rest of the tour guides -- also bare-arsed. I shot a glance around the shower at all the perfect physical specimens lathering and thrashing about like Super Fish. The women had firm, perky bodies right out of *Sports Illustrated* -- the Swimsuit Issue. The men had rippling Greek-god physiques right out of the saucy, glossy *Horse & Stud*. Alas, here, too, I was going to have to throw in the towel, not because of the dicky leg, though, this time because of a dicky dick.

There's an opinion floating around that Swedes are sexually freer and more liberated than Britons or Americans (or most of the rest of the world for that matter -- except the Danes, of course). But I don't know. One thing I do know is that Swedes are shamelessly immodest regarding taking their clothes off. If you weren't at the volleyball game, all you have to do is go down along *Mälerenstrand* (downtown beach) on a sunny afternoon where topless and nude bathing is de rigueur.

To further drive home my point, let me recount a memorable firsthand experience for you. I had a date. Surprise, I know. I met the young lady while holding open a door. Her name was Ragnhilde. No remarks, please. We made plans to go to the amusement park in the *Djurgården* and share a small beer. Ragnhilde looked a lot like the lead singer in Roxette (yes, she had the look) and had dimples like fjords. I was to pick Ragnhilde up at her mother's in the suburb of Solna. Since I've always been a bloke with a lot of time on my hands, and the sun had come out and the weather was behaving, I decided to walk the whole way, stopping only to check my e-mail at the *Stadsbibliotek* (city library). Still no mail. When I arrived at Ragnhilde's, I knocked on the door and the mother answered it. 'Oh, you must be Jon,' she sang. The mother was shockingly young and attractive and spoke that lovely trilling strain of English that so many Swedes do. 'Come right in now.

69

Ragnhilde awaits you.'

'I'm in here!' came the distant sound of Ragnhilde's voice. 'Come. Come. Come.'

I followed the sound of her voice down a long, poorly lit hall, opened a narrow door and watched in joyous horror as Ragnhilde stepped from the bubbly bath in all her glory. 'You're early!' she squealed.

About now, her gorgeous mother walked in. And here's the thing: While Ragnhilde stood there in the drop-jaw buff, *bending over* the sink and putting on her makeup, all three of us carried on a casual conversation as if we were sitting at some moody café in the *Gamla Stan*, listening to Ace of Base and discoursing the plot points in an Ingmar Bergman movie. On this, Ragnhilde's cat strolled in, rubbed up against my leg and I almost had an orgasm.

* * *

Let me close on this: If you have never been to Stockholm -- trust me on this one -- go. And go soon. But don't go as a tourist -- see if you can slip behind those recycled guidebook pages.

* * *

WHAT NOBODY WILL TELL YOU:

It's a law in Sweden that you drive with your car headlights on at all times. Even in the middle of summer when it stays light for almost 24 hours.

Up until 1967, Swedes 'drove on the left' (like they do in the UK). When the Swedes finally changed, the brave and possibly ill-advised souls did so from one day to the next. And people took picnic lunches and blankets (and expensive bottles of beer) and set up at busy intersections and roundabouts and watched as the chaos unfolded.

Imagine.

* * *

What?

You want what?

You want to know about that date with Ragnhilde?

Okay, then.

70

We spent a lovely afternoon together at the café in the tree-lined *Djurgården* -- and Ragnhilde asked me if I wanted children.

'Now?' I said.

'No, eventually. And I want a great big house and two Volvos and I never want to have to leave my great big house.'

'You don't like to travel?'

'Hate it. Hope I never have to go anywhere near a car, boat or plane.'

'What about the two Volvos?'

'I just want them,' Ragnhilde said.

'Cheque, please,' I said sadly.

CHAPTER 9 - The Basque Country: ETA terrorists blow the author out of bed and a career in *poubelle*

If you want to venture to the end of the earth, without actually having to venture to the back of beyond, you need travel no farther than the Basque Country in northwest Spain and southwest France. You see, virtually everything about the Basques is unique, distant and mysterious: their origin, their language, even their blood type.

They don't call themselves Basque, rather *Euskaldunak*. Their country is *Euskal-Herria*. Their language *Euskara*. Where they came from, nobody knows. What we do know is that Basques were living in the Pyrénées Mountains and in the foothills fronting the Bay of Biscay long before the Gauls and Iberians settled near them. Some scholars put the Basques in situ in the Pyrénées as long as 70,000 years ago. Other more conservative folk trace them only as far back as the Cro-Magnon man (for those of you who didn't get your A Levels in anthropology -- or O Levels, for that matter -- that could mean somewhere in the area of 10,000 to 40,000 years ago). However you look at it, the Basques are the oldest identifiable ethnic group surviving in Western Europe.

If you wish to peek beyond the horizons of Western Europe, you will find that the Basque language is the oldest tongue in the world and has no known origin. Scholars have tried to link Basque with Berber (northern Africa), Old Egyptian, Celtic, Iberian, Pictish (extinct language formerly spoken in Scotland), Etruscan (ancient Etruria in Italy), Minoan (Bronze Age, Crete), Sumerian (lower Babylonia), the Finno-Ugric languages (comprises various languages spoken in Hungary, Lapland, Finland, Estonia and parts of western Russia), the Hamito-Semitic languages (Afro-Asiatic), with Burushaski (spoken in the Himalayas) -- in fact, with almost all the languages of Africa and Asia, living and dead, and even with the languages of the North American Indian.

Nowadays, you may only hear Basque spoken by the older generation in the hinterlands of the Pyrénées and in back rooms and corners of smoky bistros, but there is a concerned scheme in place in Basque schools to keep the language alive and flourishing. Until recently, Basque lacked a vocabulary for talking about things like physics and engineering -- simply because nobody had the remotest desire to talk about physics or engineering.

If you would like to see what a little of the Basque language looks like, have a peep here: *zuritoa* would be 'small beer', *eguzki* is 'sun', *etxe* means 'house', *ur* is 'water', *zuhaitz* is a 'tree', and my favourite *harrijasotzaile* is 'weight lifter' (what else could it mean?).

If perhaps you think the Basque *language* is etymologically unique, wait until you check out this serology report: The Basques have the highest frequency of blood type O and the lowest incidence (virtually nonexistent) of blood type B in all of Europe. Moreover, they have the highest Rh-negative factor of *any* of the world's peoples. Simply stated, the Basques constitute a race of people different from you or me, anybody you see walking down the street, even in London (unless you are walking in front of Meson Bilbao, 33 Malvern Road, NW6 5PS), or any other peoples now in existence on the planet.

When I first visited the Basque Country, I based myself on

the French side of the Pyrénées in the sun-drenched old-world fishing town of St-Jean-de-Luz. I spent a week casing glitzy Biarritz, smoggy Bayonne and St-Jean-Pied-de-Port with its colourful outdoor market. Then, I hopped on a train and headed ten kilometres to the Spanish frontier and crossed the border into the Spanish Basque region. Here I explored San Sebastian, world-renown for its film-festival (and crime), and I hiked up into the foothills and toured a few picturesque mountain villages, frozen in time, high up in the Pyrénées. Now, upon my return, I've based myself once again in picturesque St-Jean-de-Luz.

* * *

Night was falling by the time I booked into the Hôtel Continental, so I dumped my bag and set happily off in search of dinner.

I walked over to the high street, rue Gambetta, hoping to find a Basque restaurant. I had my stomach set on traditional Basque cuisine as it is generally considered to be some of the best the world has to offer, but I had concerns about finding a restaurant open before the start of the summer season.

I strolled along rue Gambetta acutely aware that I was the only soul about. Had I come to the Basque Country too early? Not only were there no traditional Basque restaurants open, there we no restaurants of any cuisine open. In fact, there were no businesses open, so I dove down a dark alley with fog rolling up it, wondered about the crime rate in the French Basque Country, slipped through a warren of narrow lanes and ended up at the harbour.

The harbour was fronted by decaying façades, all a complimentary blend of Moorish and Spanish Andalucían, and all the cabernet-coloured shutters on all the houses were already closed for the night. The town must have looked exactly like this for the past hundred years. Lynne Ramsay could film a period piece here and nothing would have to be changed to capture the era.

Adjacent to the harbour my luck changed. I spotted the warm and beckoning Txalupa restaurant. With a name like that, it had to be Basque, and perhaps a young Basque woman would be my waitress and she would be stunning and intelligent and have somehow reached an eligible age without any suitors and would be attracted to a schmuck like me who had nothing to offer other than a fertile imagination.

I plunged in and was immediately struck by the restaurant's charm -- dark, moody, candlelit -- and it was here I heard my first Basque. But it wasn't coming from an adorable Basque lass, rather two dangerous looking men over in a shadow-filled corner. When they saw me, they suddenly stopped, and one of the men came at me in a confrontational manner -- and pointed to a great table by the front window.

I took a seat, as the other thug, with a tanned, chiselled face, approached me, lit a candle on my table and handed me a menu. Then both men repaired to the shadowy corner and discoursed in Basque once again, while eyeing me. Were they weighing if I would be a good match for that one remaining daughter?

I wanted to ask these two rogues if that was the case, but I was afraid I might end up having a testicle excised and batted about in a heated game of jai-alai.

The menu was swimming with Basque delicacies, so I wrote some of them down for you: *Makailoa Pil-Pil Modura* (Pil-Pil Cod, which is cod served in a gelatinous white sauce with garlic), *Koxkera Moduan* (Hake with Prawns and Shellfish), *Bacalao* (Salt Cod), *Marmitako* (Bonito, Potatoes, Onions, Peppers and Tomatoes), *Txangurro* (Spider Crab) and *Txirlas* (Baby White Clams). If those first choices didn't make your mouth water, there was also Pig's Feet and Beef Tongue (skinned). These entrées you will not easily find back home, I dare say.

When by the sea, order seafood, so in the spirit of adventure I ordered the *Txirlas*. They tasted heavenly. And I drank a sharp-tasting green Basque wine called Txakoli (made from under-ripe grapes) and through the wonders of alcohol I somehow felt the night was exceedingly perfect -- other than the lack of female companionship, of course.

* * *

The next morning was warm, and the fog had lifted, so I had an espresso at a stand-up bar and was about to set off to explore the town when I was drawn down a lonely street by the aroma of fresh bread. Having a keen interest when it comes to baked goods with embedded chocolate, I had no trouble finding the *patisserie*. I purchased a *pain au chocolat* and then returned to the lonely street. This is when I noticed something else. Next door was a Basque estate agent. The agency was called Agence Acotztarra and the building was hopelessly rundown. How can you flog property out of a building that is next on the list of buildings to be condemned?

This was too good to pass up, so I entered. Inside, I found a middle-aged Basque woman almost as rundown as the façade of her building. Her name was Madame Agur and she was snoozing, head back, mouth open, breasts heaving, uvula flapping. Talk about a sleepy coastal resort. When she heard the door slap shut, she sprang up. '*Mon Dieu, un client!*' she shrieked. 'Let me get you a coffee.'

You're the one who needs the infusion of caffeine, I'm thinking.

When she returned, she handed me a coffee in a cup the size of a soup bowl, and said: 'Speak.'

This wasn't part of my game plan, finding a flat through an agency, but this woman was so intriguing. Plus, I wanted her for my future mother-in-law, but chances were slim, I decided. On her desk was a family picture and she had only boys.

I told the Madame that I was in the hunt for a modest, dirt-cheap flat, something that would be easy to find if let's say for some reason I got lost. She said she had a wonderful F3 on Boulevard Thiers. It was across from the beach. 'If you can find the Atlantic Ocean, you can find your way home.'

I liked the reasoning, and I loved this woman, so I took the F3, not knowing what an F3 was.

Just so you know, an F3 has *three* bedrooms (and it was indeed 'dirt-cheap' because it looked as if it hadn't been occupied since the liberation of Paris), so the lone traveller settled into a flat the size of, well, a jai-alai court on the second storey of a traditional Basque house called Villa Pablito. The walk up the three flights could suck the life out of you almost as much as that last sentence.

I had never lived alone in a three bedroom flat. If I was bored of an evening and wanted a little domestic adventure, I would sleep in a strange bedroom. I would rotate. It's like goldfish. It is said their attention span is so short that each time they swim around the bowl they get a whole new thrill. That's the way it was with me changing bedrooms.

* * *

St-Jean-de-Luz is famous for its fishing (the Basques were the first to take up whaling, even before the Icelanders), its talented-in-battle sailors (they scared the living shit out of foreign sailors and pirates alike) and for the marriage of Louis XIV to Marie-Thérèse (temporarily delayed on account of randy Louis and his aching passion for his mistress).

Today, St-Jean-de-Luz, with its long crescent of golden sand, old port, café-lined Place Louis XIV and medieval narrow lanes, is one of the busiest coastal resorts in all of France in high season. This translates: If you are planning a holiday in July or August -- don't. The town is anything but sleepy. Prices rise by at least 50% and many hotels are booked with regular summer guests who have been summering here since the revolution. Go in September. The water is still warm, the grockles have gone back up north and the gouging has subsided.

But I wasn't going to make it to September if I didn't find employment, gainful or otherwise, so I rang up the local *bureau de placement*.

How far could I get at an employment agency without a visa or work permit? In Austria I was given a visa because the ski school needed English speakers, but that certainly wouldn't be the case here.

Surprisingly, a voice on the other end of the phone set up an appointment for the next morning and gave me directions. This was cause for celebration, I decided (in a town of 13,000 there had to be some sort of glamorous-menial job for someone illegal like me), so with security looming on the morrow's horizon I hustled down to the local market and splashed out the equivalent of one pound on a bottle of red Basque wine called Irouléguy. It even had a cork.

During the night someone blew up the police station just down the street. The blast rocked me from my bed and I didn't sleep a wink after that. Had things changed? Was ETA now operating on the French side of the border, as well? This didn't bode well.

At the employment agency, I got off on the wrong *pied* by referring to the twenty-something receptionist as 'Madame' instead of 'mademoiselle'. This apparently was about the worst thing I could have said to her except *vache* or possibly *putain*. I apologised, but suddenly I was fair game. And she was the huntress. What ruled her temperament? Pride? Vanity? Insecurity?

Why position a loose cannon on the front line?

Then, a man who resembled Truman Capote called me into his office and interviewed me. Truman was immensely friendly and radiantly nelly (and this made me feel better -- the 'immensely friendly' part) and the impression I received was that this agency was willing to enlist anyone -- visa or not -- who could fog a mirror. They didn't care that my French was crap, and they didn't ask for any identification or papers, they apparently just wanted to throw as much pasta up against the wall as they could and hope one of us would stick.

And I found this somehow refreshing.

After the interview, Truman explained the rules which went something like this: 'There's a bulletin board in the hall by the front door. At exactly nine o'clock each morning I post a list of jobs that have become available. You be here at nine o'clock tomorrow morning. If you qualify, take your interview slip and simply go apply.'

'What if there are other people here?'

'It's first-come, first-served. Whoever gets there first gets the job.'

The next morning I awoke early and headed over to the employment agency. I wanted to be the first one there, but upon arrival I was surprised to find someone had beat me to it. Dozing on the neighbouring steps in front of a taxi rank was a Basque version of Ronaldo. '*Bonjour*,' came a sleepy but distinctly cheery voice. '*Je m'appelle Iñaki.*'

'My name's Jon,' I said, greeting Iñaki, and we did the French handshake thing.

'Hope like hell we get a job today.' His usage of 'we' was not lost on me. 'Don't have anywhere else to sleep,' he went on. 'So I sleep here.'

I felt sorry for Iñaki. At least I had a place to lay my head.

Iñaki reached into the pocket of his jeans, pulled out a series of various length cigarette butts and offered me my choice on his outstretched palm: '*Tu fumes?*'

I shook my head.

I watched as he picked through his cache until he found one that seemed of special interest then with deep concentration lit the remains of the fag and inhaled the smoke blissfully. The smoke, which was gone for an awfully long time, eventually emerged from his nostrils like a genie out of a lamp. Iñaki sprawled on the steps as if he were lounging in the middle of his gran's feather bed. He might have been indigent but there was no mistaking it, Iñaki had a splendid air of dignity.

We talked for a while and Iñaki asked me why I had come to the Basque Country. I told him about being in Stockholm and how I desperately needed the sun, and I told him about how I had always been intrigued with the Basques.

Iñaki took a thoughtful drag on his cigarette, then smiled: 'Let me recount a little story.' Iñaki went on to tell me that his father had been born in Spain, in the Basque town of Guernica, and was just a boy when the Luftwaffe used incendiary bombs to destroy over 70% of the city and test their newly conceived burnt-earth tactics. Dictator Francisco Franco had been threatened by the Basque strong sense of separate identity and the flourishing Basque nationalism. Since Guernica was the most ancient town of the Basques, the centre of their cultural tradition and the symbol of their nation, Franco essentially let the Germans experiment on the Basques. After the razing of Guernica there was a mass exodus of Basques from Spain. Many emigrated to England, Belgium, Switzerland, South America, even the States. Iñaki's grandparents chose southwestern France. They didn't consider it abandoning their homeland, as it really wasn't another country, it was still the *Pays Basque*.

I asked Iñaki if his father returned to Guernica after it was rebuilt.

'My grandparents did. My father didn't.'

'Why not?'

'He met my mother here.'

'What does your father speak with your mother, Spanish or French?'

Iñaki gave me a funny look. 'He speaks Basque.'

About now, the lights came on inside the employment agency, and the receptionist-from-hell thundered over and flung open the front doors. We went in and soon after about ten equally desperate souls arrived and started circling the bulletin board like sharks. We spent the next half hour eyeing each other and jockeying for position.

At precisely nine o'clock, an office door opened and out stepped Truman. Truman was holding a single sheet of paper between his index finger and thumb as if he were carrying a dead mouse by the tail. I greeted him, but he ignored me and hurried past like a priest about to give last rites (or on his way to the rectory to molest choir boys).

Truman tacked the sheet of paper on the board. It read: 'No Jobs Today'.

An employment agency with no job possibilities?

My funds were drying up quickly, so in the spirit of conservation I hustled down the street to a Bait & Tackle shop and bought a cheap *canne à pêche*. To my are-you-shitting-me surprise, I was not only able to buy the fishing rod in the shop, but a litre of Basque wine, as well.

It was low tide, so I scraped blue mussels off the sea wall.

Then I baited my hook and cast. It was not a bad cast for a first cast. It landed in the water. And that evening, with the weather changing, I felt my luck was changing, as well, for I feasted on wafer-thin mullet and full-bodied Irouléguy.

A deepening Atlantic front swept in during the night and it was rainy and cold when I awoke the next morning. Typical coastal *Pays Basque* mercurial start-to-the-summer weather. Down along the front, force-eight winds lashed the prom, while a piercing rain drilled into the golden crescent of sand that is a hallmark of St-Jean-de-Luz.

After I showered and dressed, I wrestled my umbrella all the way down to the little *patisserie* next to Madam Agur's estate agency. I bought two *pain au chocolat*, waved at the Madame and hurried off to procure two steaming cappuccinos at the standup coffee bar.

Iñaki's eyes lit up when I handed him his breakfast. 'These are the best *pain au chocolat*,' Iñaki said. 'They are made with heaps of butter, but the secret is that it's unsalted butter. *Merci*, Jon.'

'Did you get wet last night?'

'No, I was dry.'

'I have a spare bedroom if you need a place to stay,' I said. 'No charge.'

'Thanks, *mon ami*, but I've moved onto a friend's boat.'

Soon the sharks arrived and when the doors opened we all hurried inside. At nine o'clock a door down the hall creaked opened and we wrung our hands in dreaded anticipation as Truman solemnly walked down the hall toward us carrying another dead mouse. He tacked a single sheet of paper on the bulletin board.

There was one job listed.

Because it was in French, it took me longer than the sharks to decipher. The job was at La Pergola. Hey! That was a gigantic apartment complex not far from where I fished. A little voice told me everything was going to turn out okay.

The job description was *Sortez la poubelle -- demi-temp*, which essentially meant 'Dumping the garbage -- part-time'.

I could do this!

I turned to see what Iñaki's reaction to the job was, but he was already racing out the door with the sharks. That's when I remembered Truman's words 'Whoever gets there first, gets the job'.

I ran out the door and yelled: '*Attendez moi!*' When that didn't work, I thought of the sister-aunts and yelled something that I knew would be one-hundred-percent effective, I yelled: 'Taxi!!!'

That was in the morning and I arrived well ahead of Iñaki and the sharks and I was offered the job. But later that night, Basque separatists planted a bomb in the skip and blew a portion of La Pergola and my career in *poubelle* sky high.

The sun was shinning brightly when I went back to the employment agency on the third day. Iñaki was of course already there. He was sucking on a fag and had a big grin on his face.

'That taxi manoeuvre was *fantastique,*' he laughed. 'You really got me. But *attention!* the next job will be mine!'

I told Iñaki how I became unemployed before I was even employed.

'*Oui*, I heard about that bombing.'

'That's two in one week. Thought there wasn't any ETA activity on this side of the border.'

'Here in France few favour an independent state or secession. It's not like it is in Spain. But ETA or not there are little pockets of zealots. Supposedly, they come down here from Bayonne, but I'm not so sure.'

Iñaki gently extinguished his cigarette by drawing little circles in ash on the pavement, then put the remains back in his pocket.

'You know when my father left Guernica he left everything behind except his dignity. Dignity is something my father taught me to hang on to no matter what.'

Iñaki looked me straight in the eye. 'I am Basque. And I am proud. I may sleep here on the steps or on a boat but things will turn around. We will not be beaten.'

Iñaki regarded a bird soaring free and high above for a moment, then turned back to me. 'How do you think my race has survived for so long?'

At nine o'clock the list of jobs was hung on the bulletin board. Two jobs were up for grabs this time. The first job was for a *plongeur* or *plongeuse*. This meant 'male diver' or 'female diver', which was slang for 'pearl diver' and a pearl diver was really a dishwasher. The other job was calling for a *ladanse-contact*. I didn't know what *ladanse-contact* was and didn't have time to look it up in the little French/English dictionary I always carried with me, but Iñaki quickly advised me: 'Take this *ladanse-contact* job. You're made for it! And remember, never let anyone take away your dignity.'

On that, Iñaki bolted out the door already in front of the sharks.

Curiously enough, everyone went left toward the pearl diver job. Nobody went right toward the job I wanted. This is often the way things go in my life. All the salmon are swimming upstream with serious intent and I'm cruising downstream on my way to the beach, asking 'What's up?'

When I arrived at the mystery job, I noticed that the venue was a Parisian-style nightclub and other applicants were already there sitting in an outer lounge area near the box office. I guess 'whoever gets there first, gets the job' didn't apply here.

Since I had some time before my name was called, I took out my little dictionary and decided to look up just what it was that I was applying for. I haven't learned much in life, but one thing I have learned is it's an immense help when interviewing if you know which job you are applying for. '*Lad* ... Hmmm. *Ladan* ...' I was having trouble finding it. I glanced up. For some reason all eyes in the room were on me. A big-busted young woman, trying to keep from laughing, leaned over and pointed at my dictionary: 'You're in the "Ls", you want to be in the "Ds".' On this, all the other young women screamed with laughter, then shaking their heads, went back to scouring magazines and filing their nails. What were the salmon up to?

I searched further for the word and there it was, I'd finally

found it: *D-A-N-S-E-C-O-N-T-A-C-T*. And *danse-contact* meant -
- 'lap dancing'.

I looked up from my dictionary and everyone was peeping
at me with something between deep admiration and
anatomically inspired curiosity. Up until that moment it hadn't
dawned on me that I was the only male in attendance. One
young woman, with platinum hair, was leering over her copy of
Paris-Match at me. A different young lady, in a theatrically
skimpy outfit, seemed to be inordinately amused by her copy of
Elle. Yet another woman, with almost no clothes on at all, had
to put her Basque-language daily newspaper *Euskaldunon
Egunkaria* down on the coffee table so she could gain control of
her twitching facial muscles.

Quietly, I closed my dictionary, stood up, and with great
dignity (like Iñaki had advised), ran from the room.

* * *

The following day was windy and wild and I went down to the
port and tried to get some work on the fishing boats. The
Basques as usual were friendly, but it was family and friends
who crewed and fished. It was a tight-knit group in tight-knit
sweaters. I went over to the boatyard, but there was no work
for me there, either. It was only when I was shuffling tail-
between-legs out of the *chantier* that an older Basque man,
wearing a red beret, and not the traditional black, approached.

'*Monsieur, vous cherchez travail?*' he asked, as a gust of wind
buffeted us.

I said that I was indeed looking for work.

'*J'ai quelque chose pour vous.*'

'You have some work for me?'

I asked the friendly little man if we could *tu toiyer* and he said
that he was in a particularly good mood and I could use the
'familiar'.

'How would you like to scrape the barnacles off the bottom
of my boat?'

I glanced at the surging harbour. 'Is your boat in the water?'

'The dry dock.'

'When can I start?'

It was a tub of a boat, but I treated her as if she were the Royal Yacht *Britannia* (before the decommission). After scraping the barnacles, the Basque gentleman in the red beret put the boat in the water and then asked me to bleach the teak, sand and finish all the varnish on the cabin, paint the transom and repair the cap rails, and suddenly much of the summer had passed, and I'd been working straight through. And then one sunny afternoon I was on my way home from the port when I heard a cheery voice, '*Salut*, Jon!'

I looked across the street and saw Iñaki. He was wearing a red beret like my employer at the boatyard.

'*Salut*, Iñaki. *Ça va?*

I crossed the street and we shook hands.

'I'm going to kill you for that!'

Iñaki roared.

'Hey, I got that pearl diving job and I've already been moved up to waiter. The *garçon* got sacked because he had been surfing.'

'For surfing?'

'*Oui*. The *garçon* was waiting tables and leaned over to place the entrée on the table. This is when his nosed drained from all the salt in his sinuses. Bit of a bad scene.' Iñaki became thoughtful for a moment. 'Wouldn't have been so bad if the guest had ordered the white sauce with his entrée.'

'*C'est dégoûtant!*' I laughed, then told Iñaki how I had run from my job interview *with dignity*.

'You have learned well, *mon ami*.' Then: 'Tonight, Jon. You come to my restaurant. It's Chez Pablo, at 5 rue Mademoiselle-Etcheto. Dinner, he is on me.'

Well, I went that night, and I sat at a candlelit table and dined like Louis XIV. Iñaki served me Sheepherder's bread and the Basque specialty *Txipirones*. For the discerning I should tell you that *Txipirones* is squid served in its own ink (better that than the white sauce). Believe it or not the squid was divine, but for a moment I did think I was back in Iceland.

And Iñaki kept my glass filled with my new favourite green wine, Txakoli. For dessert I had *Gâteau Basque*, and afterwards I stayed with the green alcohol theme and drank highly lethal, green Izzara (a brandy-based liqueur made from the wild flowers of the Basque Country).

It seemed too generous that Iñaki should pay, so I offered. But he would have none of it. Unlike Iceland, tipping is gladly accepted in the Basque Country, so I did leave a *pourboire*, and then when Iñaki was finished for the evening, we walked through the warm night air and over to the Pub du Corsaire just around the corner from the harbour where we drank more Izzara, my treat.

And it really didn't surprise me that Iñaki and I became friends. And it doesn't surprise me that we are still good friends. You see, those dark mornings back on the steps of the employment agency, possessing nothing, and with nothing to share but our stories, we formed some sort of bond that will last till the end of time.

As will the Basques.

* * *

WHAT NOBODY WILL TELL YOU:

In 1937, to punish the Basques for siding with the Republicans in the Spanish Civil War, General Francisco Franco not only abolished the rights of the Spanish Basques but had the very speaking of Basque declared illegal.

The word for 'beret' in Basque is *txapela*. Traditionally, the Basques wear a black beret. If you ever see a Basque wearing a red beret, it means it is a festive occasion and cause for celebration.

CHAPTER 10 - The Basque Country: My landlord tells me how he almost became the Lee Harvey Oswald of France

Iñaki told me of a job going at the Hôtel du Palais, ten kilometres up the coast in Biarritz. Apparently, anyone with the IQ of a cephalopod could telephone the hotel director and set up an interview.

(FYI: The Hôtel du Palais was built by Napoleon III as a *summer* palace for his wife, the Empress Eugénie. I guess it's good to have a little beach chalet so you have somewhere to store your bucket and spade).

Communication devices were not part of the interior decor in Villa Pablito, so I scooted down the street to the Château Basque, a three-star hotel that treated you like shit so you had the sensation of being in a snooty five-star establishment.

I entered a booth resembling a confessional and dialled the Hôtel du Palais. The phone was answered on the other end and I told some woman that my French was not all that good and the woman didn't say anything back, so I kept on talking. In my usual waffling way, I went on to say that I was applying for a certain position and that I was sincerely responsible and

87

promised not to drink on the job and that I would be punctual and that as a child I had always allowed the dog on the couch when my parents left me alone in the house. The nice lady on the other end listened and listened, responding from time to time with a kindly cooing sound and the odd *Mon Dieu!* After fifteen minutes of presenting my case, this exceedingly patient woman said: 'Have you ever thought about trying to get a job at the Hôtel du Palais?'

'You aren't the hotel?'

'No, this is a private residence.'

'Oh.'

'I wish you *bonne chance* finding a job.'

'*Merci.*'

Click.

I dialled the correct number to the Hôtel du Palais this time and heard '*Hôtel du Palais, j'écoute.*' And was told to 'Hold, please.'

I held. And held. Need I go on? Okay, I held way past that 'have-they-forgotten-all-about-me' length.

Eventually the receptionist returned and said: '*Hôtel du Palais, j'écoute.*' I asked to speak to the director. She said: 'Hold, please.'

I held.

Five minutes went by. A different voice came on the line: '*Hôtel du Palais, j'écoute.*'

In my best and most polite French, I made it known that I had been holding, growing older, forgotten, given up for dead, was calling long distance and could I speak to the director, *S'il Vous* fucking *Plaît!* Eventually, I spoke to the director's secretary and somehow I understood what she said. I was thrilled, but there were logistic concerns. I would have to be in Biarritz at eight o'clock sharp the next morning. 'The director expects all his staff to be punctual,' the secretary had stressed.

My mind was spinning with pending adventure (and once again waning funds) as I hurried across the marbled foyer of the snooty little hotel and aimed for the rococo main entrance. That's when I heard a disturbed voice screech: '*Monsieur? Vous payez?*'

88

I turned and saw an emperor penguin, with an attitude, waddling toward me. It was the concierge. He was Parisian, and he glared at me as if I were slipping out of the Louvre with Mona under my raincoat.

'*Pardon, Monsieur. J'ai oublié,*' I said, and handed the penguin my twenty euros.

'What is that, Monsieur?'

'That's a twenty-euro note.'

'*Ce n'est pas assez,*' said the concierge. 'You pay fifty euros.'

'Fifty euros! I didn't phone the bloody moon.'

The concierge fixed me with a stupid-foreigner look: 'The moon would have been cheaper.

* * *

Eager to make a good impression the following day, I took my one-and-only white shirt (funerals and interviews -- same shirt, same emotions), washed it and hung it out on my balcony to dry. Then I slid down the banister to the ground floor and asked my landlady if I could borrow her iron.

My elderly landlady and her mousy little husband were happy to help. They were always happy to help. They liked me. And I was fond of them, as well, even though they were just a bit peculiar. My landlady had clinically questionable eyesight yet she insisted on still motoring around in her Deux Chevaux. She would tool up to Biarritz or down to the frontier at Hendaye or even to the *Zone Franchise* (tax-free zone) up in the Pyrénèes near the Spanish border to purchase cases of Irouléguy and Armagnac.

And husband Martial was not run-of-the-flipping-mill either. Martial had Paul Newman eyes, and was the shy, quiet type, yet I often saw him out in the back garden doing push-ups on his fists. Yes, you heard right, on his fists. This aerobic peculiarity made me just a hair nervous (the man was not young). Mousy he might have looked but I knew in the back of my mind he was the type of guy you wanted on your side if trouble ever erupted.

'*Est-ce-que tu veux diner avec nous, ce soir,* Jon?' my landlady said.

Just what the doctor ordered. A rigorous home meal, French

elocution lessons and a good night's sleep. But please, I prayed (and I didn't want to be an ingrate here), anything but seafood!

And it was an exquisite dinner. I would say that the little Madame really outdid herself -- but I didn't know what she was capable of. There was course after lovely course of *Moules à la Poulette* (mussels with shallots and white wine, stuffed with tomato fondue), *Salade de Crevettes* (shrimp salad) and *Pâté au Saumon*. Every calorie, every milligram of cholesterol, every rubbery morsel -- from the sea. But we consumed enough Irouléguy to decimate a small vineyard, so nothing else mattered.

Then they proposed a toast. '*C'est à toi*, Jon.'

'*Moi*?'

'You know we moved here from Paris many years ago. We may be old, but we still have a good memory -- a good memory for dates. Let me recount a little history for you. The 6th of June 1944, D-Day. The 4th US Infantry Division was the first allied unit to land on Normandy Beaches. They landed at Utah Beach. They fought for 26 days and lost 5,000 boys. The remainder of the 4th US Infantry Division helped to liberate Paris. The Nazi flag was ripped down from the Eiffel Tower. We were there when the Americans marched down the Champs Elysées. We watched them. We will never forget those American boys.'

I couldn't speak.

'*Tu es americain*, Jon, and simply for that we toast you.'

I couldn't imagine this coming from the French! Certainly not now. It floored me.

'By the way,' continued the mousy husband, 'we may toast *you*, but your president is still a clown.'

The Madame gave her husband a scolding look. 'We have strong feelings and when we are appreciative we show it,' she said.

'And when we are displeased we show it, as well,' said the little man.

What did he mean by that!

The husband slipped away and retrieved a rather large, thick book from his library and a bottle of golden Armagnac. We each had a prodigious measure of the fiery liquid, and then he opened the book and pointed to a photo of a young man handcuffed and carrying thick stacks of documents. The photo was of him.

I asked what that was all about.

'For trying to assassinate De Gaulle,' he responded.

I just stared back. All I could think of was this elderly gentleman doing push-ups on his fists. I was in the presence of a would-be assassin. And one still fit at his age.

'I joined the S.A.O. because I, like a vast portion of the French population, had become disenchanted with De Gaulle.'

Hadn't they ever heard of the vote, I wondered.

'Being with the organisation, I knew the route of the *cochon*'s (pig's) motorcade and tried to blow him the hell up, but the bomb didn't fully detonate and I was caught hiding in a nearby bistro. I was in the tank for a long time.'

'May I have a few more Armagnacs?' I asked, looking down at the book. There it all was right in front of me. Monsieur Martial de Villemandy, my little mousy landlord, had almost become the Lee Harvey Oswald of France.

I stared at my landlord for a long time, and those blue eyes stared silently straight back and right through me. Then he poured me another Armagnac, and we drank a lot more that night, and it became an awfully late night -- and a night I will never forget.

* * *

As I struggled to make my way back up the steps to my rooftop flat, I remember my dear landlady yelling after me: 'Hold onto the iron. We are leaving early in the morning for the coastal village of Hossegor. We will be gone when you awake. *Bonne nuit*, Jon.'

'*Bonne nuit, Madame. Je vais faire dodo.*' (Inexplicably, I used a child's version: 'I go nighty night.')

I awoke the next morning with that gnawing feeling that something wasn't right. What was the problem? It had been a year since I set out on my quest and I hadn't found anybody to share my life with. Was that it? No, something else less important but pressing in urgency was gnawing.

I peered through clotted slits at my little travel clock. It was almost 7:00 a.m. I closed my slits, rolled over in bed again, then shot bolt upright. Seven o'clock! Bloody hell, my train left at seven-thirty.

What had I done? I'd forgotton to set my alarm. To make matters worse, my head felt about the size of a basketball and there was a slam dunk contest going on inside. Why did I drink like that? I get clinical hangovers!

I quickly showered. That would help. It didn't. I still felt like shit, only now I was wet and cold and felt like shit. I wrapped a towel around my waist and that's when I remembered my one-and-only white shirt. I had forgotten to iron it the night before. I ran to get it off the back balcony -- BUT IT WASN'T THERE!

7:05 a.m.

Panic! Where could it have gone? I looked everywhere. Maybe I had put it back in the wardrobe when I was squiffy, but no! Ah, the curse of drink! I cursed myself. I cursed the shirt. I cursed the clock.

The clock!

The clock was ticking away, and my life was going down the *pissoir*.

It must have been when I was down on my knees, looking under my bed, that I heard the noise. A noise we often hear and it is usually wondrously soothing but not this morning.

It was the wind.

And the wind was wafting at the open French doors of my balcony.

The wind. THE WIND! It was stronger than usual. I screamed a bloodcurdling scream and threw myself at the balcony. Resting down in the back garden, spread-eagle, on top of a patch of crimson bougainvillea was my brand-new, bloody-one-and-only white shirt!

I dashed down the stairs to my landlady's flat. The only access to the garden was through her apartment. As I pounded on the door I had visions of the husband coming to the door, looking at me through sleepy eyes and thinking I looked like De Gaulle. But I had no choice. I pounded again and again, and my head pounded back.

'Damn that wine! Damn that Armagnac!' I yelled, and I think it was right about then that one of the worst feelings I have ever had started to creep over me, for it was at that precise moment I remembered my landlady's angelically smiling face and her soft, cooing voice. 'Hold onto the iron. We will be gone when you wake.'

'*Merrrde!!!*' I flew back up the stairs and blew into my room.

7:12 a.m.

It was hopeless. I was hopeless. I was looking for something to kill myself with when I spotted my fishing rod over in the corner.

My fishing rod!

My five-euro *canne à pêche* was going to save my derrière.

I cast. And I cast.

7:15 a.m.

I cast some more. No luck.

7:16 a.m.

Should I try it with bait? Shit for brains! Concentrate! Cast!

7:17 a.m.

Suicide was starting to seem attractive again, when *fish on!* I snagged it. I reeled. The shirt fought valiantly back. No it didn't, I made that up.

Screw the ironing. I threw my shirt on, grabbed my money and bolted out the door. Normally people only bolt *out* the door, but no, not me. I had to bolt back *in* the door because I forgot the directions on how to get to the Hôtel du Palais.

Once again I bolted back out, took three stairs at a time and leapt out onto the street scaring the complete *crotte* out of my next door neighbour, Madame Saxifraga, and her fluffy angora cat 'Mousse'.

7:20 a.m.

As I sprinted past the Château Basque Hotel, the big grandfather clock in the foyer showed seven-twenty-three. The penguin was already at work. He was just standing there, staring at me, shaking his head. I turned and yelled triumphantly '*Agincourt!*'

I hastened down Boulevard Thiers, then along promenade Jacques Thibaud and eventually came to a shop that repaired watches. Hundreds of silly little clocks screamed at me, and they were all synchronized: 7:25 a.m.

I rounded a corner and headed down rue Gambetta. That's when I started to see clocks everywhere I looked.

TICK. TICK. TICK. TICK.

7:26 a.m.

7:27 a.m.

7:28 a.m.

TICK. TICK. TICK. It was pounding in my ears now. My life was becoming a horror movie (with a lousy storyline). Everything had become clock oriented. As I flew down the street, some heartless scamp, with a twisted mind, even had the impudence to ask me if I knew what time it was.

'To the bloody second!' I screamed.

I rounded another corner and had *La Gare* in my sights. Wouldn't you know it there was a BIG CLOCK on the front of the station and I watched in slow-motion horror as its minute hand dropped like the blade of a guillotine, KLUNK, 7:29 a.m.

I was almost there. I heard the platform conductor blow his whistle, signalling the train's imminent departure. No doubt he was looking at his flaming watch.

I could see the train. The doors were already closed and the train was moving! How could this be?

'French trains don't leave early!' I bellowed. 'THEY DON'T EVEN LEAVE ON TIME!!!' I sprinted. I had to catch it. I needed that job.

I burst past a blur of people waiting on the platform and with all my energy made a mad lunge and grabbed at one of the doors. The door wouldn't open. People stared at me now. Pointed at me. But I didn't care. '*Zut!*' I yelled, and lunged at another door. No good. One more. No use. Then I saw a door that was open. A uniformed conductor stood in the doorway.

He was my salvation. But could I make it in time?

I ran like the wind, leapt wildly --- and just made it. I held on with all my strength and tried to pull myself up. If I fell, I would be crushed by the mighty steel SNCF wheels. People on the platform stopped pointing at me and started screaming.

'Jesus, oh God help me!' I heard myself plead at the top of my lungs. And you know what? Someone with some sort of seniority must have heard because suddenly the train screeched and tons of steel ground to an abrupt halt.

I looked up at the conductor, and he was looking down at me -- and he was trying to keep from laughing. '*Monsieur! Qu'est-ce que tu fais, con?*' he said.

'What do you mean?' I said.

'The train, he is not leaving. He is just arriving. He is late this morning.'

* * *

WHAT NOBODY WILL TELL YOU:

The S.A.O or the Secret Army Organisation (*Organisation de l'Armée Secrète*), was an underground band of disgruntled French who were unhappy with DeGaulle's decision to grant independence to Algeria.

* * *

By the way, I got that job at the hotel in Biarritz. The Director of the hotel interviewed me, but he did all the talking and somehow came to the conclusion that my French was better than it was. I was put on the Reception Desk, answering phones. For the first month, until my French improved (by joking with the waitresses, who found me amusing but nothing more) all I did was answer: '*Hôtel du Palais, j'écoute.*' Then before I was asked a question that I knew I wouldn't understand, I put the caller on hold.

CHAPTER 11 - Paris: Street artists show me the ropes

I had a small problem the first time I went to Paris.

The small problem was a five-foot-four-inch train conductor. Here's the wretched story, and it begins in Nice: Owing to typically jumbled traffic, bad planning on my part and a driving rain storm, I arrived at the *La Gare*, late. There wasn't time to go to the ticket window so I dripped on board, commandeered a seat and waited for the conductor to make an appearance. By the time we pulled into Antibes the conductor still hadn't made it although I could see him punching tickets at the far end of the coach. That's when I was struck with the cockamamie idea to see if I could make it all the way to Paris *without* having to fork out for a ticket. When the train stopped in Cannes, I leapt off, ran down the rain-lashed platform, then jumped back on, but on the other side of where the conductor had already collected tickets. This charade went on until we were well past Marseilles (as did the inclement weather) and passengers must have thought they were lost in *Groundhog Day*, because every time they saw me pass by I was coming from the same direction -- and still dripping wet.

Big problems arose somewhere between Marseilles and Lyon as there was a perilously long interval between stops and I ran out of room on the train to run. Not being able to think of anything more creative, I dived into a first-class toilet and locked the door.

But I had been spotted.

Here's a travel tip: Never under any circumstances underestimate the tenacity of a card-carrying member of the SNCF, the vaunted French railway system. Like a pit bull sniffing out a luckless rat he would not cease and desist.

BANG! BANG! *'Billets, s'il vous plaît!'*

Mortified, and not knowing what to do, I made as if I were sick, but the conductor was not deterred and the pit bull kept coming back to harass the rat. By the time we squealed to a stop in Paris, I actually *was* sick to my stomach.

But that was then, and this is now.

I'm back in Paris.

It's autumn.

And it's still raining.

I found warm and dry, Left Bank accommodation at the Hôtel St-Michel, 17 rue Git-le-Coeur. The price was right, and it was just around the corner from a Tunisian *boulangerie*, the fountain where Balzac pinched water as a boy and the square -- Place Saint-Michel -- where the Resistance put up a furious fight in August of 1944 (presumably when the Germans jumped the queue at the boulangerie).

I paid for the room, one month in advance, and hurried up a winding, carpeted stairwell to the third floor to see where I'd be living. The room was small, tidy and had long windows -- ceiling to floor -- which looked down onto narrow rue Git-le-Coeur. The decor was tired and appeared to be inspired by the gents' at the Moulin Rouge. The closest showers were down three flights. The nearest toilet was on my landing and actually boasted a commode (not an evil hole in the floor), but the space was so confined the only way you could sit on the throne was to do so side-saddle. Not that I sit in these kinds of places (perhaps that was too much information?).

I unpacked my bag, soaked my feet in the bidet to warm them (don't even think about commenting), then hightailed it out of there eager to be out and about. As I left the hotel, a young demoiselle in a ground-floor room (and a diaphanous negligée) flirted with me. And let me tell you something, when a Parisienne flirts with you, you are on the receiving end of *beaucoup de* charm. I glanced back, gave the young lass a '*Salut, ma petite!*' wink and tripped going out the front door.

As I strolled down the street, I thought about the flirting interlude back there. Should I go back and rap gently on her door? Invite her for a coffee? In retrospect she was a bit rough and not exactly my type, but the way things were going, who was I to be choosy?

There's a damn good café, the 'St-Séverin', just around the corner on Boul' Mich' as the locals call boulevard St-Michel. I ordered a *café noir* and watched the usual Parisian-mix dodge puddles. It was now a hurricane outside, but the café was protected by large glass windows that could be quickly opened if the weather did something unusual like suddenly turn agreeable.

This part of Paris was always crawling with students as the Sorbonne is just right there. The area became known as the Latin Quarter because students once thought it chic to sit in the many sidewalk cafés speaking Latin. Nowadays, they think it's chic to sit in the sidewalk cafés speaking English. Many young folk of Paris have zestfully embraced the English language and now secure in their bilingualism can employ the two-pronged attack and be rude to us not only in French but in our mother tongue, as well.

The St-Séverin soon became my warm and dry home and it was good sport to watch the Parisians scurrying by or greeting one another or just kissing. An awful lot of kissing goes on in Paris. Couples just stand there, kissing, oblivious to the harried world around them.

How wonderful.

In Paris, the café is a pillar of society, as important as, say, the pub in England, so this may come as a shock of all shocks, but sipping a hot *café au lait*, cappuccino or *café crème* in a coffeehouse environment is *not* a French invention. This caffeine-infusing phenomenon started in 17th-century Vienna and even was a hit in London long before it caught on in the City of Light.

Did you know that in Paris you can go to a café, order the cheapest coffee on the menu, and then just sit there as long as you want? Nobody will move you on. No one will hurry you. (Chances are nobody will serve you.)

It's a perfect place to start and finish a novel -- even if you are writing it.

Parisian cafés are also serene venues to just chill and read your newspaper or make notes for your travel book or knock back the plonk. But most of all I think cafés in Paris are meant for the observation of unsuspecting members of the opposite sex.

As an experiment, I spent an entire rainy day in the café. I had my breakfast there. And my lunch there. And finally my dinner there. And I christened every toilet, read all the newspapers everyone left behind and watched all the people. And here's the thing -- *my waiter endured me*. And when his shift ended, he didn't rush with hands aflutter to the waiter taking over from him and scream: 'Watch out for that American in the corner, he came early and he just won't leave.'

At least I don't think he did.

One evening I returned home later than usual and found the entryway of my hotel filled with police. I feared they were there to arrest me for café abuse.

I greeted the police and then waited for them to salute me. The gendarmes in Paris always salute you when you approach them to ask a stupid question or obvious directions. But they didn't salute back.

'Hey, I thought the police in Paris always salute,' I said.

'We don't salute anymore,' said one of the policemen. 'New mayor.'

I was about to ask another question, when I peered over their shoulders. This is when I realised they were standing at the entrance to the young Parisienne's room. And something was seriously amiss. Lying face down on the bed, naked, was the young girl.

I turned to one of the *flics* for an answer.

'*Elle est morte*. Overdose.'

* * *

The sun was doing a laser show on my curtains when I awoke to a bright, crisp morning. But the lovely morning did nothing to elevate my mood. The image of the young Parisienne had ricocheted around my brain throughout the night and I hadn't slept well.

As the clock approached the crack of eight, I shivered from bed, wrapped a bath towel (that was more of a loincloth) around my waist and moved slug-like down the two flights to the shower. It was uncommonly quiet and I wondered if I was the only one staying in the hotel. Or alive.

There were two showers on the landing. One on the right. One on the left. The door on the left was ajar so I pulled it open and went inside. I flipped on a switch illuminating a startlingly bright bulb. The shower was the size of a *large* walk-in closet. I've stayed in smaller hotel rooms. Why was the shower so grand and the shitter so petite? I hung my miniature bath towel on a hook and headed east until I came to the shower head. There was no shower curtain and I felt agoraphobically exposed.

The water fluctuated between too hot and too cold, but after a while I adjusted to the *heat!* the *cold!* the *heat!* and soon felt better. When I finished my ablutions, I towelled off and strolled back to the door and turned the doorknob, but the door wouldn't open. I tried it again. Still no use. I tried once more. No go. Sod's Law at play here. Then it occurred to me: *La douche* wasn't included in the price of the room. If I had designs on showering I was supposed to go down to the reception, pay a fee and collect a key to the shower.

And now I was locked in.

I don't know about you but I'm not thrilled when countries charge for personal hygiene. 'Are you going to shower today,

Pierre?' 'No, I think I'd rather conserve the five euros for *la grande dump du jour.*'

I peeped through the keyhole and could see the landing and the stairs leading up from the floor below. I waited. After about fifteen minutes, the hunchback of Notre-Dame's mother came plodding doggedly up the stairs as if she were stomping on a cockroach with each step (in this establishement, that could have been a distinct possibility). When she reached the landing she was so winded she swayed back and forth like a metronome and I thought she was going to topple over.

'*Madame! Madame!*' I shouted. I wanted to secure her aid before she expired. '*Au secours!*'

She stopped and looked around as old folk do when they think they've heard a voice, but then decide they really haven't. Then, rocking in place to jump-start her ascent, she started toward the next flight of stairs.

'Stop you deaf old bat!' I yelled. But it did no good.

Let me cut right to the shrivelling chase here. Forty-five minutes later, count them 45 minutes, a young lovely vision heard my now faint pleas and, laughing all the way down the stairs, went to fetch a key. The only problem was when she came back upstairs and unlocked the door, I wouldn't let her push it open. You see, I was standing there floodlit and with just a swatch of muslin covering my *Honey, Who Shrunk the Kids* maleness.

After much negotiation, and a lot of giggling on the young lass' part, she assured me she would deposit the key on the carpet and repair to her room so I could decamp. When the coast was clear, I made a two-stairs-at-a-time bare-assed dash but encountered curiously familiar laughter upon reaching my landing. Leaning against an open doorway, arms crossed, was the young vision. She was staying in the room across from mine.

* * *

The cheapest entertainment in Paris (other than possibly *Monsieur* Breakfield trapped in in the shower) is *Le Show* located on the tip of the Île de le Cité behind Notre-Dame. I discovered this enchanting venue by chance. One warm evening, a local fisherman fainted (he had actually caught a fish in the Seine) and this caught my eye. When I went to investigate the rare catch of the dace-like *goujon*, I heard applause. Then I heard laughter. The peals of joy drew me farther along the island and this is when I came across *Le Show*.

Le Show is the Paris version of Covent Garden's street entertainers (or Key West's Sunset Celebration). Depending on the day of the week, and the time of the year, you can watch jugglers and fire-eaters and mimes, and listen to musicians, Edith Piaf wannabes, and a fellow from Senegal who sings into a *baguette*. These highly professional street performers come from all over the world, but really anyone who has talent (or a *baguette*) is allowed to perform.

What makes this lively stage all the more special is that the performers ply their art in front of a backdrop that just happens to be one of the world's greatest edifices, the illuminated Cathedral of Notre-Dame.

It is indeed a stunning sight.

Most nights I went to *Le Show* and soon I became acquainted with some of the performers. They worked for tips, and with home often being an old beat-up Citroën van parked down a dark, tree-lined street somewhere, there was no rent to pay and their tax-elusive earnings could be applied to the far more pressing needs of alcohol and drug abuse.

One of the fire eaters told me that before he would swallow the lighter fluid that fuelled his act (and sometimes his hair), he would drink Pepto-Bismol to coat his throat and even his stomach as some of the volatile lighter fluid would inadvertently seep down his esophagus. When he couldn't afford the Pepto-Bismol, he drank red wine. Then he didn't care if his throat was coated or not.

Monsieur Fire Eater also enlightened me to some of Paris' colour. It's good to have reliable sources with impeccable credentials.

'The Bois de Boulogne is a good place to go if you want to pull a transvestite,' he told me.

I assured him I had no such intention, but he waffled on nevertheless. 'Ensure you choose someone you can see clearly in a street lamp. If they're standing in the shadows, he/she is most likely hiding some sort of flaw.'

In an attempt to amuse, I asked what kind of flaw, a hump for instance? But I guess I wasn't amusing because I received only a look of '*Mais, oui*, that sort of thing'.

Mr Lighter-fluid-mouth went on to say that it was prudent to exercise extreme caution in the Bois de Boulogne as it was quite dangerous at night, but then there was always the Bois de Vincennes if I was interested in traditional ladies of the night. I said I wasn't interested. But he wasn't listening, only advising. Too much lighter fluid.

'In the Bois de Vincennes, the hookers work out of vans instead of hotels.'

How novel, HIV-on-Wheels.

* * *

There was a singer/piano player by the name of Paul working *Le Show*, and I became acquainted with him, as well. Paul was a carbon copy of Omar Sharif (in his early days), his style was French/Michael Bublé, and he dressed in a white tuxedo and sat at a white, upright piano. On top of the piano were a candelabra and a vase with a single rose. Street performers beware, Paul had undeniable class. What was even more impressive, Paul's upright piano had wheels and he pushed it through the streets of Paris every evening to get to work. Paul told me that he used to take his piano down the lifts into the Métro and play his way to work, but unfortunately had to abandon his lucrative commute after receiving two verbal warnings from the police and rolled eyes from the fire marshal.

Paul was one of the few performers actually blessed with talent (and mental health) and what's more he knew how to work a crowd. I asked him if he was hoping to break into the big time one day.

'Always had a knack for music,' Paul said, gesturing flamboyantly. 'But computers are my first love. I'm working *Le Show* because I want to save up enough money to buy a new

Apple and the best state-of-the-art graphics programme available.'

* * *

I ran into the young lady who had saved me from my shivering demise again. It was early one chilly morning and I was slipping the five euros I owed her under the door to her room just as she opened it. We were both wearing only towels and grins and were on a goose-bump collision course to the showers. She gave me a flirtatious smile and said her name was Sabena.

'Like the defunct Belgian airliner,' I said. 'Are you Belgian?'

Sabena froze and shot me a bad-dog look. '*Écoutez*, I thought there was only one way to offend someone from Paris. It is if you call them "provincial". *Mais, non, pas toi*, you have just found a second way!' She huffed at me as only the French can. 'And no, I am not Belgian. I was born here. In Paris!'

I meekly apologised and then introduced myself.

'*Eh, voilà!* Do I say to you, oh "John" like an American toilet!'

Colliding cultures.

When we reached the showers, we found one available and one occupied. Since Sabena already had a key, and I was in the dog house, I gestured for her to go first.

'No, after you,' she said.

'Don't have my key yet.'

'Go get one.'

'No, ladies first.'

'I am moving slowly today,' she said. 'Got a bit of a hangover.'

'More reason for you to go first.'

This went on back and forth, like a bad game of tennis on the clay at Roland Garros until she warmed up and we both started laughing. Sabena had big brown eyes -- like an owl -- and some intriguing curves hiding behind her towel.

Being French, and therefore mercurial, she suddenly shifted gears and suggested: 'We could shower together and save five euros.'

Before words of joy could dribble from my lips, the water

running in the occupied shower stopped and out of the steam stepped a tall, rippling-in-muscles French stallion. Sabena and the stallion apparently were acquainted and immediately burst into frenzied French, swapping *bon mots* or whatever it is the French swap. I was always about two verbs behind, and therefore unable to contribute, so when the stallion handed me his key, I just slipped into the shower, turned on the hot/cold water and beat my head on the tiled wall.

* * *

WHAT NOBODY WILL TELL YOU:

Napoleon had instructions issued to the bakers of France to bake breads of a peculiar shape so that his soldiers could more easily carry the coveted staple rolled up in a ground cloth atop a backpack, or even up a trouser leg. The result? A lengthy, slim loaf called -- *la baguette*.

CHAPTER 12 - Paris: Nubile Sabena shows me more than just the ropes

Autumn is a glorious time of the year to haunt Paris.

One morning I awoke to unseasonably warm weather. A high pressure system had invaded France and the humidity was low and the air dry. Clearly, the day was meant for exploring, so I fortified myself at the St-Séverin with a *chocolat chaud*, struggled through *Le Monde*, put it back on the rack with the other newspapers, and then headed up boulevard St-Michel and away from the Seine.

I strolled past St-Germain, the Sorbonne and then past a stone wall completely obliterated with garish posters of belly dancers, underground movies and Algerian food. A sign affixed to the wall above this agglutinated mess read: *DÉFENSE d'AFFICHER.*

I carried on up St-Michel until I reached boulevard Montparnasse. Here, on the corner is the celebrated bistro Le Closerie des Lilas. Paul had given me strict instructions to pay a visit, sit at the left side of the bar and order a champagne julep (as that's what the bistro is known for). Well, you know I couldn't wait to do this. I ordered a heinously priced champagne julep, leaned on a sticky transom and waited. What was supposed to happen? I looked around the bar. The place was a morgue. Nobody was exactly beating down the doors to drink champagne juleps. I glanced down at the surface of the bar, where my sleeve was sticking, and there it was. A small bronze plaque bearing a man's name. This is what Paul wanted me to see. I was sitting where Ernest Hemingway used to sit. What joy! Well, joy that is until I remembered there weren't many bar stools that have not been graced by *Monsieur* Hemingway's derrière.

(FYI: In his revealing and evocative *A Moveable Feast*, Hemingway wrote: 'The Closerie des Lilas was the nearest good café when we lived in the flat over the sawmill at 113 rue Notre-Dame-des-Champs, and it was one of the best cafés in Paris. It was warm inside in the winter and in the spring and fall it was fine outside with the tables under the shade of the trees on the side where the statue of Marshal Ney was, and the square, regular tables under the big awnings along the boulevard.'

It was a good place and a warm place where I could sit all day long on my corpulent butt and write tedious sentences that went on and on and on and employ many 'ands' and few commas while awaiting a steamer to Key West by way of Havana where I could drink real booze at Sloppy Joe's and stuff these champagne juleps and if I wrote long enough and avoided punctuation all together then perhaps I could one day come back in a second life as Frank McCourt...)

I left my champagne julep unfinished -- it tasted like a mimosa with a splash of cat pee -- and walked over to the literary cafés on boulevard Montparnasse.

There are so many wonderful sights to see in Paris. I don't know how anyone can really hope to take them all in without being born there and living to the ripest of old ages. I ambled past Le Dôme, La Rotonde, La Coupole, Le Sélect and then continued up to Rodin's 10-foot statue of Balzac where there was a prostitute union meeting going on. I looked back in the direction I had just come, said 'What the heck' and walked back past the cafés all over again.

It's almost as if you can feel the presence of all the famous people (or at least that's how I wanted it to feel) who were once habitués of these cafés and came here to drink, write, drink, sketch and did I mention drink?

At La Coupole I stopped and went in for an espresso. I found an empty table over in a corner with the best view out onto the street. I watched longingly a young couple standing in front of my window French kissing with the desperation of those who don't share a bed yet, then a snippy, snooty waiter, with a toupee that looked as if it had been removed from the shower drain at my hotel that very morning, moved me on by saying: 'That particular table is always reserved for the same individual and she could be arriving at any moment!'

As I changed tables, all eyes in the café watched me with withering subtext that read: 'We knew better than to look such a tosser.'

Picasso and Dali may have frequented this café as struggling artists, but it was clear no struggling artist could afford to make this his or her haunt now. Nevertheless, it was still goose-bump and spine-tingling to think that this had also been the haven of the likes of F. Scott Fitzgerald (until he switched to the Ritz), Josephine Baker, Henry Miller, John Dos Passos, Hemingway (see?) and hundreds of greater talents who, alas, lacked the grace of God, the marketing aplomb or the will to sleep around.

To annoy the waiter with the toupee by Hudson Reed, I beckoned him with: '*Garçon!*' A French waiter puts up with it when a Parisian calls him *garçon*, but is deeply offended if a foreigner does. A foreigner must call him '*Monsieur*'.

(FYI: If a waitress is ever serving you, *all* women, even those who are married, having Hormone Replacement Therapy or shuffling with a walker are addressed as '*Mademoiselle*'.)

The weather was turning, so I hung around the café for most of the day (I knew my rights), not only to lessen the *garçon*'s quality of life, but to possibly catch a glimpse of the enigmatic *vedette* who belonged to the reserved table. But, alas, the grande dame never materialized -- only a group of Japanese tourists. When hunger set in, I felt it prudent to escape to an eatery where I could dine without having to sell an organ.

(FYI: I found out later the table was reserved for Catherine Deneuve. *Quelle* loss.)

When I stepped outside, I was surprised to see that the morning had magically transformed from a cerulean sky with a comforting golden orb in the middle into an oppressive slate-grey afternoon *sans* orb. The good thing about Paris is, though, you only have to wait till it becomes dark, then, dismal weather or not, millions of twinkling lights flicker on and the city is once again attractive and warm and romantic.

I pulled the world's longest scarf around my neck and headed back down through the Latin Quarter and realised that the Latin Quarter was becoming more of a Greek-Tunisian-Moroccan-Vietnamese quarter. Eventually I popped back out on the lee side of boulevard St-Michel, spontaneously purchased a pair of racy Italian loafers that were on sale at a shop run by a gentleman (with many bad scars on his arms) from Sierra Leone and then stayed on St-Michel until I came to the Seine where a *bateau-mouche* was sliding silently by with a full load of blue-lipped tourists. I watched the boat cleave the placid Seine, then moved on past the *bouquinistes* wondering how they made a living when it rained or when it was too cold to stand outside all day long and sell their cheap prints and pornographic postcards.

I crossed the Seine at the Pont Neuf. Isn't new bridge an odd name to give to the oldest bridge in Paris?

Past the Marché aux Fleurs (which transforms into the Marché des Oiseaux on Sundays), I turned a corner and happened upon a *charcuterie* with a wild boar flopped on a wooden sawhorse out front. This gets a mention because as I stood there regarding the once ferocious creature the butcher himself came out and turned the wild boar around so it was facing in the opposite direction. I asked the butcher why he rotated the boar.

'In *le matin* I face him that way so he snarls at all the people going to work,' he said. 'Then, in *l'après-midi* I move him this way so he can get them again on their way home.'

'Good advertisement?'

'The best. And sometimes someone even buys the boar.' The butcher hurried back inside to help a customer and as I watched him go I realised, for him, life was a moveable beast.

Now cold and ravished, I hurried over toward Les Halles to Joe Allen at 30 rue Pierre-Lescot. It may seem a bit unhinged to want to eat an American burger in Paris (I had seen the movie), but this sort of twisted logic has always accompanied me on my travels. (Once, in New Delhi, I noticed that there was Wiener Schnitzel on the menu at the Oberoi hotel. So I ordered it. The schnitzel was authentic and scrumptious, so you can well imagine my surprise when I contracted the Delhi-belly.)

* * *

'Here's a song I hope all of you will like,' Paul announced to his audience one warm evening at Le Show and then played and sang a Maurice Chevalier number. The crowd applauded feverishly, then Paul removed his white top hat and placed it on the piano, upside down. 'Children, if your parents don't give you at least ten euros to throw in the hat,' he declared. 'It means they don't love you!' The crowd roared, then surged forward to fill Paul's hat.

After the crowd tipped Paul, they moved like a cloud of locust in the direction of the next performer. This mass exodus is called the 'blow off' and performers will scream and shout, blow a whistle or wave a burning torch to try to poach from a successful show that has just completed.

Paul saw me and beckoned me over. His eyes lit up when he saw that I was holding a bottle of wine. 'What is that you have brought with you, *mon ami*?' Paul took the bottle from me. 'Ah, *mon Dieu.* Côtes du Rhône.'

We both watched as the crowd settled in around a fellow called 'Statue Man', just down the quay. Statue Man was a Swiss performer with Adonis good looks and a Greek God body. His curly locks were powdered white. His well-muscled body, painted white. And, for the full effect, he wore white sandals and a skimpy white toga (which barely covered his Matterhorn).

As you can well imagine, Statue Man was a big success with the ladies.

Statue Man's technique was thus: He would stand on a white pedestal, point at his cheek and then with a mime's imploring eyes request an innocent kiss. When a daring young lady succumbed to his charms (and skimpy white toga), he would strike quickly and reach down and snatch his victim off the ground and haul her up on the pedestal with him. The crowd loved it and would shriek, but never quite as loudly as the young lady he embraced in his powerful arms.

'He roller-blades to work,' Paul said, as he sat down under the canopy of a chestnut tree and opened the bottle of wine. 'He puts that pedestal on a little trolley, then pulls it through the streets. Quite something to see coming around Place de la Concorde.'

Paul pulled out two glasses from inside his piano and gave me a conspiratorial smile. 'I am a man who is always prepared.'

Paul poured us each an overloaded glass.

'Tonight was good,' Paul announced, peering into the depths of his hat. 'Paris is the City of Light and tourists are drawn to that light like moths. Well-heeled moths. With so many tourists, there are enough *pourboirs* for everybody. This is a town that is good to all artists.'

We heard a scream and saw some voluptuous damsel writhing in the Statue Man's grasp. The crowd howled.

'Paris is international. That you know, Jon. But did you know we have Russians who are descendants of the White Russian refugees from the Bolshevik Revolution? *Mais, oui.* We also have Poles, Italians, Spaniards, Lebanese, West Africans (lookie-lookie), Algerians and Moroccans. Even some French. The Parisians have always been somewhat colour blind but where there may be certain undesirable ills of society it's not like in most big cities. The government is xenophobic, but if anybody destroys this city it won't be the foreigners -- it will be the French themselves.'

Paul sipped his wine, and as the wine allowed him to wind down after his show, his tongue unwound, as well.

Theme change.

Mood sombre.

Long pause.

'I was born in Paris, but my older brother was born in Casablanca. My father was a printer and he had a successful business. All in all the family had a happy, safe life there in Morocco under French rule.

'Then in 1955 things changed for my father. Morocco was struggling for independence from France. The writing was on the wall but my father didn't want to read it.

'One day, two men came to visit my father and said they wanted him to print a newspaper supporting their views -- pro-independence. My father refused. The men left.

'The next day the men came back with some muscle. They told my father they were determined to have their newspaper printed. Again my father refused. It was then that the men reminded my father that it wasn't a good idea for one of the few Jewish families in Casablanca to go against its Arab brothers. It wouldn't be a pleasant life for us in the new Arab state and out from under the protective French umbrella. My father looked the men right in the eye and again refused.

'The third day only one man returned, but he returned carrying a small cloth bag. He again asked my father if he would help. When my father told him he was refusing for the last time, and not to bother him anymore, the man said he would be back the next day to begin printing ... and, oh ... here was something for him. The man left and my father looked inside the small cloth bag. Inside was a severed human finger -- the finger of a child. Before dawn the next day, my parents and my older brother were already on a ferry crossing over to France.'

I looked at Paul. He was lost in thought somewhere, probably thinking about his family making the crossing.

'So, you see,' he said. 'This is not a bad place to call home. I will save my money and buy my computer. Then I will start a little business.'

Another scream pierced the night and we looked over to see the Statue Man with another wriggling hard-body in his grasp.

He was a like a Venus Fly Trap.

* * *

With nothing on the horizon one morning, I decided upon urban adventure. In order to expand my geographical feel for Paris, I was going to partake of each of her famous 'views'.

I strolled from my hotel all the way over to Montmartre and found a cat sunning itself in a splash of sun in front of the neo-byzantine Basilica of Sacré-Coeur. This is a view to die for. Actually, now that I think of it, Montmartre means 'martyrs mound', so perhaps this was a view to die for.

Then I took the Métro back across town to the Tour Montparnasse, rode the fastest lift in Europe and checked out the panoramic view from the roof on the 59th floor. (FYI: There's a restaurant called Le Ciel de Paris on the 56th floor, and it is possibly one of the few places in Paris where you can find wondrously uninspired cuisine.)

Eager to compare view number three, I scooted over to the Place Charles-de-Gaulle and spent the rest of the afternoon trying to ford the stream of traffic swirling round the Arc de Triomphe (there's an underground passage, but I didn't know that then, did I?). It was late in the afternoon by the time I succeeded, so I went right to the top for an unobstructed view straight down the heart of the Champs-Elysées toward the Place de la Concorde and the distant Louvre. Lights were already flickering on. Gorgeous!

Finally, I hustled over to the Eiffel Tower. On a clear day you can see 42 miles, but I now had a foggy night.

(FYI: Did you know that the Eiffel Tower wasn't meant to be a permanent structure? That's right. It was erected as the result of a contest to design a tower for the World Exposition of 1889 -- and everyone moaned when it was unveiled. Then, when the exhibition was over and it was to be torn down, everyone moaned again, so they kept it.)

Anyway, these are all astonishing views. But you don't have to do all four in one day like I did -- because you probably have a life.

* * *

I was towelling myself off on a clear, cold Saturday evening (having just returned from a bout with the shower) and wondering what trouble I might get into that night when I heard a gentle, feminine KNOCK, KNOCK at the door.

I wrapped the towel around my waist, shuffled to the door and opened it. Standing there was a rich-looking, golden-skinned woman of unknown origin. Her eyes were molten, and her hair was black and sleek and pulled back, and she was looking down at my towel -- and smiling.

'Sorry I didn't stop by yesterday,' she said, invading my space. 'But I'm willing to make up for it today.'

What the fuck?

'Oh,' she said, suddenly reading the number on my door. 'I'm on the wrong floor.'

'This is the third,' I said, noticing her perfume smelled of vanilla and had a way of wrapping itself around me.

'Doesn't matter -- you'll do.'

'I'll do what?' I said, taking a step back.

The woman's long, golden fingers reached out and caressed my chest.

'Since I'm here, won't you invite me in? You won't be sorry you did.'

Mon Dieu! Paris is nothing but a bosom of prostitution. I found myself clutching at my towel. 'Listen, I don't know how to tell you this, but I ... ah ... well ... ah ... I'm expecting someone ...' I was babbling hopelessly.

The golden-skinned woman snaked her hand down toward my towel the way a Burmese python slips along a mahogany tree in search of suckling prey. 'Three doesn't have to be a crowd.'

Holy shit! is what I was thinking, but 'Perhaps tomorrow' is what I said.

'Until tomorrow then,' sighed the golden-skinned python. 'Tomorrow, one of us will succumb.' She said this last word slowly, separating the syllables and emphasizing the *suck*. Surely it must have been her accent.

I closed the door, went back to my bed and sat down --

upright -- like I had a stick up my arse. I stared at the wall. I stared at the window. I stared at the bidet. Not knowing what to do, I opened the little drawer in the bedside table. Inside was a Bible. I flicked through the great book. Then turned to the back. Here I found a listing entitled: HELP IN TIME OF NEED.

I read the list. It went something like this:

Comfort in Time of LONELINESS, see Psalm 23.

Guidance in Time of DECISION, see Proverbs 3:5,6.

Strength in Time of TEMPTATION, see 1 Corinthians 10:6-13. Next to the word TEMPTATION someone had written in red ink: 'If this doesn't work, call "Lulu" at 42-60-38-30.'

There was another knock at my door and I ejaculated off the bed, I mean, ejected off the bed. The python was back and her name must be Lulu.

Knock, Knock. I didn't breathe. KNOCK. KNOCK. I became part of the Moulin Rouge decor.

'Jon? Are you there?' came a familiar voice.

I ran to the door and opened it. The python wasn't there, rather a soft cuddly creature with eyes like an owl. And Sabena looked adorable in her miniskirt and black leather coat.

'Are you feeling carnivorous?' Sabena asked, her eyes roving to my towel.

'What!'

'Have you had dinner yet? You're the only one I know in the hotel.'

'What about the stallion?'

'Who?'

'Never mind.'

'Are you hungry or not?'

Who can think of food? I ate *pain au chocolat* five different times today, is what I was thinking, but because Sabena looked so damn good 'I'm sort of peckish' is what I said.

'Lovely,' responded Sabena. When Sabena spoke (and wasn't angry), her lips always remained parted for a beat or two afterwards. This characteristic elicited some sort of visceral response deep down inside which I was presently trying to decipher.

'Let me just throw on some clothes and I'll meet you downstairs,' I said. Taking no prisoners, I even slipped into my virgin, racy Italian loafers.

When I got downstairs, I found Sabena standing by the front door. She was holding an umbrella.

'What's the umbrella for?' I said. 'Suppose to be clear as a bell tonight.'

'Because you dress like a tourist. I'll tell you about it later. *Allez!*

I suggested a romantic cave of a restaurant just across Boul' Mich', and with the smell of leaves burning down a lonely street somewhere, and nearly a full moon rising, we plunged into the quarter. We wended our way through the frolicking masses, passed by some stairs leading to a cellar where a belly dancer was gyrating in a distinctly Byzantine manner, then Sabena suddenly froze in her tracks.

'Where are you taking me?'

'This way,' I pointed.

'We don't want to go down there. Down there is rue de la Harpe.'

'Is it dangerous?'

'Only if you eat there. We call this area "bacteria alley".'

'*Sans déconner!*' I said.

Sabena turned her big owl eyes on me. 'What usually comes to mind when you see dead rabbits hanging in windows in the sun all day long?'

'Deadly bacteria?'

'You are so quick.'

Sabena grabbed my arm and pulled me down a narrow street that led away from the Seine. Soon we came upon a theatre with a long queue out front.

'This is Theatre de la Huchette,' Sabena announced proudly. 'Ionesco's play *Cantatrice Chauve* has been playing here for over 40 years. That's a world record.'

'Actually, Agatha Christie's *The Mousetrap* has been playing in

London for over 50 years,' I said.

Sabena gave me a smile: 'You do know something after all.'

I just smiled back, no longer looking quite the fool.

We walked on.

'By the way, I don't know how to break the news to you,' Sabena lectured. 'But back there, at that café where you spend all day, everyday, that's not even part of the *real* Latin Quarter. Tourists always think it is, but it's not.'

I am such a fool.

We walked for about ten minutes past micro-cinema after micro-cinema. All warm, beckoning holes-in-the-wall. There were films showing in Brazilian, Taiwanese, Finnish and we even spotted one that was shown in Sengalese.

'Paris is the cinema capitol of the world, did you know that?'

'I'm beginning to get that feeling,' I said.

'Some movies will be screened here first, before they are even shown in London or New York. But one must be careful in the cinemas. Thieves will wait till the climax of the film, the big chase, or some steamy sex scene and then they will steal your bag. I know that because I go *au cinema* all the time.'

'You are a fountain of information.'

'*Mais, non*, I am Parisienne.'

We carried on through littered back alleys, past a cat lapping milk from a saucer, and every once in awhile we unearthed what seemed to be a cosy little *boîte*. But Sabena seemed to have designs on something of a certain *je ne sais quoi*. She led me some immemorable, circuitous route past Greek restaurants and Moroccan restaurants and Balkan restaurants and Vietnamese restaurants. It is said that Paris has more restaurants than any other city on the planet. And of that I had no doubt. In one street alone I counted 27 different restaurants.

Finally we spilled out onto a narrow, crowded street that sloped gently up hill.

'*Voilà,* rue Mouffetard,' Sabena announced. 'Here we will find a restaurant without Salmonella.'

The restaurant Sabena chose was a dungeon with romantic

atmosphere in a smoky Belle Époque sort of way. It was a small establishment, but run by a large family. We sat at a deuce in a murky corner. A candle stuck in an old wine bottle burnt brightly and wax dripped down its sides. The table was so narrow our knees touched, sending a lightning bolt of excitement coursing through my body.

We talked mostly about food and Paris, and did I mention food? And we watched as family members kept disappearing and reappearing through a door to the kitchen. My initial estimate of twelve family members was way off, for when they all emerged from the kitchen to sing *Bon Anniversaire* to a group of Russians, I could only count five.

Sabena said she wanted to order for me, so we started with *belons* and a carafe of *vin ordinaire*.

'The *belons* are brought in from Brittany,' Sabena said.

'Sounds great,' I said. 'What are *belons*?'

'Brown-fleshed oysters.'

'To brown-fleshed oysters,' I said. We held up our glasses to toast and our knees touched again.

Sabena told me the restaurant was known for its *cuisine du marché*. *Cuisine du marché* demands only the freshest market produce. Sabena had some sort of a fish casserole and I had *sanglier* in sauce with a mound of *pommes frites* as big as Montmartre.

The meat I was eating was delightful and had a familiar, distinctly wild flavour. Could it be? 'What's *sanglier*?'

'Wild boar,' Sabena said. And we toasted to wild boar.

I was becoming a fan of wild boar, and of touching knees.

It seemed every time we were running low on wine, the proprietor of the restaurant would appear with another carafe. It occurred to me that this was Sabena's doing.

'So do tell 'bout thish umbrella,' I slurred.

'When I'm alone, I look Parisienne. But when I'm with you, we look like tourists. It is for self-defence against all the gypsy pickpockets.'

I wanted to dig deeper into this umbrella-protection plan, but just then an inebriated patron rose shakily from the table next to ours, wobbled over to a railing and with complete impunity, heaved his empty wine bottle down onto a stone subfloor. The bottle shattered in a frightfully loud crash, and everyone in the restaurant shouted: 'Hey!!!' Immensely pleased with this destructive act, the drunk tottered back to his table, winked at his date and collapsed in his seat.

What an exotic atmosphere!

Throughout the course of the evening, this unusual phenomenon occurred time and time again. A ripped diner would stagger to the railing, the empty bottle would smash in a splintering of glass and then be followed by a drunken chorus of 'Hey!!!' I never wanted to leave this enchanting environment, but then there was Sabena's knee. That, and the subsequent lightning bolt. Lightning bolt...'Hey!!!'...lightning bolt...'Hey!!!' It all made the evening somehow erotic, and I was slowly being wound up like some spring-loaded sex toy.

Later in the evening, after we had polished off two carafes of cabernet, the proprietor suddenly sprang from the ceiling: 'Would you care for a cappuccino?'

'No, I don't want to mess up my buzz,' Sabena said, smiling playfully at the old man. 'Please bring us another carafe of wine.'

Okay, now it's really late and I don't remember ever being quite so happy (I'm chatting with the Russian Mafia at the neighbouring table and asking: 'What's it going to be, Moscow Rules?'). I paid for the dinner, then to impress Sabena, slipped away with our now armful of empty carafes and flung them down onto the stone subfloor, and 'Hey!!!' shouted it out at the top of my lungs. I turned to face all my new Russian friends (rough folk who have seen it all) but saw only sincere horror on their faces. There had been no rounding accompanying chorus, only deadly silence. I looked around. The restaurant was a tableau of shock. All the patrons, including the staff, had their mouths open wide like baby birds feeding.

I shot a glance over to Sabena. She was trying to slip beneath the table. 'I can't take you anywhere!' she hissed. Then as I sought refuge back at our table: 'What are you trying to do, put this poor family out of business? You can only do that if you buy one of the expensive wines, not a house carafe!'

Oh.

I handed the weeping proprietor some euros to cover his loss, and then we scarpered up the stairs and took a long walk through the *real* Latin Quarter. We could see stars twinkling through bare trees against the black sky, and I really didn't know where we were other than the streets were teeming with students and professors and tourists and litter and dog shit, and it was all somehow exceedingly perfect.

'*Regard!*' Sabena said, as a funny little motor scooter swept slowly by. 'That's a *caninette!*'

(FYI: A *caninette* is sort of a hybrid cross between a motor scooter and a giant vacuum cleaner. These little joys of ingenuity are known colloquially as *motorcrottes* or 'turd-mobiles'. There are upwards of 75 of these nifty marvels tooling around Paris hoovering up, get ready, dog shit. As we all know, there is a certain amount of poo decorating each and every *rue*, avenue and boulevard. Cue the turd-mobile. It is estimated -- and who counts, I don't want to know him -- that somewhere between three and 11 tons are excreted on Parisian streets, by man's best friend, daily.)

On a curiously optimistic note, it is considered good luck in Paris if you step in dog shit with your *left* foot. 'Oh, look, Jean-Claude, it's our first date and you've just stepped in a big pile of dog doo-doo with your left foot. Now during dinner I will be sick to my stomach because your shoe smells of puppy poo. My parents are in Biarritz for the weekend, but later I will refuse to let you come upstairs to my room to make heated love to me because your foot smells of canine excrement. But, hey! The shit is smeared all over your *left* foot. Aren't you the lucky one, Jean-Claude?'

On an allied theme, if you are shit upon by a bird in Paris, that is considered good luck, as well. I guess it's commendable to make light of a desperate situation. Every dollop of *merde* has a silver lining?

We left that part of the quarter behind and swayed down

neon-rich boulevard St-Germain, past sophisticated cafés and avant-garde fashion shops, and soon came to the café Deux Magots. We were in the heart of legendary St-Germain-des-Prés. The night was now chilly, yet for some alcoholic-induced reason, startlingly sensual. I looked at Sabena, and she was looking up at me with those lips parted. I smiled and she put her arm through mine.

'*Allez!* Let's have some more wine. It's our national drink, you know.' And she pulled me in the direction of the Deux Magots.

The Deux Magots was festively packed. Sabena seemed to be on a first-name basis with everyone in attendance and room was soon made for us at a table on the sidewalk. Sabena motioned to the waiter, and I waited eagerly to see if she would address him as *garcon*, but she didn't. She addressed him as 'Henri' -- then ordered wine.

My, the girl certainly knew how to enjoy the national beverage.

We blubbered through a rich bouquet of burgundy and watched a street performer juggling chain saws entertain the patrons of the café (and a large crowd that had gathered, but not too close).

After we finished our bottle, we strolled back down toward the Seine, brushing against one another and laughing probably a bit too loudly. Secretly, I was walking Sabena around and around, waiting for the ethers to get just right. When I felt the ethers had to be at their most imposing, I popped the question: '*Tu veux aller et observer la lune éclat hors les toits de Paris?*'

Sabena stopped in her tracks and gave me a quizzical look. 'Your French is an adventure, but I think you're asking me to accompany you to watch the moon sparkle off the rooftops?'

'*Oui.*'

'Where?'

'*Mon balcon.*'

'You don't have a balcony.'

'*Tu as raison.* From the window of my room, then.'

'I would like that very much,' Sabena responded tipsily. She had a look in her big owl eyes of simply wanting to please.

Sabena wanted some more wine, so we bought a litre from a dark form with a Lebanese accent working out of a hole in the wall and aimed in the general direction of our hotel.

As we turned the corner at rue Git-le-Coeur, I caught a glimpse of someone standing in the shadows. It was the python lady, and she was smiling lustfully at me and holding up three fingers with a hopeful look. I scooted behind Sabena, madly waving my arms 'Nooo!' the way an errant F-18 is waved off an aircraft carrier.

We wobbled up the stairs to the third floor and laughed nervously as I inserted the key into the lock and swung open the door to my room. Both Sabena and I hurried over to the double windows and past the bed as if it were radioactive.

And the moon did, indeed, sparkle off the rooftops that night, and we stood there for a long time just tingling with the excitement of being where we were, with whom we were. I opened the bottle of wine and splashed a few fingers in each of our glasses. I made a toast. 'To tonight, Sabena. It's a night I know neither one of us will ever forget.'

'To tonight, Jon.'

We drank and then threw our wine glasses out the window and down onto the street below. They bounced because they were plastic. We heard a voice, with an accent of unknown origin, protest: 'Zut alors!'

'Sabena, why do you live in this hotel?'

'No background check,' Sabena said, or something to that effect, and she lifted her face to mine. 'Not tonight.'

I put my arm around Sabena's waist and pulled her hips to mine. The ethers beckoned. I kissed the owl.

'Let's go sit down,' Sabena's parted lips said. 'I'm feeling the wine just a bit.'

We went to the bed and as if by some blessed unwritten code silently began to take each other's clothes off. I was about to cross the Maginot Line of sex. It was cold in the room, but I could feel the heat coming off Sabena's body in lustful wave after wave. Sabena lay down on the bed, invitingly, and said to me with those parted lips: 'Yes, Jon, this will be a night we'll never forget.'

And you know what? Sabena was right, because she rolled over onto her stomach, leaned over the side of the bed -- and projectile vomited into my racy new Italian loafers.

I guess it's no surprise the relationship suffered. We decided it would be better to be just friends. And we both made bogus resolutions to 'never drink that much again'.

Did you know there is an acronym for when you abuse yourself as we did? Yes, that's right. It comes from the expression: 'Such A Bad Experience Never Again'. S-A-B-E-N-A. Same as the defunct Belgian airline.

* * *

On my last night in Paris, I went by *Le Show* to say goodbye to Paul. During a break, he said: 'There's someone I want you to meet.' It was his big brother.

I shook hands with Paul's brother and I will never forget the two of them. Paul, because he looked like a young Omar Sharif. And his brother, because he had one missing finger.

* * *

WHAT NOBODY WILL TELL YOU:

It is said on a good night, in high season, Paris can field over 50,000 prostitutes. By comparison, Amsterdam can only scramble 5,000.

In 1815, during the Russian occupation of Paris, Russian officers impatient for a quick meal in their favourite restaurants shouted in Russian '*Bystro! Bystro!*' for the cooks to hurry up -- and the term for a moderately-priced French restaurant, which served meals quickly, was born: the 'bistro'.

CHAPTER 13 - Venice: Locals show me how to build a gondola

Henry James once wrote: 'Almost everyone interesting, appealing, melancholy, memorable, odd, seems at one time or another ... to have gravitated to Venice ...'

I identified with only one of the above, but decided to gravitate to Venice, nevertheless.

And I did so in deep, late autumn.

Nobody with at least the intelligence of a *panini* visits suffocatingly hot Venice in summer when the Eau du Canal (or the 'pestilential air' as Horace Walpole referred to it on his Grand Tour) is at its most malodorous, the mosquitoes are their most voracious and Venice's 100,000 resident pigeons are in mid-season shitting form.

I booked a room at the train station, well, not at the train station, itself, but from a cheery fellow with a name tag that said 'Luigi'. Luigi was a rogue tout and, as you know, I don't usually succumb to a tout's charms. But I felt sorry for Luigi. He wasn't cut out to be a tout. He was shy and seemed to be in a constant state of embarrassment. I found him standing in the shadows just outside 'APT' (the room-reservation office), feeding off the overflow. He was the lone dog at the pound that nobody wanted. I couldn't help myself.

Luigi recommended the not-so-Italianate-sounding Hotel Messner and said it wasn't far. But guess what? Everything in Venice is far because you get tortuously lost trying to get there.

I headed off through a labyrinth of narrow streets, *direction Accademia* (as Luigi suggested). To be able to provide you with some fairly useless information, I counted how many times I had to make a right turn and how many times I had to make a left turn before arriving at the Messner. And this is what makes Venice so unique. I turned left 57 times and turned right 62 times and somehow still made it there.

The Messner was located at Madonna della Salute 216/217. If you aren't up for the walk, or have heavier bags than my one satchel, you can always convey by *vaporetto*. Take *Linea* #1, the 'Grand Canal local', and jump off at *fermata* #14. The waterbus only makes one right turn and one left turn and you will pass nearly 200 Renaissance and Gothic palaces along the way.

Upon arrival don't forget to check out the Messner's brochure. It proudly offers: 'Modern Dining Room with Air Conditioning Inside' (thank goodness the air conditioning is inside!).

I have to tell you I was sincerely relieved when I found my hotel, you see, I had trouble finding Venice in the first place. I'd booked my journey in Paris, but the little man behind the window only booked me as far as Venezia-*Mestre*, which was still the mainland and two and a half miles short of my goal, the real Venice. But I didn't know that, did I?

When the train arrived in Venezia-Mestre, I jumped off, watched it clackety-clack out of sight and then stood there dumbly looking about as Robert Redford, Paul Newman and Katherine Ross did in *Butch Cassidy and the Sundance Kid* when they disembarked in Bolivia. No one else detrained and I was left leaning into an icy wind, watching the Italian equivalent of tumbleweed roll by. When it occurred to me that this Venice lacked such fabled icons as basilicas, gondolas and a Grand Canal, I hijacked the next train that came through and travelled ten minutes into Venezia *Santa Lucia*. For being uninformed, I was penalized with a plump *supplemento*.

* * *

My room at the Messner was on the second floor and it had Italy's smallest balcony. If you had larger than size-ten shoes (or size nine with those pointy toes), you were unable to venture outside.

I opened begrimed double doors and peered down at an astonishingly green canal below, a dozy cat sunning itself on the adjacent *fondamenta* and the most gorgeous *signorina* retrieving frozen laundry, just opposite. I knew that women in Venice were known to be flirtatious, so I yelled '*Buon giorno, principessa!*' to get her attention, but only got the attention of an Italian in an undershirt who was picking his teeth with a switchblade.

Machismo the Knife appeared behind *principessa* and then drew her back inside (for stormy Latin love making, no doubt). With now no need to dally, I headed out to the Piazza San Marco to infuse caffeine, embrace Venetian history and window-shop for undershirts.

(FYI: Did you know that the pigeons in Piazza San Marco know when the clock is going to strike at their feeding hour and they start to get antsy as the joyous moment approaches? Just like a pet? Or a husband? Then, when the gong sounds, a blizzard of feathers swoop down like extras in a Hitchcock film searching for the little man who feeds them -- and anyone resembling Rod Taylor, Tippi Hedren or Suzanne Pleshette.)

The walk from my hotel to Piazza San Marco only took ten minutes. But it was the longest ten minutes of my life (other than, of course, that time at the proctologist's), you see, when the wind comes in off the Adriatic, Venice can be the coldest place on earth.

I took a brisk tour around the piazza and spent a moment in front of the 323-foot tall *Campanile* (bell tower of St Mark's) pondering its 1000-year-old history: In the 15th century, clerics found guilty of immoral acts were suspended in wooden cages from the tower as punishment. Then during the reign of the Austrian Emperor Frederick III, Frederick rode his horse up the 37 flights of stairs to the top. Our Freddy was taken with the view (you can actually see the Alps on a clear day), but his horse was unimpressed.

And then on 14 July 1902, at precisely 9:47 a.m., weakened by age (and no doubt emperors riding horses up the stairs), the entire bell tower collapsed, killing a cat.

It took ten years to build a new tower.

The bitter wind swept the square clean of pigeons and I decided that I had best make an executive decision. Do I plunge into the oldest café in Italy, the garishly ornate Caffè Florian (since 1720), do I retreat back across the piazza and patronise the snobbish Quadri (a café even the Venetians won't frequent, because the Germans do) or do I slip around the corner to Harry's Bar and forgo the caffeine?

I ruled out the Quadri right off on account of the Germans. That left the Florian and Harry's. The Florian was once the den of literary lions, philosophers, composers and libertines: Lord Byron, Goethe, Dickens, Proust, Bruce, Weeks, Wagner, Stravinsky, Rousseau, Casanova. And Harry's had liquored the likes of Truman Capote, Hemingway (see?), Onassis, Orson Welles and a whole lot of others who were just as decanted but not nearly as famous. When I remembered that a small Bellini in Harry's costs about a tenner, I deleted Harry's from my list.

That left Florian's.

Caffè Florian, or Florian's as it became known (the original owner's name was Florino Francesconi) is made up of different sized rooms, some small, some not so small, but all shamelessly opulent. I peeped into a few rooms, but they were occupied by professional smokers, so I searched until I found a room where I could breathe. I sat down on a seat of soft velvet and was immediately set upon by an elderly, tuxedoed waiter with hair by henna. The waiter told me I was not allowed in that particular room as it was the *Sala del Senata*. I asked if one needed to be a senator to enjoy its ambiance, but the schlemiel did not see my humour.

Signor Henna personally escorted me to a distant chamber, and I felt like a prisoner crossing the Bridge of Sighs. As punishment, I was seated next to a pretentious Teutonic couple wearing sunglasses. Just so you know, I am not particularly fond of pretentious folk of any nationality who wear sunny-specs *indoors*.

Then they both lit cigarettes and took life-threatening drags.

My waiter bleated: '*Prego?*'

I ordered a *caffè dell'Imperatore* off the menu (as that was all I could afford on my budget), and my waiter seemed deeply disturbed by this choice. What was he like in the height of summer?

The waiter was gone for so long Venice sank another inch. Finally, *Signor Adagio* returned, with a grin on his face of suspect subtext, and I had the most awful feeling that he had deposited bodily fluids in my *Imperatore*.

My *caffè dell'Imperatore* consisted of a *piccolo* silver panniken of coffee, a dollop of cream, a tiny glass of water and a silky *zabaione*. A *zabaione* is an eggnog of sorts and it was served with *baicoli*, which are typical Venetian biscuits.

I was still cold, so I wrapped my hands around my silver cup and received a withering glare from the 40-a-day couple. Evidently, I had broken the rule of finer cafés. The coffee ended up being the least enjoyable of my entire life -- and by far the most expensive.

Thrown into an uncharacteristic state of malevolence, I considered purloining the silver pannikin and bolting, but then I remembered how ol' randy Casanova, a Venetian himself, had been unceremoniously tossed in the slammer for 'unbecoming behaviour' (read: porking the mistress of one of the city fathers). Casanova ended up literally in deep shit over this dalliance for at high tide his prison cell would fill with two feet of faecally enriched Adriatic. To make matters *peggio*, when Casanova was fed his rations, he had to fight off enormous, hunger-emboldened rats for the right to eat a mouldy brick of bread with suspect breakfast spread. With the image of large rats in mind, I forked over a small fortune to cover the cost of a modest cup of coffee -- and 280 years of Caffè Florian history.

Other than my henna-haired *cameriere*, Venetians are generally friendly, if you can find a Venetian nowadays. You see, many Venetians have had their fill of damp palaces, chilly baths and mouldy boudoirs and have moved to the less expensive mainland where they can live in warm comfort.

This brings us to that ever-gnawing question: How did Venice become Venice in the first place? Let me take out my canvas and paint you a little picture: Envisage churlish barbarians from the north of Europe coming overland to your hometown to rape, pillage and plunder, and generally beat the absolute crap out of you, far too frequently. When you come to your senses and realise you've had enough of raising blond, blue-eyed children, you get your act together and move to the one place northern European barbarians can't get you -- the middle of the lagoon. You build on muddy humpbacked islands called *barene* by pounding millions of 12-foot-long tree trunks made of oak or larch down into the blue clay for support. Then you dredge canals so your fellow Venetians will have somewhere to dump their garbage. Pleased with your work, you elect a *doge* (who gets to live in the Doge's Palace) to govern, and then you patiently wait 1000 years for the tourism to kick in.

Okay, now get this. Just when the Venetians have the place set up the way they want it, industry starts to develop over on the mainland, and industry needs water -- freshwater -- so they drill 70 wells down into the water table and this virtually sucks the underbelly out from under the Rialto Bridge (and the store where Shakespeare's Shylock kept shop). In wisdom that can only be political wisdom, the lagoon has landfill added to it which upsets its ecological balance and tidal flow. Then the natural channels in the lagoon are dredged so large ships can reach the mainland to service the industry. What someone failed to mention, with deep channels and a mucked up lagoon, the high tide would lay siege to Venice's 118 islands like, well, churlish barbarians from northern Europe. The result? A city that had sunk at the gloomy rate of one inch every five years (they swear the subsidence has bottomed out) and is now susceptible to the same tidal *acqua alta* that a millennium ago left it alone. Guess how deep the water gets in St Mark's Piazza in the winter when the *bora* (sirocco) blows across the Adriatic and compounds this nightmare by stacking sea water in the geographical cul-du-sac that is 'Serenissima'. Go ahead. Guess. Do you want a clue? If you are up on your Cockney, think *daisy roots*.

I'm not a very religious person, but I did find myself praying for Venice -- for the city to stop sinking, the waters to recede and perhaps just a little for the prices to go down.

Don't you find Venice a bit overpriced? You could finance a Bertolucci film for the price of a bottle of fine wine from Friuli, a hearty seafood meal from Fiashetteia Toscana and a *gelato* from, well, any canal-side stand. Did you know in many restaurants, if you order the fish, the price on the menu is per 100 grams? Now, isn't that just a trifling deceptive? Stop and think. You are on your first date with *principessa*. You want to make a good impression so you order the hammerhead entrée for two, *assuming* that the price is for the entire entrée. Do restaurant owners really believe we will ever again frequent an eating establishment that responds to '*Il conto, por favore,*' with '*Sorpressa!*' We have a right to be brought out of the deep-sea dark, don't you think?

* * *

It was the start of December when I ran into Luigi again. I had just exited the Messner and I froze him in his Bacco Buccis.

'You're still here!' Luigi said, then blushed. 'I feel so bad. I put you in that hotel, but it's too expensive to stay so long.'

'But isn't that your job?'

'Afraid I'm not very good at my job.'

Then Luigi's eyes lit up: 'Listen, if you are staying on, you come stay at my mama's. She rents rooms. One just became available.'

'Where does she live?'

'I take you. It's council housing, therefore cheap.'

Council housing! I've seen council housing in Liverpool and Glasgow.

Luigi guided me back through the rabbit's warren that is Venice all the way over to the palaces along the Grand Canal. Then he pointed across the canal at a three-storey palatial mansion with gondolas docked out front, tethered to tall blue-and-white stanchions.

'*Ecco!*' Luigi said.

'*Ecco*, what?' I said.

'*Ecco*, your new home.'

'That's council housing in Venezia!'

'*Si*, what you expect?'

I couldn't believe my eyes. Was I really going to be living in a 15th century Venetian Gothic *palazzo* on the Grand Canal?

'Say, Luigi, you don't happen to have a sister, do you?'

'I do. Half-sister.'

'Married?'

Luigi just laughed. 'She three.'

And then Luigi took me to the *palazzo* and introduced me to his mother and I was shown to a bachelor apartment with twenty-foot ceilings, and Luigi's mama told me the interior was one hundred percent authentic Venetian with Murano chandeliers and antiques dating back hundreds of years. Then she threw open double windows and I stared gobsmacked out at the Grand Canal below and watched as *vaporettos* and gondolas glided slowly by.

Talk about a room with a view!

That night, to celebrate my good fortune, I went out for a glass of Chianti (ended up having a litre) and then I splurged and took a gondola right to my front door, and my Gondolier stopped under a bridge, so he could make use of the acoustics, and sang 'O Sole Mio'.

When I stepped out of the gondola, I could see the lights of the Rialto off to the left and stars in the sky nearly as bright -- and the night was magical.

And I desperately wanted to share this with someone, and I was thinking that I was *O Sole Mio* until I remembered the song is not about being 'lonely', rather about the 'sun'.

* * *

Our next subject is gondolas, so let me ask you a little question. Is there truly anything in this whole wide world as romantic as a moonlight serenade in a gondola? Anyway, let me explain how I've come to this topic and it has nothing to do with my ride home.

I was on my way to the church of Madonna dell'Orto. The Madonna dell'Orto is in the unfrequented northern quarter of Venice, a bit distant, but well worth the effort if you want to go to a part of Venice few visit. Here you can view Tintoretto's tomb or pay homage to St Christopher, the patron saint of travellers (the church is dedicated to him) and I had to do that. Anyway, I was headed to the church when I happened upon a boatyard where two workers were building gondolas!

I hung around for a while and when the two workers saw that I wasn't going to go away (and after I bought them each an espresso) they agreed to show me how gondolas are built. Their names were Benedetto and Burano, and I learned quite a few juicy titbits about gondolas: For instance, did you know that all true gondolas are made from eight different types of wood, are 36 feet long and four feet wide? That's what I thought. And did you know that the shallow keel is curved to counteract the sweep of the gondolier's oar? (If the keel wasn't curved, the gondola would go around in circles and getting anywhere would be even more expensive.) Or at the bow there is the *ferro* (the iron) which is indeed iron and looks like a musical clef? The *ferro* has six points, which stand for the six *sestiere*, or districts, of Venice, and its considerable weight helps balance the weight of the gondolier. In the old days, a gondola would last 30 years, but now owing to pollution, menacing wakes from motorboats and overweight tourists from America and the UK, only 20 years. Back in the 1500s there were over 10,000 gondolas, but sadly less than 400 service Venice today.

* * *

Have you ever visited a city somewhere and the weather was crap and you thought the city was, say, crap, as well? Then the next day you awoke to sun streaming through your hotel window and the whole world seemed a better place (except for the hangover)? Well, dear traveller, you don't have to worry about that happening in Venice. You see, Venice retains its romantic charms when a curtain of mist drifts in from the Adriatic and enfolds the row of gondolas docked in front of San Marco, or fog does the cat's paw thing across the lagoon, or the canals are peppered with rain and you have to take shelter in an old-world café (and wrap both hands around an overpriced cappuccino).

If you are like me, and you don't mind walking in all types of weather, you can just stroll aimlessly about Venice discovering places you otherwise might never have known existed. You see, walking in Venice is comparable to walking in an open-air museum.

It was so cold and grey one morning I thought it was going to snow. I took a long stroll to catch the icy air and to work off, alas, 300 grams of fish I had dispatched the previous evening. And I don't know about you, but once I find a place that I like in Venice, whether it be a new café, unknown airy square or public toilet -- I can never seem to find it again. Anyway, this one particular morning I had an espresso at the Gritti Palace, where Queen Elizabeth, Greta Garbo and Winston Churchill once stayed, and then set out to find a little-known church I'd stumbled into the day before. I had ventured in just before noon and never having lit a votive candle in a church decided to light one. I popped a handful of coinage into a little slot and lit the candle. I had been there for only a moment, considering the holy procedure, when some winged harridan flew out of the shadows, rudely shouted '*Mezzogiorno!*' in my face, blew out my candle and unceremoniously threw me out on my *culo*. That's not so very Christian, is it? This may not seem so earth shaking, but it was rather earth shaking, indeed. I had entered the house of God with divine intent and was tossed out because I was clearly nothing more than a tourist and I was encroaching, not on someone's beliefs, rather their feeding time.

That evening I went for *penne alla arrabiata* with Luigi and told him of my eviction. And once again, Luigi became embarrassed, embarrassed for his fellow Venetians.

'Tomorrow I take you somewhere few ever see.'

Early the next morning it was bone-chilling cold and drizzling when Luigi took me to that place 'few ever see'. And it was called the *gèto*.

Luigi was smitten with history and here's what he told me: In 1516 the Republic of Venice decreed that all Jews living in greater Venezia must live in a deprived area known as the *gèto* (this is 39 years before Pope Paul IV confined the Jews in Rome). The term was derived from the medieval Venetian word *gèto*, which meant foundry, as this was where the commune's foundries were once located. It was the vilest and unhealthiest part of the commune and it was here the Jews remained until Napoleon (carrying a baguette) invaded Venice in 1797, put an end to this segregation and tore down the *gèto* gates.

It is from this Venetian neighbourhood that the term 'ghetto' was adopted to designate the place where Jews were forced to live. Nowadays, Venice's Ghetto is quaintly picturesque and definitely worth a visit, so I'm glad I had Luigi as my guide.

Finally, it did indeed begin to snow, an occurrence that is somewhat rare in Venice yet enchanting when it does.

'What else do you want to see?' Luigi said. 'I am at your service.' Then he looked at his watch: 'For another hour.'

I told Luigi that I wanted to go back to the church I got thrown out of, and he knew exactly which one I was talking about and he took me right to it. My candle wasn't there from the day before so I purchased one for Luigi and a new one for me. I lit it and then for some reason said my second prayer in a week. I said the prayer to St Mark, the patron saint of Venice, and I asked him to protect this most splendorous of cities, not from the sucking mud, not from the engulfing seas, not from the fierce siroccos, but from the bureaucracy that moves like a snail across the lagoon and lets too much time pass while it tries to decide what to do to save Venice.

* * *

WHAT NOBODY WILL TELL YOU … UNLESS YOU

KNOW LUIGI:

Many families from around Italy come to live in Venice to escape the violent crime that plagues their hometowns. Venice is the safest of major Italian cities and violent crime is rare, you see, escape, for the perpetrator, is risky at best.

In spite of the aforementioned influx, Venice has lost more than half its population since 1945. The young people of Venice are fleeing in droves and in doing so are leaving behind a city where the average age of the remaining folk is the highest in Europe. I know this because I spent the winter and spring in Venice and I saw an almost weekly pilgrimage of Venezia's youth shifting to the mainland. I would not recommend Venice as a place to go to find available members of the opposite sex -- unless you are an OAP.

CHAPTER 14 - The Republic of San Marino: Home to insufferable shits

This will be a short chapter, not because San Marino is such a small country, rather because San Marino fields the highest number of patently arrogant, flatulently rude locals, per capita, on the face of this earth.

And tourism is their main industry. *Faccia di culo! Porca miseria!* Even animals have enough sense not to soil their own beds.

San Marino is a nipple of a country protruding from the bosom of the Romagna farmlands of surrounding central Italy. Almost as tall as it is wide, and the Old Town not much larger than Lord's Cricket Ground, San Marino is stuffed with 29,615 stuffy, disagreeable inhabitants. It is the smallest independent state in Europe -- after the Vatican City and Monaco -- and until the independence of some far-flung coral atoll called Nauru was the smallest republic in the world.

For reasons I simply cannot fathom, 3.3 million tourists visit San Marino, annually. Most are day-trippers. And when they arrive, they are met with the welcoming cry of 'We want your money, we just don't want you.'

San Marino was not always like this. Years ago, the people were handsome and gay -- now they are handsome and insufferable shits. Perhaps the country was just having a bad year, but the locals were so ill-tempered and condescending, I lost all interest and desire to get behind their guidebook pages.

What was I missing?

I was missing the oldest country in Europe. I was missing a country where on a clear day you can see Croatia from the top of Mount Titano (749 metres). I was missing a country that prides itself on its culture. I was missing a country that celebrates its founding day, September 3rd, by playing bingo. Such culture. And I was missing the only country in the world to host a Formula One Grand Prix race every year that is not held in its own country. San Marino is too minuscule and too mountainous to enjoy a proper Grand Prix circuit, so the San Marino Grand Prix is held in Italy (a country and its people the Sammarinesi have little time for except when they need a race course).

Yawn.

Enough.

Chapter over.

That's more than they deserve, the buggers.

* * *

WHAT NOBODY WILL TELL YOU:

During World War II, San Marino was neutral and its, then, good and kind citizens offered shelter to over 100,000 refugees fleeing the holocaust. How soon we forget to be thoughtful and considerate to others.

San Marino had a fleeting moment of glory when they faced England in a World Cup qualifier on 17 November 1993 and took the lead after just 8.3 seconds -- still the fastest goal in World Cup competition. Must have royally pissed off the English side as they came back to score seven straight goals (Ian Wright four of them).

137

CHAPTER 15 - Hamburg: Katarina asks me to marry her

Hamburg, a city with, oh, so many faces.

You have fashionable, cultural and industrial Hamburg. You have cosmopolitan and prosperous Hamburg. And (cue the mood music) you even have Mephistophelean and hormonal Hamburg.

Wait!

No, really. Wait.

I need to stop for a moment and confess something. I didn't really believe I was going to find my soul mate in Hamburg. Anywhere in Germany, actually, but I'm a hopeless romantic when it comes to the Beatles, and I just had to see where they got their start.

John Lennon once said: 'I might have been born in Liverpool, but I grew up in Hamburg.'

And that was enough for me.

I decided to rent a flat in the heart of the St. Pauli district and within walking distance of the Beatles' original venues. Alas, what I didn't know was that the old haunts of the Fab Four were located on or near a colourful street called the 'Reeperbahn'.

And the Reeperbahn was considered 'the world's most

wicked mile'.

* * *

I arrived on the night train from Italy, detrained and stepped out of the vaulted and echoing *Hauptbahnhof* to a bright and sunny morning, and a town awash with besuited, worryingly serious businessmen and businesswomen.

I asked a bespoke-suit directions to the St. Pauli and was ignored. I asked a couple of yards of Dolce & Gabbana directions and he snapped '*Ich bin im Stress!*' and hurried off.

My, wasn't everyone in 'big industrial northern German city' mode.

Eventually, a nun (who resembled the Reverend Mother in *The Sound of Music*) told me: 'Follow the scent of sin.' And jabbed a crooked finger in the direction of the harbour.

I headed through the Old Town and then the New Town and in the general direction of the harbour and eventually found myself in St. Pauli. St. Pauli is charming in an 'old world architecture allied bombs must have missed this part of Hamburg' sort of way.

I stuck my nose in the air and didn't smell any sin, just beer and sausage, so I carried on.

Near the Reeperbahn I spied a boutique which sold prisoner's garb -- made by prisoners -- and espoused such attire was the new 'in' look for trendy locals. Such a trend.

Then something else caught my eye and it made my eyeballs grow stalks. It was a sign in the window of the shop next door and it said: *Zimmer Frei*. I have always believed just a bit in fate (in hindsight, mind you, when things turn out of a positive nature), so I opened the door and stepped in.

The shop reeked of last night's drink and something I couldn't put my finger on. I looked around. I was standing in the middle of a sex shop. Hmmm, hadn't paid attention to the wares on offer in the window, had I? Just saw the 'Room For Rent' sign and plunged right on in.

Have you ever been in a sex shop? You don't have to answer that if your mother's in the same room. If you're curious, though, let me just whisper these three words: 'Yikes!

Ouch! Wooohooo!'

And have you ever had the feeling that someone was watching you? When you are standing in the middle of a sex shop, it is not a feeling you want to experience twice.

I heard a noise just over there to my right and spied a hunched crone observing me from behind the Trojan display.

'*Gruss Gott*,' I said, but my Austrian greeting was ignored and a gruff German '*Guten Tag*' barked Linda Blair-esque my way.

I approached the old woman and saw that she had warts on her hands, and I feared she was responsible for the stench of last night's drink.

I stared at the crone and the crone stared back. Then she did something utterly disarming: She made a circle with the thumb and index finger of her left hand, then repeatedly jabbed the index finger of her right hand back and forth through the warty opening.

Need I go on?

Suddenly my stay in the St. Pauli had lost much of its appeal. I was about to bolt for the front door when a young gay (who made Andy Warhol appear to have good colour in his face) slipped from behind a purple curtain and stepped in front of the crone/mime: '*Wollen Sie das Zimmer vermieten?*'

How did he know that I had come in the shop to ask about the room for rent rather than had entered in pursuit of inflatables? The man may have resembled a week-old corpse, but he knew how to read clientele!

As you can well imagine, I wasn't so sure about the room, what with Andy as the intermediary, but the rent was only 250 euros per month. And money was a concern. So I took the room and within the hour I had a really great bed-sit with a rusty hot plate and a half fridge that was down the hill, around a corner and not all that far from the river Elbe.

And here's the thing: I had always fantasized about doing something daring and misguided like this in a wretchedly large city -- thought it somehow romantic -- but now that I was doing it, I didn't see the romance. Just squalid living conditions and danger leering from every lace-curtained window.

And it wasn't even dark yet.

* * *

Before we embark on my journey behind the Hanseatic guidebook pages in search of the Beatles, I need to give you a little background on a certain delightfully twisted person who will be leading me behind those pages. Her name is Katarina and she lives next door.

It's probably best that I tell you right off that Katarina grew up in the nearby Davidstrasse and just around the corner from where she used to live was Herbertstrasse. Now get ready for this, Herbertstrasse is a refuse-riddled street of legalized prostitution where a menagerie of strumpets, mostly from the Eastern Bloc, sit in bespattered windows and do the Amsterdam thing. But here's the difference between tolerant Amsterdam and uptight Hamburg: The street is fenced off at both ends and if you want to enter you are free to do so as long as you are an adult and a male and you have a pocket stuffed full of euros (Translated: no sightseeing and serious enquiries only). With this sort of nurturing environment you can well understand that lower life forms were nothing new to Katarina.

Where Katarina lived, and where I now lived (in fear), was a rat-infested brick tenement house with a lift licensed for no more than three persons. Our neighbourhood was rife with drug addicts, connoisseurs of the flesh and feral cats that would rip your arm off if you came too close to stroke one.

If you didn't live in our St. Pauli hood, or have first-blood next of kin, it was best not to enter. If you did enter by mistake, or ill-advised design, ferociously protective locals -- fucked up by years of toking, tooting and shooting every imaginable cocktail of drugs, would greet you with psychologically challenged leers, cold steel or perhaps just a joint.

The first words Katarina ever uttered to me in her life were: 'Wanna take a bath?' The flats where we lived were sort of daisy-chained together and not all of the flats had bathtubs. I, for example, had a shower with an attitude. In the spirit of good neighbours, Katarina offered me her bath water after she had finished with it.

Katarina was the spitting image of the ice skater Katarina Witt, so imagine my surprise when I tippy-toed goose-pimpled over to her flat wearing a towel (and, NO, I wasn't going to bathe in her bath water, rather draw a fresh lot, thank you very much), only to find out she was a lesbian. Katarina had short red spiked hair, was just a bit butch, could beat me at arm wrestling and could spit farther than I (thus the spitting image...).

After about a week of annoying Katarina with scores of questions, she said: 'Tell you what, Jonny. I think you need a tour guide, and that would be me. Let me take you to this museum.'

'I'm not doing museums this trip,' I said. 'Like to see where the Beatles got their start, though.'

'The Beatles can wait.'

Katarina delighted in showing me around Hamburg by foot, by boat and on her 'crotch-rocket'. Her crotch-rocket was a motorcycle that you sort of made love to as you drove -- just like the bike Tom Cruise tooled around on, in *Top Gun* -- and it was fast, hair-raisingly fast. I would straddle the sleek machine, hold on to Katarina's waist, then she would explode away from the kerb like an F-14 Tomcat scorching off an aircraft carrier. After a few hours of being thrust forward and raked back, I would invariably be dressed right even though I had left home dressed judiciously left.

Hamburg is a monumentally glorious city and I was fascinated with its architecture, its rich thousand-year-old history, its watery layout, everything except the locals themselves.

Excluding Katarina, the Hamburgians always looked as if they had just received really bad news.

Katarina was one of those people who felt perfectly safe in the most god-awful bowels of the city (probably because we lived in the most god-awful bowels of the city), but she also felt just as much at home in the backyard of the super rich -- although, the feeling wasn't mutual. One balmy autumn evening we were walking along the handsome Binnenalster (or Inner Alster) -- I was pleasantly surprised to find a fairly good-sized lake with trees, a promenade and benches, right downtown in a big industrial city -- and Katarina, who was a horror film buff, was pointing out some of the stately hotels on the waterfront. She was telling me which ones she thought would make great locations for a chain-saw massacre movie, when we came upon the anally swank Hotel Alster. Here we crossed paths with two snooty, *nouveaux riches* couples who had just slithered out of the hotel, thinking they were God's gift. The stuffy faux high society of Hamburg stopped in their tracks and blatantly gawked in mute ill-will at Katarina as she was wearing a miniskirt with prisoner stripes. (The Germans have no sense of shame when it comes to staring and in fact almost rival the Austrians.)

Never one to run from an opportunity to offend the rich, Katarina said something to the effect of: 'If you're going to stare, stare at this!' On that, she showed them her backside, hiked up her miniskirt and, since she never wore any underwear, gave the New Money a view of a real St. Pauli moon. For added effect she wagged her bum rudely, leaving nothing to the imagination. The two bejewelled women were clearly shocked and incensed by the impudence -- but in a quandary -- should they be outraged by the likes of us or upset with their husbands who had been unwittingly excited by Katarina's upper-class ass.

* * *

Katarina loved speaking English, said the German language was suited for the building of a BMW but otherwise unromantic, so sometimes we would tool all the way out to the larger of the two lakes, the picturesque Aussenalster, or Outer Alster, and then along its shore where we would just talk about everything under the moon and watch the diminutive passenger steamers ply the waters. When the steamers unloaded we would fall silent and wait to see if we could catch a glimpse of George Smiley stepping off the boat from the Jungfernstieg. But we never did.

In case you're wondering, Katarina did indeed drag me off to that museum. I only went with the proviso that she would accompany me, and protect me, on a pub crawl in the Reeperbahn afterwards and finally show me where the Beatles got their start. Well, surprise of surprises. The museum turned out to be Claus Becker's (no relation to our Boris) stimulating Erotic Art Museum. And if you've never been, I guess I can heartily recommend that you purchase a pair of nose-glasses and hump it on down to this lofty five-storey brick gallery. If unsure about the nature of art on display that uncertainty is quashed the moment you step in the front door of the former warehouse for you are greeted face to face (or head to head) by a frightfully large penis.

(FYI: Besides displaying graphic photos, nifty ancient dildos, and fertility icons by unknown, traditional erotica-themed artists, the museum also displays some works by Picasso, Henry Miller and even John Lennon. Well, aren't we impressed!

There is also a gift shop on the premises that has not only the traditional museum kitsch on offer but also a fairly impressive display of vibrators and an extensive selection of sex toys -- batteries not included. Please note that the museum has curious hours -- open until midnight on Friday and Saturdays. Think about that. Upon closing, hundreds of aroused art connoisseurs are set loose on already radiantly randy Hamburg.)

After the museum I had an extra-strength Tylenol and then we walked the short distance over to the Reeperbahn for a *Bier*. By day, the Reeperbahn is just a bit tawdry and depressing but by night with all the humming neon lights, hundreds of slabbering sailors and local colour, it transforms into a wickedly exciting venue. And somehow attractive once you realise you won't be mugged, pressed into slavery or forced by some amphetamine-driven tout to go down into a smoky *Keller* to listen to bad German rock 'n' roll.

Katarina told me that the image-unconscious municipal authorities of Hamburg consider the Reeperbahn to be one of Hamburg's pre-eminent cultural treasures What kind of people consider a red-light district a cultural treasure, let alone pre-eminent? Okay, the Amsterdammers, but who else?

Katarina was a good tour guide. On the surface, with her perforated black-leather evening attire, chains, and changing hair colour, she came off somewhat kinky-cum-punk (I had decided to find it all charming) but under the rebellious outer core, an amateur historian was trying to get out.

You can well imagine I was over the moon when we started our pub crawl at the deliriously raucous Top Ten Club at 136 Reeperbahn. This is where the Beatles were playing when George was deported for being under age, and Paul and Pete Best were thrown out of the country for purportedly torching the room they lived in at the back of a sleazy cinema called the Bambi Kino (in reality, they had only set fire to a used condom). Many Germans are still wildly mad about the Beatles and lucky for me Katarina was one of them. This is when I realised our pub crawl was going to be more of a magical-mystery pub tour.

'Finish your beer. I got some crash-hot clubs to show you before the crack of dawn. Don't have to work tomorrow.'

I did a double take. 'You have a job?'

'Of course, I have a job, Jonny. Hamburg may have a high rate of unemployment but this girl will not live off the state.'

'So where do you work?' I could just picture her in some punk, underground club.

'You used up your quota of questions for today. *Los, Bier trinken!*'

Katarina led me through a pulsing jungle of primal sounds and vile smells to Grosse Freiheit 34.

'See this building? This is where the Indra Club used to be located. Right here is where the Beatles first played when they came to Hamburg. The club has long since been moved down that way to number 64 Grosse Freiheit. Everyone goes down there thinking it's where the Beatles first started, but they didn't. They started here.'

Katarina went on to say that the Beatles made quite an impact at the original venue. They were so boisterous, the little old lady who resided upstairs repeatedly complained to the *Polizei* and the joint was eventually closed down. The building that once housed the Indra has changed over the years and in the spirit of not offending anyone, especially little old ladies, has been painted a memorably gaudy pink and tenderly renamed the Funky Pussy Club.

'C'mon, let's go in.'

The Funky Pussy Club was good crack. We listened to absolutely awful German rock here, but drank a damn good beer called St Pauli Girl.

'See where the stage is? When the Beatles played it was over there in the corner and the setting was much more intimate. John Lennon used to strut around the stage doing goosesteps and shouting "Heil Hitler!" or yelling "What did you do during the war?" Pissed off a lot of Germans, but they kept coming to see them. Perhaps because he sometimes performed in just his underwear.'

I looked around the bar. It was dark and on the seedy side of moody. And it was chocka with good-looking women. Good looking in an 'I can suck a golf ball through a fifty foot hosepipe' sort of way.

'What's going on, Katarina?'

'What do you mean?'

'The male to female ratio. It's just me and those two guys over there.'

'Those aren't guys.'

'What?'

'They're women. This is a lesbian club.'

'No shit.'

'You know, I really should take you over to number 19 Reeperbahn, to the Café Keese.'

'I'm not so sure I want to hear this.'

'Oh, but you do, Jonny. They have what's called a "Ball Paradox" there. This is where the women ask the men to dance.'

'Tell me more.'

'It's a good place to get--' Katarina froze and watched a

146

young Anne Heche look-alike cruise by our table. '--laid, but you've got to be careful. Many women are sex addicts and you could even run into the odd he/she.'

Holy shit.

I weighed what Katarina just said. I remember reading somewhere what Ian Fleming had said regarding Hamburg and the Reeperbahn: 'Except to the exceedingly chaste, it is all good, clean German fun'.

Either my values were different or I'd grown up in a biosphere.

Under cloak of drunkenness, and blasted by loud music from all ends of the block, we made our way back out onto the street and I was immediately accosted by a prostitute who grabbed my arm and tried to lead me away. Katarina grabbed the lady of the night by the hair and yelled, '*Er ist mit mir!*' Then she put her arm through mine and led me the short distance to Grosse Freiheit 36 and we fell downstairs into the Kaiserkeller.

'This is where the Beatles relocated after being thrown out of the Indra.'

The Kaiserkeller is small and smoky and raucous and smelled like someone had been peeing on the walls. But what history! I was thrilled to be there, but I think we were the only ones not ingesting voluminous amounts of banned controlled substances. We listened to German rock 'n' roll (By now I had decided that German rock 'n' roll was an oxymoron) and for added diversion watched a shining example of the improvidence of youth at the table next to ours pop new designer Ecstasy tablets, which sported little pictures of the Smurfs. The future of Germany offered us a few tablets, but we declined saying that we generally steered clear of brain-crushing drugs doled out by teenagers who were total strangers in clubs that smelled of pee.

Katarina went on to tell me that the Beatles enjoyed enormous success at the Kaiserkeller and this is where the band rotated sets with another band from, yes, you are so clever, Liverpool. The band was called Rory Storm & The Hurricanes, and when one band played the other band would just chill, swill and take uppers. Weeks went by and the Beatles became acquainted with the members of the other Liverpudlian band and became particularly fond of the spunky drummer -- a lad by the name of Ringo Starr.

It was late when Katarina and I stumbled back home, arm in arm like two drinking buddies, and it had turned evilly damp and chilly as it only seems to do in a city climatically influenced by a combination of the North Sea, the Baltic Sea and about 20 square miles of polluted lakes, rivers and canals. As we walked down the hill and neared the Elbe, we spotted huge flames from an industrial site shooting up in the air along a tiny portion of the harbour's 25 miles of quays. Katarina watched the billowing flames lick at the underbelly of an oppressively foggy sky then became uncharacteristically subdued. That's when she recounted a hellish night in Hamburg's past: On 28 July 1943, Hamburg became the first city to ever suffer a firestorm. A firestorm is a wildly intense and destructive fire where strong currents of air are sucked tornado-like into the conflagration from the surrounding area. The firestorm was born when incendiary bombs transformed over 12-square miles of city centre into a massive suffocating oven. Hurricane-force winds snapped trees in half and actually sucked fleeing citizens into the fiery hell. The heat was so intense, the tarmac on the streets actually burned and 'cooked' thousands of citizens who had taken refuge in underground air raid shelters.

In that one night alone, 42,000 residents of Hamburg died.

Then Katarina said: 'As you sow so shall you reap.'

We were silent for a long time, just watching the flames blowtorch the sky then, magically, Katarina was back among the living: 'Y'know, you told me you're looking for someone to share your life with. Why don't you just marry me? We really get on well.'

I just stared at Katarina for the longest time, speechless. When I didn't respond, she just smiled, took me by the arm and said: 'C'mon, I'm buying breakfast. I'll take you to the Café Möller. It's where the Beatles used to go after they finished their gigs.'

148

Well, for the month that I hung out in Hamburg, Katarina showed me a lot and taught me a lot. She even taught me about how important it is to just be yourself -- at the very least when you are home and away from your place of employment (Translated: the girl really knew how to let her short hair down).

Early one Monday morning, I think I had only three sleeps remaining in Hamburg, I opened the door to my flat to throw something at two cats that were wrestling in the hallway. I heard the morning news in German coming from somewhere down the hall and then saw a gorgeous young creature emerge from Katarina's flat. I guess I shouldn't have been so surprised that someone had spent the night. After all, Katarina was human just like the rest of us. I'm not the nosy type, but curious I am, indeed, so I gave the young beauty a good long look. The young lady was dressed in a business suit and high heels, and she was carrying a briefcase. But what was weird, she could have been a respectable double for Katarina. People do this, don't they? The Mick and Bianca thing. Embarrassed, and possibly, I admit, a little jealous, I threw my copy of the *Hamburg Morgenpost* at the cats, then ducked back inside my flat. Immediately there was a knock at the door. One of the cats ticked off? I opened the door a crack. It was the young, gorgeous woman. I was wondering what to say, when she beat me to it: 'Aren't you even going to say *"Guten Morgen?"*'

I said 'good morning' and it was only when I heard the laugh that I realised I was standing there talking to Katarina.

'B-B-But?'

'A lot of us in Hamburg live secret lives. I work at the Deutsche Bank. What can I tell you?' She walked off laughing, then turned: 'I know this great little place for tonight, if you're game?'

'Only if it involves good German beer or bad German rock 'n' roll?' I said.

Laughing, Katarina raised one finger in the air and was gone into a lift licensed for no more than three persons.

Then the lift door slid back open and Katarina was standing

there with a funny look on her face.

And then the door closed again.

* * *

WHAT NOBODY WILL TELL YOU: In 1998, a Hamburg man was found sitting in front of his telly. He had been dead for five years. Cause of death was never determined, but I believe he was most likely bored to death by German television.

Hamburg has 2,302 bridges. That's more than Venice and Amsterdam, combined! (Venice has 401 bridges, Amsterdam 1281.)

When the Beatles popped uppers, they would pop Preludin or 'Prellies', as they called them back then. The Prellies were often purchased in a tube. Before leaving for work, one Beatle would invariably say to the others: 'Taking the tube tonight?'

The name 'Beatles' was originally considered too risqué in Hamburg, for a similar sounding word, *Peedles*, in local dialect, means 'little willy'.

Jon Breakfield

CHAPTER 16 - Istanbul: This is where the circumcisions took place

Over the centuries, the city of Istanbul has been ravaged by fire (60 worth noting), earthquakes (50 and counting) and invasions (barbarian and touristic). The above are all undeniably frightening, but there was a time when it wasn't such misfortune that struck sincere fear deep into the hearts of the young men of Constantinople, rather the Circumcision Chamber in the fabled Topkapi Palace. Yes, indeed. You see, according to Turkish tradition, the male Istanbulians were not circumcised at birth, rather when they reached (author clears throat) manhood.

(FYI: The above penile practice raises some immediate questions, wouldn't you say? What makes more sense, to go under the knife at a tender age when pain à la foreskin is a surprising and frightening experience -- yet quickly banished from the memory banks -- or have your patently adult member filleted when it's raging with teenage hormones? You tell me. What would you prefer?)

If possible, this excursion into circumcision hell gets even more ludicrous. Occasionally, ah, headstrong Turks, with an

151

appalling sense of timing, wait to have the dastardly delicate procedure performed, get ready, just before marriage. What would possess any individual with at least the intelligence of a Döner kebab to partake in such an ill-timed endeavour? I'm sure it's comforting to enter your future with the new, sleek model but, I mean, really.

How about a little foreskin foresight!

These thoughts (and the razor-sharp image of the famed Emerald Dagger) were flashing in my head as I took leave of the opulent Topkapi Palace and stepped out into the thrilling chaos that is the defining signature of Istanbul. Immediately, I was swept in a direction I didn't want to go by a crush of steamy, sweaty humanity.

It's often like this in Istanbul, you see, Istanbul is chaos in its purest form. People rushing, cars honking, scooters zooming, muezzins wailing, babies shrieking, vendors imploring, touts cajoling and beggars clamping on who just won't let go (sort of like ASDA on a Saturday morning).

As if this isn't disconcerting enough, Istanbul is unbridled capitalism run amok. Down by the waterfront, in one short block, I was besieged by a coffee vendor selling a glutinous aromatic substance with the viscosity of streaky bacon, a flurry of dirtbags who attempted to foist off expensive cigarettes and cheap watches, and three entrepreneurial lowlifes with pornographic postcards, lottery tickets and an inflatable Madonna (the singer, not the Virgin).

I had flown a national airline, which shall remain unnamed (so as not to offend the British) into Istanbul's Yesilköy Airport. The flight gets a mention on account of what happened onboard. The captain made an announcement, sounding sincerely authoritative, and then forgot to turn off the intercom button and the entire aircraft was privy to his real self and immediate concerns: 'What I could really go for now is a coffee and a blow job.' Shocked by what she had heard, a young trainee stewardess, dutiful nevertheless, bolted through the cabin toward the cockpit to inform the captain of his X-rated faux pas. As she ran through economy, one alert and conscientious passenger was heard to yell: 'Hey, don't forget the coffee!'

My fist digs were unconventional. I slept in steamy heat on a laundry-bedecked rooftop for two dollars a night (you can do that over there, so I wanted to try it -- don't). Eventually, I found more luxurious accommodation down at the harbour on, yes, a houseboat. I had wanted to live near the Golden Horn, and now I was actually living on it, straddled by water buses and historical ruin.

My rent was an agreeable twenty-five dollars per week.

During week two, I awoke to streaming sun, the usual honk of shipping in the harbour and the summer miasma of raw sewage. I got out of bed, stretched like a cat and stumbled out onto the afterdeck. Standing there on the dock, smiling at me, was a man with a nose like a scimitar. Rhino Man informed me that he was the Harbour Master and that I was living onboard illegally. He also informed me that he would gladly stop sniffing around if I paid <u>him</u> twenty-five dollars a week, as well. 'You pay me now,' he said, holding out a grubby hand.

'My landlord didn't say anything about me being illegal.'

'You pay me now!'

'Let me talk to my landlord first.'

'You pay me now or I go to police!!!'

Police? Turkish jail? I had seen the movie. So I paid.

Eventually, I discovered that the Harbour Master was in fact not the Harbour Master, just another entrepreneurial slug, so I threatened to renew his vows of circumcision and my rent dropped back to twenty-five dollars a week.

The houseboat didn't have a shower or toilet but did have a pre-Byzantine fan that had two speeds -- dead, and dead slow. I would go to bed sweating and I would wake up sweating. My morning ablutions had to be performed from a perforated hosepipe. When I needed to tend to pressing bodily functions, I had to discreetly pee overboard or hustle up a steep hill to where a sign proudly proclaimed: 'Modern WC'. Let me tell you right off, Modern WC does not translate into 'Armitage Shanks with the push button dual flush'. It may have had tiles to rival the Blue Mosque but it still had a steaming, evil-smelling hole in the floor -- and an air force of flies.

**Author's Clairvoyant Observation: I know what you're thinking right now, you're thinking: 'I hope he doesn't think he's going to meet the woman of his dreams living in a hamster's nest.' Well, you're right. You see, I've given up looking. Yes, you heard right. I've given up. If I'm not looking perhaps something will happen.

At sunset, I would often sit out on the deck of the houseboat. The early evening light made it easy to see that the water in the harbour was a sluggish, oily cauldron, and I was always afraid it would catch fire if one of the local fishermen perchance tossed a cigarette in. Creatures resembling fish were caught in these waters and even sold down at Galata Bridge (most likely to the blind) but, fish with boils on their heads or not, it was still said that the water 'possessed nothing so alive as its place in history'. Supposedly an effort is being made to clean up the harbour but I didn't see any effort being made, just a never-ending parade of faecal matter and distended condoms.

* * *

I think it's time I drew you a little map -- a somewhat rough map. Envisage a big dog bone lying on your kitchen floor. The round bit at the top is part of the Black Sea. The round portion at the bottom is part of the Sea of Marmara (which leads to the Mediterranean). The narrow bit where your hand would go, if your dog would let you pick up the bone, is an 18-mile strait called the Bosporus. Now, when your dog isn't looking, quietly pick up the bone with your right hand and stick your thumb out to the left. Your thumb is the harbour area of Istanbul called the Golden Horn (where I live). To the right of your hand is Asia. To your left is Europe. Istanbul rests on both sides of the Bosporus, in Asia and in Europe -- and your dog is now eyeing your carotid.

The Bosporus is unquestionably stunning to look at but did you know it is one of the busiest and trickiest waterways in the world? I kid you not. To make it even more of a titanic task to navigate, pesky passenger ferries crisscross in front of north and southbound freighters and cruise ships, get ready, 1500 times a day. If this doesn't turn a skipper to drink, a ship trying to slip through the Bosporus, from let's say the Mediterranean to the Black Sea (top of the dog bone), also has to contend with sucking whirlpools and conflicting currents. The current at the surface of the Bosporus is cool and flows from the Black Sea southward, but beneath those waters, the salty warm waters of the Mediterranean rush northward as a powerful undercurrent. To make maritime matters even more exhilarating, vessels on the Bosporus, unlike those on most waterways, pass starboard to starboard.

Here's one for you: In 1994 an oil tanker collided with a freighter up near the Black Sea. The oil tanker exploded, killing 28, and burned out of control -- for a week! If the accident had occurred just a few hundreds metres farther south, the strong currents pushing from the Black Sea would have carried the burning tanker right into the heart of Istanbul. (Both the freighter and the tanker were of Greek-Cypriot registry. Oh, dear)

* * *

Istanbul by night is romantic -- darkness tempers the chaos and conceals the filth.

Often, when it was a steamy tropical night, which was, well, often, I would venture from my houseboat, tingling with pending adventure, and slip up the hill to some dive of a bar to murder a cold beer. And it was on one of these sultry nighttime sorties when I was off wandering blindly about Istanbul that I noticed it. It was a building that looked like a cross between a Bronx tenement and an up-market crack house, if that is architecturally possible. But these were not the principle characteristics that caught my eye -- the main eye grabbers were the fence, the police and a long queue of men in a highly anxious state. Does this sort of setup sound familiar? I thought so. What I had stumbled upon was a designated *genel ev* -- a house of dastardly ill repute.

In these designated surroundings, prostitution is legal and moreover these digs are actually protected by the police. If you want to enter, all you have to do is simply present your ID to the crack Istanbul constabulary. If you are drunk, which is rare as the price of drink in Istanbul tends to sober you right up, the police will not let you enter. And, no, I did not enter. But I did hang around. And get ready for this next bit, I learned through the lowlife grapevine (my people) that *foreign* women who are thrown in Turkish prisons for drug offences sometimes can get their sentences significantly reduced if they go to work in a *genel ev.*

And why am I telling you this you ask? Isn't this just another big city character flaw? Isn't this just a sleazy mirror image of Hamburg? Well, there's a difference here in Istanbul, you see, members of the Turkish military are awarded three entry passes each month as part of their pay.

While we're hovering around this topic, I have an allied theme I would like to toss your way, if I may -- it's harems. But first some clarification: The word *harem* referred not only to the women themselves but also the separate part of a palace -- or even small household -- where the women lived in seclusion. A harem could even be a back room in your house.

In the Topkapi Palace, which was the former *Seraglio*, or residence of the sultans of the Ottoman Empire, the harem was guarded by a stable of eunuchs whose job was to ensure that no stray males gain, ah, illegal entry. One of their other coveted duties was to make sure, and I tell the truth here, no cucumbers found their way behind closed doors, *unsliced.*

The big boss of the eunuchs was the chief Black Eunuch. Some of these eunuchs, as if they hadn't already been hit below the belt, had their eardrums punctured and even their tongues slit. This went a long way in cutting down on the gossip and most assuredly various other leisure pursuits.

The physical harem, in the aforementioned Topkapi Palace, consisted of a dark, secret world of opulent luxury: elaborate buildings, silky salons, steamy baths and fragrant boudoirs. And there were dancers, musicians, jesters and even botanical gardens where lions and tigers and bears romped.

This world of excess was also where the sultan and his

adoring mother resided. The sultan's mother was the second most powerful person in the empire and undeniably the biggest pain in the tuchas. The harem was also Home Sweet Home to, the sultan's wives, brothers, children, concubines, odalisques, eunuchs, Christian female slaves and male pages (not unlike the Clinton White House). You would have thought it a good deal to be related to a sultan but if you were a younger brother it was a dicey situation at best. You see, the sultan's younger brothers were kept under lock and key lest they have premature designs on the throne. To avoid any disputes over succession, the sultan occasionally partook of fratricide to cull competition.

Harems existed at all levels of society but the major-league numbers were posted by the Ottoman sultans. To give you an idea, these randy lads had between 1,000 and 2,000 women cooped up behind the closed doors of the Topkapi Palace. Is this perhaps a classic example of your eyes being bigger than your stomach? And what sort of condition were the women in by the time one of these fellows got around to one of the higher numbers on his dance card?

(FYI: We've come to a delicate issue so, if you don't mind, I'm going to have to whisper again: Left without a heck of a lot to do other than scarf vast mounds of sherbet, consume copious amounts of mind-numbing opium and play backgammon, many of the young lasses of the harem would take turns grooming one another. You see, it was a sin to have hair on one's private parts -- which in those days meant everything from the eyes down. Hair was removed from the legs, underarms, the genital area and even the nostrils and ears. While washing one another the women soon became friends, *close* friends -- and sometimes, dare I say, even lovers.)

* * *

WHAT NOBODY WILL TELL YOU:

One of the reasons the odalisques weren't serviced by the sultan as often as they would have desired was because besides having to compete against all the gorgeous 17-year-old members of the harem, they had to also compete against all the gorgeous 17-year-old *seferlis*, or male pages. And it was well

157

known that the pages were not chosen for their writing skills, rather their oral.

It is a little known fact (and perhaps it should be kept that way), but here, at the glorious crossroads of Europe and Asia -- this great civilization gave us the fork.

CHAPTER 17 - Istanbul: A bacchanal night of belly dancing and lust

I found a part-time job at the Grand Bazaar.

The Grand Bazaar is a tangled labyrinth of delightfully tacky shops, moody cafés and restaurants of questionable cuisine. Here in this vast bazaar, artisans pound old tin things into new tin things, and you can buy everything from frying pans to Ray-Bans. There are over 4000 of these higgledy-piggledy shops/stalls, so your choice of kitsch is unlimited. I soon surmised that no Istanbulian with any common sense shops at the Grand Bazaar. The locals shop at the nearby Egyptian Bazaar.

I worked in a little shop with no front door, and I sold leather coats to English and German speaking tourists. Often, I was late for work, not because of the commute (which was unimaginably awful in its own right), but for the simple fact that I was always getting lost in the bazaar's muddled maze trying to get to work.

I had been hired because of my haggling acumen (which I didn't know I had). It all began when I bought a leather coat from my future boss, Podrum. Podrum had tried to sell me the coat for the equivalent of 300 dollars. Knowing that negotiation was a coveted tradition in the bazaar and that one should never encroach on a vendor's dignity by countering with an offer less than half of the original stated price, I purposely encroached on Podrum's dignity and countered with just three dollars.

'Three!' Podrum shouted in my face. 'That is ridiculous!'

'No, three hundred is ridiculous!'

Podrum looked at me for a long time, the way someone sizes you up to either kill you, or hug you to death. 'You get coat for thirty dollars if you come work for me!'

And I had a job in the Grand Bazaar.

Many of the tourists were English or German and ended up being mainly flight crews. Soon I made the acquaintance of two stewardesses, Muffy and Corolla from British Airways. Muffy was a Geordie and spoke what I found to be a most unique patois. Corolla was from Belfast and could handle her tongue like a gun.

The first time I set eyes on Muffy and Corolla, they were trying on knee-high leather boots at the adjacent stall. Muffy had leaned back to thrust her foot into a boot and her skirt went halfway up to Hadrian's wall. She caught me staring.

'Stop lookin' at me knickers in giv' us a hand, ye wanker!'

'Is that the Queen's English?'

'Divint givvus any i ya cheek, ye little bugger!'

Corolla laughed. As did I. Finally Muffy.

Now, owing to the latest nightmare in the Middle East, airlines from around the world were being diverted to Istanbul, and hotels that weren't usually designated as layover hotels were being pressed into service. One of these hotels that suddenly found itself thrust into the premiership was the Hotel Cinar, a decidedly modest establishment at best but with a stunning location right on the Bosporus. The staff at the Cinar wanted to accommodate and impress, so they threw a big shindig. It was to be an evening of entertainment and diversion in the form of wining and dining and belly dancing.

Muffy and Corolla got wind of the impending fiesta and invited me. 'There won't be many lads,' I was told.

'You'll be surrounded by randy women.'

'You'll feel like a sultan.'

'Can you come, bonnie lad?'

(**Would you mind terribly if I interrupted this chapter for a moment and had a word with you? Yes. Yes. Yes. I realise I do this a lot, but you are all I've got. What do you think the chances are I might meet a young lady this evening who works for an airline? If she works for an airline, and is flying internationally, then there is a good chance she's besotted with adventure and languages. Right? If the pot wasn't going to boil, perhaps I could at least get in some hot water.)

The plan was for everyone to meet in the ornately decorated, Byzantine-inspired nightclub as the clock struck nine.

At the crack of nine I stepped into the room and saw something that made my stomach do a triple flip with a half twist. In my short time working at the bazaar, I'd become acquainted with a handful of young flight attendants who had caught my eye and, so okay, I admit it, perhaps I had flirted with them a bit. Now, as if by divine intervention (with a devilish sense of humour), every last one of these young lasses had been on these diverted aircraft. What was I going to do? What would you do?

'*Bonjour*, Jon!'

I turned and saw Yvette from Air France waving at me.

'*Tu prends une verre vin avec moi, oui?*'

'But, of course,' I said, sounding like Inspector Clouseau again. Who wouldn't have a glass of wine with Yvette? Yvette had long firm Moulin-Rouge legs and thick, *pain-au-chocolat* hair and that accent, oh, that accent, need I say more. It made me go all crème caramel inside.

'G'day, Jon,' came the greeting from Rory of Qantas. 'What about that pint you promised me?'

'No worries.' Oh, how could I turn down a sheila like Rory? She was always so tanned and fit. Her Aussie accent was like fingernails on a blackboard, but when I was looking at her fine brown frame, I didn't notice the blackboard.

161

'Hej! Hej! Jon!'

I heard the trill of a libidinous Swede by the name of Inga from SAS.

'Jag drika med dig ikvell!'

'But of course we'll have that drink together.' Those Scandinavians, oh, those Scandinavians. Inga with polar-bear hair and blue eyes like the Baltic. She always entered my space when she spoke. I was worried she could hear my heart pounding.

What was I going to do?

Oh, there's something else I think you need to know. When we arrived for this enchanting evening of belly dancing, there were fifty-four of us -- and fifty-two were female. That's right, the odds were leaning heavily one way. There would be a plethora of cunning lingual young crumpet. I was delirious. Hormones thought extinct were erupting, and I was thankful I had been circumcised as a wee babe.

No cockpit crews attended the evening and the only other male in attendance turned out to be a rather effeminate steward who was innocuous at best and made such a lasting impression on me that night that as I write this chapter damn if I can remember his name, only his features. He resembled, in unimaginably vivid detail, a vulture: hunched narrow shoulders, sharp-beaked face, dressed in black. It was just going to be me and a gay predatory bird.

Okay. Okay. As you read this let's not get carried away thinking I'm some sort of chauvinistic, sexist, opportunist hoping to get laid. I graduated from university with an unopened box of condoms, okay? Opportunities didn't come along like this all so often. It was a chance of a lifetime. When was the last time you were thrown into a closed room with fifty-two sexually parched members of the opposite sex and the competition was only one hollow-boned buzzard who dined on same-sex carrion?

And you can imagine how happy the belly dancer was to perform for us. This many flight crews probably hadn't laid-over at this hotel in the jet-age and she was only used to dancing for three narcoleptic guests and the kitchen staff. The belly dancer sensed the atmosphere and her zaftig body undulated sensually and set the mood of erotica.

Enough already. Stop yelling. I know you're all dying to know what happened, so why don't I just jump right to the sordid highlights (I'm dying to know what happened and I was there).

After watching the rotating, gyrating, pulsing pelvis of the belly dancer for a few hours, I set out like a cheetah stalking. I moved from table to table, casing the entire group. Then, slowly, I closed in. Who would be the most tasty? Who wouldn't put up a fight? Who could I drag back to my lair without needing a sherpa?

To warm up, I commenced with Giovanna from Alitalia, but all she could talk about was her impression of *signor* Right (I was her impression of *signor* Wrong). I slipped over to Heike from Lufthansa, and she told me her dream man would have to look like former Chancellor Schroeder (or at least have his power, influence, and unnumbered Swiss accounts). Undaunted, I transited to Lauren from Swissair, but she was, as you've guessed, neutral about everything. So I honoured the drink with Yvette from Air France and then Rory from Qantas and Inga from SAS. I circled. I sensed. I sniffed. I received a coquettish smile here, an innuendo there -- a bill for six cocktails.

The cheetah was ready to pounce -- but he needed directions. I was waiting for someone to send off some sort of signal.

Finally, near the end of the evening, after dancing the night away and losing Kamiko of Nippon ('I go meet captain, now.'), the signal came from Roye, a dazzling beauty from Denmark with wrap-around legs. Ah, those Danish. Ah, those Nordic women. I think the clincher, I mean when I knew it was going to be safe to set my claws, was when Roye pursed her lips and whispered oh so deep in my ear: 'You know, some say Denmark -- that's where it all began.'

'It?'

'Yes,' purred Roye. 'It.'

'It -- what?'

'You know -- it -- sex.'

Meow.

I made my move. I asked Roye to dance the last dance. The air was electric. The music was pounding. The belly dancer was vibrating like a sex aid. My loins were on fire.

It was a slow dance and we danced wrapped around each other as if we were one -- with four arms and four legs. I looked into Roye's eyes. Roye looked into my eyes. She was melting. I was melting. The heat was rolling off us in undulating, sweaty waves. There was no time like the present I thought to invite her back to my houseboat for uncensored, unbiblical sex. I opened my mouth to close the deal, but heard instead: 'Mind if I cut in?'

I looked up to see the predatory bird swipe Roye out of my clutches. I stood there and watched them go off, arm in arm, gazing lustfully into each other's private parts. I heard a noise behind me. I turned and saw Corolla and Muffy sitting at a nearby table. Corolla was shaking her head in disbelief. Muffy was giving me a major eye roll.

'Was wonderin' why you were spendin' so much time tryin' to pull Roye,' Corolla said.

'Ye coudnt see the forest for the bluddy trees, bonnie lad,' Muffy said. 'Roye's his lass.'

'You knew they were an item?'

'They both work for British Airways.'

'Why didn't he say something to me?'

'Guess he didn't think you were a threat,' Corolla said, and even though she was sympathetic I could tell she was trying to keep from laughing.

Now Muffy was trying to keep from laughing. Her quivering lips sent Corolla off, then they both exploded. As Corolla and Muffy rolled back in their seats and gestured for me to pull up a chair, Muffy presented me with these painfully lingering words: 'A lad like ye shud be gettin' more arse than a toilet seat.'

* * *

WHAT NOBODY WILL TELL YOU:

One of belly dancing's original purposes was to aid women in labour.

CHAPTER 18 - The Canary Islands: Tenerife and the North

One titbit the guidebooks fail to mention is that it's geographically rewarding to sit on the *left* side of the aircraft the first time you fly into Tenerife.

If you sit on the left side of the aircraft, and depart from Gatwick (I was transiting from Istanbul), as I did, you cross the Channel, hug the western coast of France and fly past Bordeaux, the French Basque Country, Spanish Basque Country, Portugal, Gibraltar and then you are over open water for 650 miles.

And I defy you not to be goggle-eyed the first time you set eyes on Tenerife, for the four-hour flight will reward you with the breathtaking sight of a vast volcano (Mount Teide) rising out of the Atlantic Ocean to a height of 12,198 feet. If you do this in the winter -- you will see a volcano rising out of the sea capped with snow.

I had heard a lot about the island of Tenerife: about its humid, deeply fertile north ('Some say it resembles the Garden of Eden.') and its arid, vastly barren south ('What a dusty shit-hole.'). Could this really be true? Could somewhere on this earth be so intoxicatingly diverse?

I had to see for myself.

Besides, you know what transpired in the Garden of Eden.

* * *

As the aircraft closed on Tenerife, I could actually make out the plush, leafy city of Puerto de la Cruz in the fertile north and soon after the man-made beaches of Los Cristianos and Playa de Las Américas in the desert-like south.

But that's the last I saw of the grandeur of 'the island of the two faces' as it's known, owing to the fact that I had booked a package holiday at an *unnamed* resort and ended up halfway between the arid south and the verdant north, stuck in a cultural no-man's land with the appeal of suburban Kabul. Trapped miles from all sights worth seeing -- and out of walking distance from all decent watering holes -- my days were spent prone on a Lilo, and my evening entertainment came in the form of karaoke, bingo and Mr & Mrs.

Not only was I missing the ethnic experience, I missed the whole point of going -- Tenerife's diversity.

So I checked out of my hotel early and took the transfer bus back to Reina Sofia airport and headed directly to the rental-car counter where I rented a dented Kia that looked like shit, ran like shit and drove like shit.

I nicknamed it the '*Caca-coche*'.

Other than the multitude of floral memorials alongside the road reflecting the Canarians' ability to take command of a motor vehicle, the short drive (45 minutes, *mas o menos*) from the south to the north is utterly spectacular with the shimmering Atlantic off to your right and majestic foothills off to your left soaring up toward the volcano. Then just as you approach the outskirts of the north's largest city, Santa Cruz (population 224,000), you turn inland and away from the sea and climb toward the Anaga mountain chain (the spine of Tenerife) and the university town of La Laguna (population 142,000).

I parked the *Caca-coche* and took a stroll. And guess what? It was cooler here. And walking through the immaculate old quarter of La Laguna is like stepping back in time. The old quarter is preserved much as it was centuries ago. The tranquil streets, many of which are now completely pedestrianised, lead you through a veritable wonderland of traditional architecture hailing from the 16th through 18th centuries: traditional Canarian houses with their intricately carved balconies and courtyards, beautiful churches, impressive convents and noble mansions. Make no mistake, La Laguna has serious old colonial charm.

And few tourists go there, so you might consider doing so.

I jumped back in the *Caca-coche* and climbed higher up into the mountains. Just past La Laguna is the Los Rodeos Airport. Here the weather changes rapidly. Windy. Cool. Misty. Exciting.

Los Rodeos rests at 2000 feet and has the worst weather on the island. It's the last place on earth where an airport should have been built. But they built one here nevertheless. A lonely runway stretches between a series of worryingly high mountains, and if the weather turns suddenly sour, the venue becomes a disaster waiting to happen.

(FYI: On March 27, 1977, a Pan Am 747 collided on the runway with a KLM 747 in dense fog, killing 583 people. The accident still has the highest number of fatalities of any single accident in aviation history.)

As you leave Los Rodeos and the foul weather behind, you slowly enter another world -- a tropical world of flourishing greenery, vast leafiness and exotic flowers.

And it's startling how quickly you are over the spine and on the other side of the island, rocketing downhill toward a jewel of a city nestled on a verdant volcanic promontory. This is what I had seen from the air. This is Puerto de la Cruz. 'Puerto' is the oldest resort in the Canary Islands -- and it is the Garden of Eden, indeed.

As you descend through lush banana plantations, gnarled vineyards and sprawling fields of geraniums and exotic orchids, you can peep up through the clouds and catch a glimpse of the misty eminence of mighty Mount Teide rising high above the florally lush Oratava Valley.

This is an immensely beautiful sight. And I was excited to be here.

I found a charmingly well-worn Canarian hotel in Puerto de la Cruz by the name of the Xibana Park. I chose this particular hotel because of the central location and the fact the coloured brochure offered a car park. Parking in downtown Puerto is not recommended to anyone without a lot of time on his or her hands. You could say I fell into this category, but it didn't matter today. I had done my research.

'We don't have any parking,' a young woman (with dark, burning eyes) at the front desk told me. This, after I'd paid for a week in advance.

'But it says so in the colour brochure.'

'Perhaps, but we still don't have a car park.'

'Where can I park my car?'

'On the street.'

'Where on the street?'

'Don't know. I never drive to work.'

'Why not?'

'Too hard to find a place to park.'

As you know, when I arrive in a new town, I take to the streets and roam and explore and people watch. I skulk around moody back alleys, creep through beckoning narrow lanes and linger interminably in cafés. This really is a great way to get to know your new home. And sometimes you are privy to a bit of local colour: In front of the parish church of Our Lady of the Peña de Francia, I spotted five nuns walking along eating ice cream cones (I found this charming -- a first with nuns); behind the church, I startled two teenagers who I presumed had deigns on gaining employment at airport security as they were briskly frisking each other all over; then alongside the church, I came upon a priest nitrogenating a tree. When he saw me he adjusted his cassock and fled.

Puerto de la Cruz by night is exotically romantic. It has oceans of humming neon lights, ornately tiled pedestrian zones (where some people park their cars) and quaint, beckoning restaurants. One balmy evening I had a stroll around the leafy, raised square of Plaza del Charco. Here's a tip: If you ever see someone you fancy in Puerto and don't know where he or she lives, go to Plaza del Charco. Your fantasy will eventually turn up here whether it's for an after-siesta coffee, an evening stroll or a late nightcap.

They always do.

Anyway, I was creeping about the square one evening when lively salsa music came wafting along with the erotic fragrance of night-blooming jasmine. The music drew me (like a cartoon character) up a narrow lane that led away from the square. Here on the right side, I found the source of the salsa seeping from an older white building with little blue tables and little blue umbrellas out front. I had happened upon one of Puerto's sincerely romantic venues, the typically Canarian restaurant of El Pescador.

El Pescador is in the oldest building in Puerto and you can sit outside at the blue sidewalk tables, inside at the bar, or deep in the loaded-with-atmosphere dining area. The restaurant is known for its fresh fish and seafood and you can even procure authentic Canarian food here, cuisine that is hard to come by in the restaurants in the south of Tenerife.

The bill of fare at El Pescador is exquisite, but the true draw is not the *paella* or *mariscos* (seafood) or *papas arrugadas* (small potatoes still in their skins, boiled in heavily salted water and served with two types of mojo sauce), rather the two musicians who play nightly.

One of the musicians was a vertically challenged fellow by the name of Chano. Chano (think Ronnie Corbett) sang like an angel, but that was not his real talent. His real talent was with the women. Somehow during the course of an evening, Chano would lure all the attractive ladies up on stage to sing the choruses with him. Knowing the words or being able to hold a tune was not a prerequisite, only a good body. Chano felt that getting a woman up on stage with him was the equivalent of foreplay. How he did it I don't know for *GQ* material he certainly was not, but he did it nevertheless. And as I was soon to find out, he did it regularly.

When there were no members of the opposite sex within sight, and Chano was beyond bored, he would sometimes waddle over to my table. He would sit with me and rabbit on about his lovely wife and his frisky kids and, then, just when his eyes would well with saltwater out of devoted familial love, he would spot some curvaceous creature slipping in through the front door and he would be off like a stud horse who had been locked in the barn all winter and had just been turned out to the spring grass.

Chano preferred the north of Tenerife over the south: 'At least you can find a local here.' He also mentioned that the Canarians are still struggling to find their own identity: 'We sing music from Mexico and South America, we holiday in Cuba and Venezuela (nobody from the Canary Islands holidays on the mainland of Spain as the Canarians find the mainland Spaniards insufferable and condescending), and we have one of the most beautiful islands in the world yet we put pictures of Hawaii on our walls. What does that tell you?'

I started to say 'It tells me you are still struggling to find your own identity,' but Chano no longer knew I existed. His eyes were fixed (like a cat on a canary) on two zaftig birds who had just appeared at the front door. The young ladies were British and, yes, later that evening he had them both up on stage singing a sexy chorus of 'Guantanamera''.

* * *

One essential element Puerto de la Cruz always lacked was a decent beach. There was the odd black-sand beach, but nothing that made you want to run to the sea and throw off your clothes until the renowned Canarian artist (whom none of us have ever heard of), César Manrique, had his vision over 25 years ago. You see, he decided to build the *mamasita* of all swimming pools, and he wanted his realised vision to blend in with, yes, Mother Nature. To get an idea of the scope of this beast, envisage an area about the size of a football stadium. Now fill that entire area (including the seats) with crystal-clear sea water, place seven islands made of lava in the middle (to represent the seven Canary Islands) and then build a restaurant and a few bars on the islands, bridges to connect some of the islands (others you must swim to) and plop a humongous fountain in the middle of another island that absolutely erupts like a volcano. Then flesh out the islands with swaying palm trees, tropical flowers and thorny cacti. And then name it the Lido Martianez.

This is a swimming pool.

I had to check this venue out, so I went early one morning and the water was frighteningly cold. Infinitely colder than that outdoor swimming pool in Iceland.

Okay, stick with me now, I'm going to take you on a wee tour around Puerto de la Cruz. If you depart from the Lido and walk along neighbouring Avenida de Colón, you will soon come to the Ermita de San Telmo (hermitage dating from 1780) on your right. We are now on a promenade of sorts known as Paseo San Telmo. Carry on down the hill and the sea reappears on your right. You are now walking in the direction of the Old Town. Down below you and off to your right, you can see the natural black-lava rock pools where young nubile men and women lounge about endeavouring to upgrade their already golden tans (and endeavouring to lure any passers-by). Keep on moving and now you are walking uphill once more -- as everything is uphill or downhill in Puerto. Here you dodge a restaurant tout (from Ecuador) and suddenly feel a brisk wind. Did you feel the temperature drop? This is the *Punta del Viento*, or Windy Point, as it's facing the prevailing wind. But don't ask me why the wind buffets us here but back all of 100 metres it is decidedly tranquil.

Cross the street here, but don't be mowed down by the crazed Canarian drivers approaching from the left. When they approach a zebra crossing they are more likely to speed up than slow down. We are now standing at the entrance to Calle Quintana. This is a pedestrian zone and vehicular traffic here is either nonexistent or benign (early morning delivery). Before we start down the *calle*, look to your right. See the BBV, the Banco Bilbao Vizcaya? This is where you *don't* want to change your pounds into euros). Now look to your left. See that Bureau de Change? It's called the Euro Cambio Exchange. This is where you *do* want to change your money. But be forewarned, the little man working in the cage (he looks like a young Elton John) possesses a wicked sense of humour.

Now dive down Calle Quintana. There are people of all sizes, shapes and nationalities milling about. This walkway is another one of those areas with a 'place to be' feel to it -- restaurants, hotels, boutiques.

Farther on the right, you will soon see the Hotel Monopol with its traditional Canarian balconies, and here you must stop and have a squizzy inside (the hotel has been managed by the same family for the past 80 years -- so you can imagine how tired they are). As you enter the main doors you step over a carpet of fresh geraniums, orchids and hibiscus. These flowers are placed on the steps each morning by a gorgeous young damsel (in a bright-red, traditional Canarian dress) to give you a warm, colourful and fragrant welcome. This I really liked, the flowers *and* the dress. Then as you step into the lobby you realise that it's comparable to going to the other side of the wall in the movie *King Kong*. Stop here and look up. You are in the middle of an indoor jungle. Long leafy vines tumble down from three storeys above and the entire lofty expanse is one rich arena of tropical flora. Who the job of watering this tangled boscage belongs to I don't know, but I reckon there's a fair amount of job security here.

(FYI: The climate in the north of Tenerife is considered a 'spring climate all year round', and perhaps that's why the plants and flowers grow to seemingly nuclear-irradiated sizes and heights. Have you ever seen an elephant ear plant? Well, they are enormous, aren't they? Wait until you see them in Puerto de la Cruz. An elephant would be proud to be associated with something of this stature. All the plants in Puerto seem to be super-plant. You'll find travelling palms as wide as the screen at your local cinema, poinsettias as tall as your garage and hibiscus as deep as a pint of beer.)

Now, let's walk farther on down Calle Quintana. (You

thought we were finished with our walk, didn't you?) Here, on the right, is the Hotel Marquesa. The Hotel Marquesa has been welcoming guests since the late 19th century and it is awash with old-world charm. This is where you want to come one evening and sit outside on the terrace and drink something tropical and listen to the soothing, live music. This evening there is a young woman playing a harp, and I don't think I want to leave.

Canarians dress well. This you will notice if you now partake of *paseo*. *Paseo* means 'get up off your lazy behind, throw on some fresh clothes and take a walk after dinner instead of sitting glued to the telly'. That's loosely translated. When the Canarians go *paseo*, they wear their Sunday best. Everyone strolls about the town appropriately kitted -- except the tourists, of course.

You see, most people who go on holiday buy the clothes they plan to wear -- back home. And does this make much sense? If you were going to Key West would you buy your clothes in Glasgow or South Milwaukee? If you were travelling to Orlando would you buy your clothes in Troon or Detroit? Doesn't make it, does it? And yet, the unfortunate answer to the above question is, yes, I buy my clothes at the Houndshill Mall in Blackpool when I plan to holiday in Tenerife.

Actually now that I think of it, you could easily find what you're looking for at the Houndshill Mall.

Keep walking! We are still strolling on Calle Quintana. On your right should be the Iglesia de San Francisco. I wanted to go inside and light a candle, as this is what I now do. I went over to the rows and rows of candles, but they were not for sale -- rather for rent. Here you throw a small coin into a little slot and a miniature light, which is supposed to simulate the flame, illuminates. What kind of twisted holy technology is this? Have you ever seen this before? I haven't, and I am -- besides an international beer taster -- an international candle lighter. (FYI: Just so you know, the above church, the Church of Saint Francis, was built between 1599 and 1608, by Juan de Tejera -- a Tax Collector.)

Farther along Calle Quintana, you can often spot some illegal street theatre. I don't know about you but I love street theatre, illegal or otherwise. Today we have Statue Lady (no relation to Statue Man in Paris). Statue Lady is a young, exceedingly attractive woman in a long, white, diaphanous gown. She's standing on a pedestal, but her gown flows over it so her nakedness appears about eight feet tall. Now look down at her feet. The feet, I said. See the blue gossamer and the shells? They represent the sea. Isn't she lovely? She appears to have emerged from the ocean just for our very own voyeuristic enjoyment.

As you continue down Calle Quintana (don't do what I did, I was looking back at Statue Lady and fell down the steps at the bottom of the walkway), you go literally downhill and guess where we've come to? Why, Plaza del Charco, where else? C'mon! I'll buy you a *con leche,* just on the other side of the square is my favourite sidewalk café.

The café is called the 'Restaurante Mario', and it features authentic Canarian Warsteiner beer umbrellas, wicker tables and a vile toilet.

I took a seat in the shade and looked around. This glorious square, with its Indian laurel trees (brought over from Cuba in 1852), is the part of Puerto de la Cruz I love the most. Beneath the laurel trees, children laughed and played. Nearby, a guitarist serenaded the tables of a neighbouring café. Curled up on a bench, a young couple canoodled in a roving embrace. In the middle of the plaza, tourists and locals sat in blissful harmony (even with the Germans). At a corner, a policeman on his beat stopped and kicked a football back to a group of youngsters.

And right now, at this very moment, I couldn't imagine anywhere else on this great earth of ours where I would rather be.

I ordered another *con leche*, but my waiter didn't bring it, Chano did!

'What are you doing?'

'I saw you sitting here. I know your waiter.'

Chano pulled up a seat. 'You coming tonight?'

I told him of course I would come.

I looked around the square. Other benches had filled with lovers. Couples strolled arm in arm. An older married couple sat under a laurel tree holding hands. Everyone seemed to be in love.

And I was falling in love, as well, with Puerto de la Cruz and its mild climate, picturesque setting, explosion of floral colour -- and colonial square full of romantics.

And I'm not supposed to be looking for someone any more, but after seeing all this, it sure would be nice to have someone to share it with...

* * *

WHAT NOBODY WILL TELL YOU:

Puerto de la Cruz is, price-wise, surprisingly reasonable -- inexpensive actually. A room, petrol, and a pint of beer -- three definitive measures of a town -- were all refreshingly reasonable.

Most buses have A/C. Most hotels don't.

Admiral Nelson became left-handed on account of a visit he paid to Tenerife. In 1797, Ol' Horatio endeavoured to come ashore in nearby Santa Cruz and kick some arse, but a musket ball shattered his right elbow and any plans he had for that evening. Back onboard his ship, the crack ship's surgeon amputated the right arm, and you know the rest of the story.

CHAPTER 19 - Tenerife and the South, the author is roughed up by Romanians

Do you fancy a bit of adventure?

It's warm and sunny today and we have a great view of the volcano, so let's jump back in the *Caca-coche* and tool back down to the southern part of the island, to the resort town of Los Cristianos.

If you drive down the other side of the island (from the way we came up), and you are not faint of heart, you can take the hair-raising road up into the mountains and through the village of Masca.

Once upon a time, Masca was a virtually inaccessible haven for hippies. Then in 1988 the pothole-riddled dirt road leading to the mountain hamlet was paved. Now it is an accessible haven for hippies.

There's a restaurant in Masca perched on a precipitous cliff with a sweeping view of the surrounding jagged peaks. And here something strange happened -- I ran into Chano. And he was with a woman. And he had his arm around her.

'I would like to introduce you to someone.'

I was all ears.

'I'd like you to meet my wife.'

I was very pleased to see this.

'I often come here to enjoy a little day trip,' he said. 'And to see if we can hear the whistling language.'

'The "whistling language"?'

Chano went on to tell me that long before the hippies planted their seeds in Masca, it was the home to the aboriginal people of the Canary Islands called 'Guanches'. When the Guanches lived up in these hallowed heights, they employed a 'whistling language' so they could communicate over the deep ravines and from one jagged peak to another. *The Canarian equivalent of yodelling*, I was thinking.

The language consisted of nearly 3,000 words and entire sentences could be 'spoken' across great distances.

Chano had a wonderful sense of humour and he joked: 'I can just picture it now, some young *chico* whistles over to his *novia* (girlfriend): "Do you want to go out tonight? I know this great little ravine ..." And the girlfriend whistles back: "Not so loud, José, my father's just on the next peak."'

Then Chano said: 'Are you in a hurry?'

'Never.'

'*Bueno. Vamos*, let's take a hike.'

The weather looked to be changing as Chano and his wife led me up a narrow path higher up into the mountains. After about an hours' slog, we came to a small farm hanging on the edge of a deep ravine. Here Chano knocked on a heavy wooden door and an older woman in traditional Canary dress emerged. Chano gave me a wink, then turned to the woman, introduced me and mentioned that we were hiking farther up the mountain.

The older woman regarded me for a moment, then smiled. 'Let me call my sister. She lives higher up the mountain. You'll be thirsty by the time you get there.'

I waited for the woman to pull out her cell phone, but she didn't. Instead, she let go with a series of shrill high-pitched whistles. I shot Chano a look, then the old woman pointed to a path leading uphill. It was a steep climb and Chano and I reached the sister's house first. We were immediately greeted by a friendly older peasant woman: 'So you made it,' she said to Chano. 'Come inside for a refreshing drink. But where is that wife of yours?')

* * *

After Chano and his wife and I returned to the restaurant, the weather did indeed turn sour. Chano gave me a hug. I thanked him for enlightening me to the enchanting world of whistling language, then I drove yet higher up into the mountains through a thick fog. And the road was awful. It snaked its way back and forth and was frighteningly narrow and steep.

From time to time the clouds lifted and I could peer down into absolutely unfathomable depths to distant verdant valleys streaked with sun. It would not have surprised me if a Pterodactyl had come swooping up just to make my day even more exciting.

At one point, I looked up ahead and counted six treacherous switchbacks with harrowing hairpin turns. These, I still had to conquer. And then the clouds moved back in.

Every once and a while, fighting the impenetrable fog, I rounded a corner and stared straight into the terrified face of some white-knuckled driver crawling slowly down the mountain. We were so close, we would look right into each other's eyes, let out a small whimper and then slip silently by. Just when I thought it couldn't get any worse, I came face to face with a tour bus. How they got a tour bus up here I'll never know.

What a road!

It was dark by the time I reached Los Cristianos and I was now hungry enough to eat, well, even imported beef. But first I needed a room.

I stopped at numerous establishments that appeared to be hotels (as overly sunburnt tourists carrying packets of digestive biscuits were coming and going in great waves), but I was wrong, these weren't hotels -- these were time-shares. For the next two hours I scoured the town. I drove out to the golf course, over to the port, back to the Old Town, and guess what? Other than the pricey, budget-killing five-star Hotel

Gran Arona, not only could I not find a hotel with availability - - I couldn't even find a hotel. Every single sleeping establishment was linked to time-share hell.

Eventually, I made a wrong turn and happened upon salvation in the distinctly towering form of the Hotel Princesa Dacil.

'You want a what?' Hugo the front desk clerk asked. Hugo was a Canary version of Ricky Martin (albeit heterosexual), tight pants, all legs, all bulges. And he spoke beautiful English with an American accent.

'A room.'

'At this hotel?'

'Don't tell me you're time-share.'

'Not at all. It's just that we don't get walk-ins. Our guests are always part of a package tour.'

'So nobody just arrives in Tenerife and walks in your front door?'

'Other than you, no.' Hugo gave me a searching look: 'Say, are you American?'

'That I am. Is that bad?'

'No, just different. We never get Americans here.' Another searching look, then a big MTV smile. 'I used to live in Cleveland. I loved it.'

(FYI: Just so you know, nobody loves Cleveland, not even the people who live there. You live in Cleveland only under duress -- marriage, demotion, serious jail time.)

'And since I used to live in Cleveland, I'm going to give you a room -- a "special" room.'

'I like your logic but, pray tell, what's so special about a special room?'

'You get A/C.'

'Such a deal in a desert environment. Are you telling me that if you're on a package holiday you don't get air?'

'That's exactly what...' Hugo was about to finish, but his attention was breached, mid-sentence, by two hard bodies in bikinis (more like floss, actually) on their way out to the pool.

These Latin males certainly are devoted connoisseurs of the

opposite sex.

Hugo burned holes in their backsides, then turned his attention back to me: 'God, I love this job.' Then: 'Where were we?'

'I was in here. You were out by the pool.'

Hugo shot me a conspiratorial smile, then slipped me my special key.

My room was on the 16th floor and it was special, indeed. King-sized bed (in case the unthinkable happened). Marble floors. Balcony looking out onto the charming, croissant-shaped bay of Los Cristianos and the Atlantic beyond. Massive bath. Pub-sized telly. And the A/C. What's more, when I inserted my key (which was actually a stale slice of Emmentaler cheese posing as one of those perforated plastic magnetic cards) into a slot by my door, all the lights came on and so did the A/C. Decidedly up-market for decidedly down-market south Tenerife. My hotel room in Puerto de la Cruz hadn't even had TP, let alone a TV.

But here I had it all *and* CNN!

I also had a Hotel Info sheet with the following pearls: 'Welcome to the Princesa Dacil Hotel. We wish you a very pleasant stay with us, we work for it day by day.' And: 'Please take a shower before entering the pool and do not play with balls.' And finally: 'We feel very proud of our gardens. Do not mistreat the plants.' (I can just hear it: 'You are a very naughty aspidistra! They'll be no Miracle-Gro for you tonight. Now, go straight to your flower bed. Do as you're told. You're grounded!')

Don't you just love to flip on the telly in a strange country? Watch all the incandescently bad programming? X-rated game shows? Disgraceful talk shows? Sexy commercials? Comatose news readers? I just love doing this. In fact, I would have spent the whole evening in front of the telly if Los Cristianos (and my stomach) hadn't beckoned. You see, I love exploring new towns even more than watching bad programming on foreign TV.

I threw some water on my face, surfed once more through

the channels, caught the UK weather on the Beeb (sunny and hot). Why does the weather suddenly turn glorious the minute you leave the country? I flipped off the telly, slipped into my flippies and plunged into the fragrant night air.

What a nice temperature. Warm and dry. Low humidity. A perfect night for a stroll. Some folk were even on their way to dinner -- at least those who hadn't booked half-board and were forced to spend their entire holiday in the same monumentally boring dining room, night after night. (Half-board -- *half-bored* -- isn't a holiday ...it's a hostage situation.)

I aimed toward the harbour. And it's easy to find the harbour in Los Cristianos as the town is set in a vast natural amphitheatre. If you want to go to the beach, you go downhill. If you want to go home, you go uphill.

I proceeded down Paseo Maritimo. My plan was to dive into the first restaurant that wasn't displaying plastic colour pictures of plastic colourless food. I walked and walked. Where were all the Spanish restaurants? Where could I sink my teeth into some authentic *paella*? I saw a sign in front of the El Bote bar that said: *Se habla Español*. What was going on here? I scampered up moody back streets and slunk along the edges of the Old Town, but damn if I could find a restaurant that wasn't British or German or Italian.

It was getting late -- even for Spain -- and I was feeling faint and edgy. Breakfield deprived of food is a dangerous animal!

Now, having lost the use of most of my faculties (such as they are), I lowered my standards and plunged into a plastic place with plastic tables out front. It was right across from the beach. And it was mobbed.

I wrestled the last remaining table away from a family of Germans and sat down next to a family from Birmingham (England, not Alabama). Now hypoglycaemic, I looked through foggy eyes at my surroundings. The last thing I had wanted to do my first night in Los Cristianos was to eat in a non-Spanish establishment. I wanted the ethnic experience.

I read the name of my restaurant off the menu. I was at a restaurant called 'Chicago's'. This was too bizarre for words, so the ones below will have to do.

Chicago's is an American hamburger joint -- run by Brits. Somehow I found this curious. But at that time of the night and at that stage of my condition who was complaining? Not me. Who really gives a hoot if there's a chippy run by a cowboy from Dallas? A Tandoori restaurant operated by a family from Oslo? A Vietnamese restaurant owned by a couple from Motherwell -- or Des Moines?

Nevertheless, Chicago's had an agreeable ambiance. And my Scouse waitress was delightful. In fact, everybody at this American restaurant was agreeable and delightful and decidedly British -- the other waitresses, the bartender even the Mackam singing: 'We are the champions, my friends ... And we'll keep on fighting, till the end ...'

After dinner I walked along the prom. The entire resort was out now (towels had already been placed on the sunbeds at the pool so the Germans couldn't reserve). Children were playing on the beach, caricature artists were making people look foolish and getting paid for it, and a local (I actually found one) down on the beach was carving a behemoth sand sculpture of a whale.

Los Cristianos had some charm, I decided.

I was in the mood for a nightcap, so I walked back to my hotel and set about testing San Miguels at the bar. The bar was dark and moody and exotic and a Spanish fellow was singing pop tunes, in English: 'Sex bomb ... sex bomb ...' He was a Tom Jones look-alike, and he was just awful, worse than the local telly even, but it really didn't matter, nothing could tarnish my first evening in Los Cristianos.

Have you ever heard the sound of someone walking in high heels on marble? CLICK CLACK. CLICK CLACK. CLICK CLACK. Have you ever heard it at 5:00 a.m.? I can assure you it's a sound you will not soon forget. Especially if it rips you from your sleep and your fantasy dream of hitting a wedge out of a sand trap on the first try.

The woman who was staying in the room directly above me had just returned to home base. And wasn't she a busy little beaver? For the next 45 minutes this nocturnal creature paced back and forth across that marble floor, CLICK CLACK, still in those noisy high heels. What was she doing up there, modelling lingerie?

I awoke late the next morning, so I quickly showered and hurried straight downstairs so I wouldn't miss breakfast. There's nothing like a good breakfast, I always say. But why do they have such a narrow window of opportunity? You can't afford to have a lie-in on holiday lest you miss your feeding time.

I entered the expansive breakfast room and what a sight! Everyone was hung over. Droopy faces. Slumped posture. Even the children were quiet -- at least the ones not chugging the Red Bull.

And the breakfast was sumptuous: bacon, bangers, fried bread, fried tomatoes, black pudding, beans, mushrooms, eggs of your choice, toast, jam, cereal, coffee, tea and a whole raft of delightful cereals. It was all surprisingly tasty and it was all quite English. And this, too, I found interesting. Wasn't the south of Tenerife still part of the Canary Islands? Why was it I could find a full English breakfast, a traditional carvery, an American burger, but not an authentic Canarian dish?

But I wasn't complaining. No, not me. In fact, I was trying to wolf a second helping of beans-on-toast before the 9:00 a.m. breakfast-cutoff time, when I was interrupted by a frighteningly familiar noise. Sort of CLICK CLACK, CLICK CLACK. It couldn't be. I looked up. Strutting in was the irksome, late-night clubber, and she was still in her sequinned, tight, murderously plunging evening gown.

Breakfast kit this wasn't!

'Breakfast is finished for the day, you noisy inconsiderate slut!' I wanted to shout it out loud, but I didn't. The whole dining room froze in mid-bite, even the children. We all watched in staggering disbelief as she crossed CLICK CLACK, CLICK CLACK and with shaky hands fumbled for the bangers. Yes, we all knew what she had been up to the night before. You could surmise by the way she handled the bangers.

* * *

It's no secret that Los Cristianos has changed dramatically over the last 20-plus years. What was once a sleepy fishing village and port, from where tomatoes were shipped, has transformed into one of the most hopping resorts in the Canaries. And with growth has come aggression in the form of greed run amok (translated: let's sucker the tourists). I was about to cross the street and head down to the harbour one morning when a car screeched to a halt in front of me and a young woman leapt out: 'Mind if I take a quick survey?'

I adopted a defensive karate pose. I thought I was going to be mugged. 'Just let my pulse drop back below a hundred,' I said, 'then go ahead.'

But the woman wasn't interested in surveys, this was part of her come-on, you see, she was a time-share tout on wheels. When this reptile realised I was less than interested in buying a piece of property -- so that I could trade it for a week in Florida (and pay for an upgrade) -- she ceased and desisted. Then, when I told her I found her spring-from-the-vehicle approach a tad offensive, she became a tad indignant.

'I have all the proper licenses and permits,' she hissed.

'Perhaps, but do you have any sense of dignity?'

Miss Reptile sprang into her getaway car and scorched about a hundred metres of rubber. Boy, did she show me.

I once again commenced my descent along the Paseo Maritimo, but oh, no, not again. Up ahead, lurking in a darkened archway, was another tout. To avoid this troglodyte, I cut across the street. I don't know about you, but when I'm walking down the street -- alone -- I prefer to avoid mankind. I want to be left to my own devices and my own silly thoughts. I avert my eyes. I cross the street.

But the tout was tenacious and he sensed my slipperiness.

'Aren't you a friendly Brit?' he yelled aggressively after me, trying to embarrass me into submission. I was taken aback by this behaviour. Suddenly, my day was going downhill -- and fast. Not good in a town that is fifty-percent downhill.

The guidebooks will tell you that there is still a semblance of pre-tourism life in Los Cristianos, but I'm not so sure. Can you truly feel the days of old when an 18-year-old Swedish tout implores you to patronise her restaurant, and if you don't, she whines that she won't be paid? Can you gaze in wonder at local crafts while a Brownshirt with a menu under his arm marches you off to a German restaurant? Does it do any good to try to absorb the history of this once cosy corner of the world when someone sticks a flyer in front of your face advertising those venerable Canarian institutions such as: Burger King, Pizza Hut and KFC?

Have you ever heard the expression 'It's a tough room'? This is how it is in Los Cristianos for the locals. They are doing their best, but it's just not working. It's not their fault. They've had tourism jammed down their throats and up where the light doesn't shine. In some ways, against their will. And now they are weary. I don't think most locals understand what has hit them. One day you are packaging tomatoes and the next day you are packaging tourists. They tolerate the invaders, but you have to seriously dig around to find a local who doesn't wish all the tourists would just go away and drop dead.

Ouch, I've been saying a lot of not so nice things about Los Cristianos. But wait. I've thought of something of a positive nature: Los Cristianos is an ideal place to go if you want to sit by the pool all day long and sit in a pub all night long. How's that for good news?

Just for the research aspect (and perhaps just a little to give the vile curs enormous grief) I went to a time-share meeting of my own volition. Yes, I let them rope me in. I had been stopped on the street by a female French tout with dirty fingernails. Given a scratch-off card. Told I'd won all sorts of wonderful prizes. Then whisked off in a taxi -- gratis -- to time-share-hell headquarters. The place was crawling with sharks, remoras and impressionable holiday-makers. The victims were writing cheques, popping champagne and wondering what in the hell they had just signed. I let the sales force lead me on for close to *four* hours (I had been assured it would only take 90 minutes). When 'sales' thought they had me just where they wanted me, they brought in the Big Gun. A fellow from Glasgow, of all places, and he was dressed like a banker and there to close the deal. 'So what's it going to be ... the £12,000 deal ... or the £6,000 deal ... or the £3,000 deal?'

'Could I ask you a question first?' I said.

'Anything you want, laddie.'

'This could be a deal-breaker,' I said.

'Ask away.'

'It's just that I need to know, before I sign on the dotted line, you understand, ... which football team do you support, Rangers or Celtic?'

He shot me a look. 'Och. You serious?'

'Completely.'

'It would be Rangers, then.'

'Sorry, mate. I support Celtic.'

And on that I stood up, finished my glass of champagne and walked from the room.

And that was the first and only time I've seen time-share-hell barracudas speechless.

* * *

I ran into Hugo one evening. He had spent the day on the neighbouring island of La Gomera and was returning from the ferry. I invited him for a beer.

'You're on,' he said. 'But let me show you my favourite pub.'

Hugo took me to La Bohéme, a hole-in-the-wall of a bar five minutes from the harbour. The bar was smoky and stuffy and heaving and good fun. We ordered *dos jarras* of Dorado beer.

I asked Hugo what it was like to live in a town where the majority of the people were foreigners.

'Same as living in lots of cities nowadays, I guess,' he said. 'You get used to it. Besides, I like to practice my English. That's why I work in the hotel business. I like the Brits.'

'Do any of your countrymen share your enthusiasm?'

'Sure, some do,' Hugo said, eyeing the front door. 'You have to have the right attitude. You know, Britain has a lot of good-looking women. Let them come all they want. Anyway, if I need to escape, I just go over to the neighbouring island of La Gomera and go hiking.'

'So you went hiking today?'

'No, I went to see this girl.'

Our beers arrived and Hugo and I toasted.

'To Cleveland.'

'To Cleveland.' Clink.

'Will you go back there one day?'

'Where, La Gomera or Cleveland?'

'Cleveland.'

'I would like to. Before I get married.'

'You're getting married?'

'Yeah, soon.' Hugo eyed the front door again.

'Who is the lucky one?'

'Don't know yet. But I'm sure the right person will come along.'

'Maybe she's in Cleveland.'

Hugo gave me a long look. 'Y'know, I've never even considered that.'

'What about you? When are you going to get married?'

I was about to respond when Hugo's attention was breached: A young curvaceous creature stepped into the dim, billowy-blue light of the bar.

Hugo waved to the girl. 'Gotta go.'

'Two in one day?' I said to Hugo, but he couldn't hear me. He was already walking out the front door, and as he and his bodacious date stepped onto the tiled pavement out front, all I could hear was the frightening sound CLICK CLACK, CLICK CLACK.

I had to laugh. Hugo didn't mind the weekly tourist invasion. In fact, he lived for it. If he moved to Cleveland, Cleveland could only become a better place.

Before heading back to the Princesa Dacil, I walked down to the harbour. What a scene! A man was juggling fire. A bloke playing the guitar. The sand artist was carving a 15-foot shark. I watched the juggler, listened to the music, then dropped a handful of coins down onto a towel the sand sculptor had placed next to his shark for *propinas*. 'Tomorrow, I'm doing a unicorn,' he yelled up to me.

'Then I'll see you tomorrow,' I yelled back.

I turned to leave and saw a sozzled lad standing there wearing a Stoke City strip. He was admiring the sand artist. Then he turned to me: 'I'm an artist, too,' he said, with an alcohol-induced glint in his eye. 'I draw the dole.'

I actually laughed out loud. I just love the British sense of humour.

I looked around. What a gorgeous setting. The Hotel Gran Arona twinkled in the distance, swarms of happy tourists milled about, a feral cat slunk across the beach with a fishy prize. But I couldn't get a handle on Los Cristianos. Did I like it here or didn't I like it here? I didn't know. For sure, I was put off by all the touts preying on the tourists. I would have to sleep on it.

* * *

I was having breakfast the next morning, when Hugo walked in. He saw me, waved, and came over.

I offered him a sausage: 'Banger?'

'No, she just wanted to talk.'

* * *

Los Cristianos is wheelchair friendly. And that's a good thing. And there are lots of golf courses within minutes. And that's a fun thing. And there are lots of massage parlours blatantly advertised right out along the harbour where the children play. And that's a weird thing.

But here's a bad thing: I was walking along the prom one scorching afternoon in the direction of the Hotel Gran Arona, when I came upon a crowd of tourists. They were huddled around a dark, shifty-looking fellow who was standing over an overturned cardboard box. He was shuffling three black objects that resembled large hockey pucks. It was the shady yet seductive peanut-shell game. I had read about this in *Island Connections*, one of Tenerife's English-language newspapers. There were groups of illegal immigrants from Romania, and they were making hundreds upon hundreds of pounds a day by ripping off the tourists.

I looked closer at the seven tourists forming the scrum around the dealer and surmised that these weren't tourists. These were shills, working together, trying to lure unsuspecting holiday-makers. Not good, this.

Dangerous even.

But I was curious.

So I went up and watched. Suddenly everybody was winning and they were all encouraging me to splash some money out. But I didn't and this incensed the man dealing. What pissed him off even more was when I warned some wide-eyed younger English couple to not get involved. And do you know what happened? After the young couple moved off, the man dealing looked straight at me and said in German: '*Du bist Arschloch.*'

I didn't respond to being called an arsehole. Just kept observing. And I guess this didn't endear me to my new friends because three of the larger miscreants dragged their knuckles over to me and started pushing me around, and then, get ready, Mr Dealer ran up to me and spat in my face.

Seven of them and one of me. Even I could do the maths. What was I thinking mucking around with lowlife Romanians? It seemed prudent to pursue other diversions, but before I did, I left them with this thought: 'What are all seven of you fine gentlemen doing in about five minutes?'

'What do you mean?'

'Well, that's when I'll be back with the entire Los Cristianos police department.'

Of course I couldn't find a cop to save my life -- which, in fact, is why I was looking for one in the first place.

(FYI: I have since learned that these Romanian scum would be just as happy to stick you with a knife, as spit in your face. Either way, they don't mind.)

Cut to a few nights later.

I was walking along the prom still trying to decide if I liked Los Cristianos when I spied two members of the crack police force walking my way. (Where's a cop when you need one?) One was older, the other younger. Maybe a rookie even. I went up to them and said in my most polite tone: 'I do believe that there might be a problem here in Los Cristianos.'

'Oh, and what is that!' the rookie replied with a bit too much brio.

I told them about the Romanians. I told them about the article in *Island Connections*.

And do you know what this upstanding member of law enforcement said? 'Where's the problem? You don't play. There's no problem.'

'But they're ripping off the Brits, and the Brits are the ones paying your wages ...' I tried to present my case, but he was not interested in what I had to say.

'You don't play -- you have no problem,' he snapped.

I countered with: 'Your theory is misguided. If you had heroin dealers all along the prom would you say that it's not a problem as long as I don't buy?'

Well, the case was suddenly closed. The rookie cop said something to the effect: 'You come here. You tell us what to do ...'

The police took leave. I watched as they walked off, then they suddenly stopped. They had spotted the man sculpting in sand. He had sculpted 'The Last Supper', and it was, if I may say, a masterpiece. To annoy the police, I went over and stood behind them. They were reprimanding the sand sculptor, telling the artist, who was a local, that this sort of *tontería* (nonsense) wasn't permitted and he damn well better not be caught sculpting the dirty, kitty-litter, man-made sand of Los Cristianos into stunning religious tabloids if he knew what was good for him.

God help us.

(FYI: Here is a titbit that really has nothing to do with this chapter or my journey, but I just have to share it with you: Leonardo Da Vinci wanted to use live subjects as models for Jesus and the Apostles when he painted his most sublime work -- The Last Supper.

Hundreds of young men were interviewed for the part of Jesus. Da Vinci wanted a face 'unaffected by sin.' No easy trick to find back then in 15th-century Italy. After weeks of searching, a 19-year-old man was selected as the model for the portrayal of Christ. Da Vinci painted his Christ, then over the next seven years suitable individuals were selected and one by one Da Vinci painted each of the Apostles. The final face to be painted was that of Judas Iscariot. For weeks Da Vinci searched for a face 'marked with the scars of avarice and deceit'.

But no such face could be found.

Eventually word came from Rome of an imprisoned murderer, a sociopath of unimaginable degradation sentenced to death for a life of heinous crime. Da Vinci travelled to Rome. The prisoner was brought from the dungeon and up into the light of day. Da Vinci saw before him a face that personified viciousness, evil and complete ruin. He had his man. Special permission from the King was granted. For six months Da Vinci painted the face of Judas. As he finished his last stroke he turned to the guards and barked: 'I have finished. You may take the prisoner away.'

'Look at me!' cried the prisoner. 'Do you not know who I am?'

Da Vinci, the master artist, with a master's eye, shot back: 'I have never seen you in my life!'

'Wait, Da Vinci!' cried the prisoner, as he was dragged off. 'Look at me again, for I am the same man you painted just seven years ago as the face of Christ.'

A true story.)

And perhaps Los Cristianos, too, has two contrasting faces.

I looked back over at the sand sculptor's masterpiece then went over to my old bar at the Princessa Dacil, swilled a medicinal dosage of lager and endured Tom Jones as he sang 'Delilah'.

And I still don't know if I like Los Cristianos.

* * *

WHAT NOBODY WILL TELL YOU:

I saw this notice. It was in a market frequented by Britons. I couldn't resist sharing it with you: GOOD HOME WANTED FOR 'JASPAR', A VERY HANDSOME BORDER COLLIE.

MOVE BACK TO THE UK FORCES RELUCTANT
PARTING. JASPAR IS A GREAT COMPANION. HE
NEEDS A LOVING HOME WITHOUT HENS OR KIDS.
WOULD LIKE TO EAT ONE AND TERRIFIED OF THE
OTHER. HE WILL BE YOUR BEST FRIEND. RING...)

CHAPTER 20 - Benidorm: At language school I meet an English lass named 'Kinkie'

Benidorm.

The very sound of the name conjures up a myriad of frightening images, doesn't it? Too British. Too German. Too Dutch. Too concrete. Too high rise. Too young in the summer. Too OAP in the winter.

I was told the streets of Benidorm were lined with English pubs, Scottish pubs, Irish pubs, German Kneipes, Dutch taverns and comatose lager louts. Spain was in there somewhere, but nobody seemed to know exactly where.

The first time I visited Benidorm I stayed on the outskirts in picturesque La Cala de Finestrat. I didn't hang around long enough to see what Benidorm was all about, but I certainly found nothing wrong with its aquamarine waters, pristine beaches and long promenade lit at night by a thousand twinkly lights.

When I visited the UK the next time, I ebulliently announced to all my friends that I had been to 'Benidorm!' and they suddenly got the look you get on your face when you step in dog shit.

My dear friends went on to tell me unbelievable horror

story after unbelievable horror story about Benidorm. In fact, they were all so unbelievable, I just had to ask: 'Say, have any of you actually been?'

No one had. That's right, no one had, and yet they all had clearly defined opinions.

Something wasn't computing so I decided to make a return journey to Benidorm and spend some quality time there so I could get to the bottom of this prejudicial conundrum.

I went at the end of sun-drenched September. And I enrolled in language school. If I didn't come home with a positive opinion of Benidorm, then at the least I would come home with a deeper respect for the subjunctive.

Plus, isn't the classroom a great place to meet someone (even though I'm technically not looking)?

To enliven the full ethnic experience, the language school placed me in a two-bedroom flat, with a local felon, on the twenty-second storey of one of those high-rise eye sores. My roommate's name was Mateo. He was Benidorm born and bred -- a Costa Blanca Russel Brand.

Mateo was just a bit twisted, as are the majority of people I seem to spend time with behind locked doors. He owned a rapacious pet called a Tokay Gecko. I'll never forget Mateo's first words to me: 'I should tell you right up front, I have this pet.'

'I love animals,' I said.

'You won't love this one. It's a Tokay Gecko.'

(FYI: Tokay Geckos look like a cross between a gremlin and Vladimir Putin, and they are slate blue with rusty orange spots. The little buggers come from the humid climate of Southeast Asia. They grow to 14 inches long and have a wrestler's build. And they are aggressive -- startlingly aggressive.)

'I have to keep the heat turned way up in the flat or he gets annoyed,' Mateo told me. 'He likes it warm, the little brat.'

'He sounds fun.'

'Tell me that in a week.'

'Where is he now?'

'Dunno. Probably hanging upside down from a ceiling.'

I looked out at the shimmering Mediterranean twenty-two floors below, then I looked back at my new roommate with a questionable disposition and a Tokay Gecko. My stay in Benidorm was off to an inauspicious start.

I cast my mind back to my arrival at Alicante airport earlier that day. This should have been a clue. We had landed so hard the Air 2000 aircraft had nearly cracked the runway (near-fatal landing and everyone had still applauded).

I rented a Ford Feckus from Centauro Rent-a-Dreck and headed north for about 30 desperately disillusioning minutes. The first time I came to Benidorm I arrived during the night, but now I was arriving in the blazing heat of the afternoon and what I saw from the slightly elevated A-7 *Autopista*_was anything but idyllic: barren hills, mountains of questionable eminence and leering over the coast, the most higgledy-piggledy forest of concrete rising toward the heavens.

All heat and dust -- and nary a green patch. Dog shit, indeed.

Night one in Benidorm was not meant for immediate or restful slumber. First of all, Spanish beds are crap. Second of all, Spanish pillows are shaped like braunsweiger -- and therefore, crap. And third of all, it was hotter than Hades in the flat, which reminded me that I still hadn't seen the rusty orange spots of a certain predatory beastie with a wrestler's build. Visions of the little blighter filing his teeth on the legs of my bed kept me from dozing right off, so I got up, looked under the bed, then tiptoed to the front window and peered out. Wow. Over the Mediterranean the stars were putting on a show for free. To my right and below was the teated sprawl of high-rise Benidorm. I could see why some people thought Benidorm might resemble a miniature Manhattan (especially if those people had never been to Manhattan).

Benidorm has a population of just under 70,000, but it looks significantly larger than that when you are standing in your bare feet viewing it from the twenty-second floor. To get an idea of Benidorm, geographically, envisage a crescent shaped beach to the left and a crescent shaped beach to the right. Separating the two is a rocky cliff-like protrusion that contains the artists' quarter and abuts on the Old Town. Jam as many high rises as you can along the beach, intermingle the odd, noisy, dusty construction sight -- complete with 30-storey crane -- and you have Benidorm.

I heard a strange noise behind me, sort of a cross between a Jurassic-hissing sound and something trying to move the refrigerator. I froze. Stopped breathing. A toilet flushed upstairs somewhere -- the Doppler Effect -- cascading loudly towards my floor and beyond. I took a breath. Evil, foreign, kitchen smells wafted up from below. I decided to go for a walk.

The temperature outside was lovely and warm and the streets were heaving with tourists who were showing an awful lot of skin. Benidorm is known for having one of the most equable climates summer and winter in all of coastal Spain. The balmy night air and the crowds surprised me, but what surprised me even more was how startlingly noisy Benidorm was. Horns honking, sirens wailing, scooters whining, lots of laughter.

Laughter?

What was this?

I peered through two dancing palm trees and spotted a lively little venue over the road with live entertainment. There were boisterously merry sounds oozing from within and I wanted to be part of this mirth (and now I wanted a beer). I strained to read the name of the establishment: Wankers & Punters I thought at first, but then when my contact lenses floated back to the centre of my eyes I realised it was called the Wheeltappers & Shunters.

I entered through a carcinogenic haze and the place was wall-to-wall, cheery, sunburnt faces. A Blackpool-esque comic up on stage had an appreciative crowd in stitches: 'When I die, I want to go peacefully in my sleep like my father ... not screaming like his passengers.' And: 'I went to the library to get a book on suicide, but they were all checked out -- they don't return them, do they?'

Everyone howled. I guess the fine folk were happy to be in Benidorm and out of a country where there are hose-pipe bans one month and floods the next.

When the show was over, which I enjoyed very much, I walked around the neighbourhood and this is what I saw. I spied a Dutch bar called 'Kansas', and an English pub called 'Mississippi', and then a Liverpuddlian pub, a Yorkshire pub, a Geordie bar and a Scottish bar that had a sign out front that distinctly delineated: 'Authorised Access for Glasgow Rangers Fans Only'.

I didn't think this could get any worse until I walked by a hotel with a large Welsh flag hanging over the third-storey balcony. Who takes a Welsh flag on holiday -- a *large* Welsh flag?

Only my first night and my opinion of Benidorm was already forming in, well, cement. Benidorm was package-holiday heaven.

* * *

My first day at language school was intoxicating, invigorating and frightening. Have you ever gone back to school? You are over the moon to be there, but you soon realise that your brain had closed to all new stimuli years ago.

My school was *Inlingua*, at Calle Rioja 5. And my instructor was an attractive local girl, with mane for hair, by the name of Sylvia. I was given a short test to determine the extent of my Spanish linguistic ability. Apparently it was nonexistent. I had understood *nada* on the test and had even written my name in the wrong corner.

There were five of us in the class, and Sylvia prattled on at the speed of light. She made it patentedly clear that we were in Spain, we were there to learn Spanish, and Spanish was the only language to be spoken once we stepped through the front door ... or else. I glanced at my watch. I had two and a half more hours to endure today, four more days this week and then four more preterite, past-historic, pluperfect weeks after that. *Dios mio*, what had I done?

I looked around at my classmates. They were all female. Two were Russian. One was German. And one was English, from Hove. (Don't you think Hove should be renamed 'Hove-Actually' because whenever you hear that someone is from down that way, and you politely ask: 'Where are you from, Brighton?' it seems the response is always a slightly affected: 'No, Hove, actually.')

I glanced back over at my classmates. The two Russians and the German looked as if they had just stepped off the boat. The lass from Hove (her name was 'Kinkie') looked as if she shopped in the Lanes and had just come straight from the Brighton Festival, the fringe bit: Long skirt made from her gran's curtains, hairy colourful top, hair by Medusa, vegetarian shoes. She was gorgeous to look at in a North Laine sort of way and I would have said something along the lines of 'All Things Brighton Beautiful,' but she was from Hove, actually.

When I left language school for the day, I had a headache and I got lost. But guess what? I may have been lost but I found Spain. It was hiding in Benidorm's bustling Old Town, and it was a different world back here. There were no lager louts, no Glasgow Rangers fans and no Welsh flags.

I heard Spanish accents not package-holiday accents. Even the names of the bars and restaurants were in Spanish. Moreover, the Old Town was quaint. Narrow streets snaked uphill and downhill and around tight corners. I discovered a small leafy square, a large ornate church (next to the artists' quarter), an amphitheatre where José Carreras was performing that night and a glass-enclosed club with Flamenco dancers.

It was sunny and warm and lovely, so I allowed myself to get lost some more and I happened upon sprawling outdoor cafés with elegantly dressed folk enjoying various Spanish coffees, not rough pubs with the lads sitting around with their shirts off deep-frying their skin and massacring their brains and livers. I saw happy tourists sampling the baked delicacies of *gofres* and *ensaimadas* and other pastry delights, not punters with the critical selectiveness of locusts stuffing their faces with plates of chips and beans-on-toast and bacon sandwiches,

Chuck. I was captivated by the Old Town. I loved it here and didn't want to go back to my flat -- not that I could anyway, on account of being lost.

What was going on? Everyone had told me Benidorm was ugly and trashy, but now that I think of it, everybody I asked had been British. Could the Britons have one section of Benidorm that was decidedly down-market and the Spanish have another part that was, say, Spanish? Stay tuned.

When I returned home I found a note on the kitchen table: 'I'm at the beach in front of the *Biblioplaya*. C'mon down -- Mateo.'

I changed into my Speedos (which had stretched and didn't look all that speedo on me), grabbed my towel, SPF-45 BULLFROG MOSQUITO COAST SUNBLOCK and INSECT REPELLENT, Spanish homework and jumped into the lift. At the 19th floor the lift stopped, the door slid open and two heavily muscled women -- who looked like poster girls for Eastern European steroid abuse -- thundered in (faces only a mother could love). I greeted them in my best Spanish and received an icy glare through the acne and facial hair. We rode in cryogenic silence the rest of the way down. Don't you just hate that suffocating awkward silence that occurs only in a lift? (And some of my first dates when I mentioned I might want to live in Europe.)

I found Mateo at the beach, which was a miracle. I don't think I have ever seen a stretch of sand anywhere in the world, French Riviera, Miami Beach, Waikiki, Bournemouth, Paignton (when the razor-fish aren't on the attack) with more roasting oiled bodies. Every square centimetre of blazing sand had been commandeered by sun-worshipping herding animals bent on activating their melanin.

I greeted Mateo, but he gave me a befuddled look, then: 'Oh, it's you, Jon. I didn't recognise you at first. I've never seen you in the daylight.'

I laughed, then tried to determine where I could stake claim to a modest patch of molten sand. The sand was so hot, I had to do something between the burning-feet dance and the 'haka' until I finally moved some of Mateo's 'toys' and plopped my towel down.

Apparently, Mateo didn't go to the beach unless he was well prepared: beach umbrella, towel, sun block, Lilo, cooler, radio, newspaper, crime novel (*DEATH BY GLASGOW*), deck of cards, binoculars, mirror, hair brush, mobile phone, postcards, snorkel, mask, fins and one of those little fans that runs on batteries and spits mist at you.

'Why the binoculars?'

'Girls.'

'Mirror?'

'Girls.'

'For them?'

'No, for me.'

We hung out on the beach for quite some time. I did my homework. Mateo took inventory and flirted with every female that came within his postal code. And they all seemed to find him carnally irresistible. 'My flirtations set off chemical reactions in women,' he told me.

When there was a lull in the parade of women stopping by to greet Mateo, I asked him about the two female weightlifters in the lift.

'Oh, those two. They're Russian. The building is loaded with Russians. Benidorm is crawling with Russian Mafia.'

'Mafia? I have two Russians in my class!'

'We're being invaded. They're buying up property all over Spain. Aren't the friendliest people in the world, are they?'

'I greeted them, but they just flung icicles with their eyes.'

'They're cold fish, those two. If they get on at the 19th, I get off on the 18th and then walk down. Women who have a heavier five-o'clock shadow than I have frighten me, and I'm Latin.'

As the day wore on and the sun scorched our skin, it became more and more obvious that Mateo was a fountain of information. I asked him if there was a part of Benidorm that was predominantly British.

He shivered slightly, then lit a cigarette. 'Scarier than the

Russian women. The Brits call it the "Square", but we call it *La Zona Giri.*'

'What's *Giri* mean?'

'A *Giri* is short for a *Girufo*. It's what we call the Brits.'

'Is it rude?'

'It's like calling you a Yank. If I say: 'A friend of mine is a Yank,' it's not rude. If I say: 'He's a *fucking* Yank,' that's quite something different, isn't it?'

'So what's the problem with *La Zona Giri*?'

'Everyone is always drunk or looking to pick a fight or spewing up all over the place.'

Mateo took a hefty drag on his cigarette and its glowing tip raced toward his mouth (how could he smoke in this heat?). 'Listen, if you order a coffee around town make sure you say you want "Spanish" coffee, or they will give you *Giri* coffee, which is just instant coffee. Local people presume that if you are from Britain, you won't want the real deal.'

'Why does that sound racist to me?'

'Oh, but it's not. They have learned over the years that most Brits just want everything they're used to back home. Except the weather, of course.'

I asked Mateo if the Spanish have a good opinion of Benidorm (or actually any opinion at all). Mateo extinguished his fag, then pulled out two chilled bottles of *agua mineral* from his cooler. He handed me one then went on to inform me that Benidorm is a huge destination for the Spanish as it offers something for everyone. Families love it for its clean, safe beaches and the Terra Mítica (Disney-esque) theme park on the outskirts of town. Older folk adore it for its cafés, restaurants and dancing venues. And teenagers think it's cool because there are numerous clubs where they can listen to live *Bakalao* music and drink *Calimocho* (red wine and Coca Cola!) without having to venture out of the mosh pit.

'The *Bakalao* music incites drugs,' Mateo said. Perhaps not the proper choice of words, but I got the drift.

Mateo watched a curvaceous young thing waddle by, took a lap around the deeper recesses of his mind, then gave me a friendly smile. 'If you ever need a car for a date you can borrow mine. It's really a hot little number. It's a Lada Baltic GL.'

* * *

In the mornings, before language class started, I would venture off into the Old Town -- or *Casco Antiguo* as it is called -- and let the wake-up process take place in warm and sunny Spanish surroundings. I would go early and sit under the umbrella at my favourite café, the Café Brasil, and sip a steaming *con leche*. It was a great place to people watch and make notes. The young ladies working at the café soon learned that I was in language school and that somehow endeared me to them. I was a stranger in their country, but I was trying to grasp their language and they appreciated the effort. When they would see me coming down the street each morning, they would quickly prepare my *con leche* and have it ready for me when I took my favourite seat at my favourite corner table. This was an immensely wonderful way to start the day.

The *camereras* would often giggle as I sat there madly trying to decipher a children's book (in Spanish) with large, colourful pictures, and they would even help me if I got stuck on a tough name like, say, *Ricitos de Oro y Los Tres Osos*. While other patrons were enjoying the great works of Tolstoy or Steinbeck or Bright, I was struggling with *Goldilocks and the Three Bears*.

* * *

Early one evening Mateo suggested we go to a topless bar in the Old Town. It was called the Méson Alameda on Carrer de Martínez Oriola, and it was not to be missed. Mateo said I had to go as he had a little secret for me. 'Y'know the short *camerera* at your Café Brazil with the perky *chi-chis*? She works there. Let's surprise her.'

When we arrived on the scene, though, I found that it was not a topless bar, rather a *tapas* bar. I was sincerely disappointed -- until I tasted the *tapas*, that is: *Calamares a la Romana* (squid), *Verduras Plancha* (fried mushrooms, aubergines, green peppers), *Magro de cerdo con Tomate*, (loin of pork and tomatoes), *Espárragos a la Plancha* and something called *Ropa Vieja* (which translated to 'old clothes', but in reality was the Spanish equivalent of bubble and squeak).

Mateo made me order in Spanish from 'my friend' and each time I did so, five diminutive Spanish ladies who were sitting adjacent to us laughed. The Spanish ladies reminded me of the sister-aunts. We were all sitting outside under sprawling umbrellas almost in the middle of the narrow street and it was difficult not to be privy to each other's conversation.

The night air was hot and dry and the ladies were drinking small beer after small beer. My friend the *camerera* had to tend bar, so Frederico ('You may call me Freddy'), the owner, became our waiter. Freddy was tall and handsome and a clown, and he brought us a carafe of red wine to wash down the *tapas* when we weren't washing them down with small beers (don't mix the grape and the grain!).

Filled with the zest of life (and possibly too many small beers), the ladies started ordering *tapas* for Mateo and me and for a few monetarily disconcerting moments I thought that perhaps they were in league with Freddy as there were no prices on the menu.

The ladies laughed when I tried to pronounce the names of the various dishes and laughed even louder when I realised that *Espárragos a la Plancha* was fried asparagus and I told them I hated asparagus as a kid, but they sure were damn good as *tapas*.

Eventually Freddy presented us with our bill and including all the alcohol and all the tasty *tapas* the amount only came to the equivalent of about ten pounds for the two of us.

Can you keep a secret? I was just a bit sozzled when Mateo and I returned home, and I apparently placed my contact lenses in my *spare* contact-lens case by mistake -- and thus on top of my reserve pair of lenses. This meant that when I awoke the next morning and put my contacts in, I put *two* lenses in each eye. You can well imagine my horror when I staggered out to the local chemist's to procure some paracetamol.

* * *

It happened during my third week at language school, I was standing on the tree-lined Avenida del Mediterráneo reading a flyer someone had pinned to an oak tree. It was a picture of an attractive young woman. The flyer was in Spanish, but it went something like this: 'Lonely young girl in need of gratification. Last days of being single. Searching for a *chico*. All interested parties telephone 646 819 459.' Obviously the poor girl in the picture was having a pre-wedding prank played on her by her mischievous and soon-to-be ex-friends. I thought the entire idea to be quite amusing, and I wanted to be able to share it with you, so I was standing there writing down all the details when I heard a voice say: 'You're not that desperate, are you?'

I spun around, embarrassed. Standing there was Kinkie, from Hove, actually. We had a good laugh, then I invited Kinkie for a coffee. 'Great idea,' she said. 'I want to hear how you get yourself out of this one *and* you have to do it in Spanish.'

I suggested a Parisian-style café just down Avenida del Mediterráneo called, oddly enough, 'Le Café de Paris'.

'Absolutely not!' Kinkie said. 'Haven't you learned anything about Benidorm yet?'

'Apparently not.'

Kinkie held up three fingers: 'Here are three reasons not to go there: it's tourist city, a cup of coffee costs 2 euros and the waiters are from Morocco. Come with me. We'll go into the *Casco Antiguo* and have the best coffee in Benidorm for half the price.'

Kinkie's hideaway café was in an area of the Old Town known as 'Champagne Alley'.

'How did you find out about this café?' I asked.

'Sylvia told us about it the first week of class. I figured you didn't have a clue what she was saying.'

Kinkie went on to tell me that on Friday evenings the Spanish flock to Champagne Alley so they can sup bubbly and enjoy *tapas*.

About now, our teacher Sylvia walked up. 'Hey, what a coincidence!' I said.

'No coincidence, Jon,' Kinkie said. 'We planned to meet here. We're going to the fitness centre.'

'There's a fitness centre in Benidorm?'

205

'You don't remember?' Sylvia said. 'I told everyone about that the first week of class.'

Kinkie gabe me a look and just laughed.

Sylvia sat down and somehow the topic went from language school, to Sylvia's old boyfriend, to the different types of coffees that are served in Benidorm. I don't remember much about Sylvia's old boyfriend -- except that he stole her heart and her cat and was a world-class dickhead -- but I do remember what Sylvia told us about some of the coffees found in Benidorm (before Sylvia qualified as a language teacher she worked in a café and was Benidorm's fastest barista). A *con leche* is half coffee and half steamed milk; a *cortado* is a short coffee served in a short glass with three drops of milk; a *solo* is served without milk and in a small cup (sort of an espresso); an *Americano* is a watered-down espresso served in a large cup with or without a little milk; a *Carajillo* is a *solo* with three drops of cognac; a *Café Irlandés* is, yes, an Irish coffee; and a *Bombón* is in a small glass like a *cortado*, but it's served with condensed milk. So there you have it. A whole bunch of new ways to infuse caffeine.

After we finished our coffees, we strolled in dappled sunshine through a leafy park called Parque de L'Aigüera. Here, I spotted a bust resting on a sturdy plinth. And guess whose bust it was? Juan Carlos? Wrong! Cervantes? Wrong! It was none other than ol' silver-throat himself, Julio Iglesias. I asked Sylvia why Julio and why here? Sylvia said our Julio got his start in Benidorm back in 1968 when he won the competition at the Festival de Benidorm, and he often returns to give concerts and clean the pigeon shit off his bust.

(FYI: Did you know that Julio was born in Madrid? And that the only thing he wanted to do in life was play football? And that he realised his dream and became the goalkeeper for junior Real Madrid? And did you know his career was cut short as a footballer when he was nearly killed in an automobile accident at the age of twenty? And that he was partially paralyzed and spent 18 months in hospital?

When Julio was in hospital, late at night, he would listen to the radio and write sad, romantic poems. One day a nurse lent Julio a guitar to cheer him up, and so he could put his verse to music. Julio never considered himself a singer, so when a career was born -- in Benidorm of all places -- he was more than appreciative, and he will never forget the town that gave him a new lease on life.)

Just beyond Julio's presence is the outdoor amphitheatre where José Carreras had performed a few weeks earlier, and the amphitheatre is called the *Auditorio* 'Julio Iglesias'.

We carried on through the cool depths of the park and crossed under the hectic, and lethal, Avinguda D'Alfonso Puchades and guess what we came to? The *Plaza de Toros* -- the Bull Ring.

The Bull Ring was oval and about the size of a softball field. Painted on the outside were signs instructing prospective spectators which seats were in the sun and which seats would be in the shade (*Sol y Sombra*). Some blood-sport aficionado, clearly unimpressed with the ferocity of the bulls presently being teased, tormented and summarily slaughtered had spray painted a little succinct graffito to capture his sentiments: *Plaza de Vacas*. 'Plaza de Cows'.

Just behind the Bull Ring was a barren and wind-swept dirt field with old mattresses, a burnt-out rusted car and mutant weeds. This area was devoid of tourists and only a few local kids were kicking a football around. I named this area the Gaza Strip (as 'Blackpool Pleasure Beach' was already taken). Leading up and away from the Gaza Strip was a dizzying set of concrete steps which, if you survived the climb, dumped you out on a higher street, and up here was the fitness centre called 'Navarro's Gold Gym'.

I followed Kinkie and Sylvia into Navarro's to see what the facilities were like, and this is when I realised that not only did Benidorm have a well-equipped fitness centre, but Kinkie had a well-equipped body, actually.

* * *

WHAT NOBODY WILL TELL YOU:

Benidorm boasts Europe's tallest hotel, the 52-storey, 776-

room Gran Hotel Bali, which is nearly as tall as One Canada Square (the Canary Wharf Tower). Bit lofty for a beach town, but you can see Ibiza when it's clear.

Julio Iglesias studied English in Ramsgate and then at Bell's Language School in Cambridge.

CHAPTER 21 - Benidorm: My European travels come to a screeching climax -- with Kinkie

Benidorm has received its fair share of bad press over the years, and deservedly so, but the town is making major efforts to clean up its image -- along with its beaches (this new found pride possibly had something to do with everyone from the UK donning mouse ears and pissing off to Orlando).

Benidorm's two beaches, Playa de Levante (where the sun rises) and Playa de Poniente (where the sun sets -- and the Germans hangout) are among the cleanest in Europe. While you are enjoying dinner or quaffing drinks or possibly even slaking your sexual desires, the hardworking beach crew of Benidorm is grooming and tidying and primping the rich, golden sands, preparing for your arrival the next morning.

A lot of topless bathing goes on in Benidorm. And so does -- shock of shocks -- a lot of *flaunting*. This playful display of attributes is performed by hordes of fledgling nymphets. If you are taking notes, you may want to jot down that it's vogue to wear a skin-tight one-piece cossie and then roll it down to a skimpy string bottom in front of the boys.

Oh, those Spanish girls.

Oh, those girls from Benidorm.

Here's a tip: If you want to ogle the cream of the Costa Blanca you can do so from the discreet confines of the *Biblioplaya* (where Mateo hangs). The *Biblioplaya* is an open-air canopied *library* right there on the sizzling sands of Levante beach at the foot of Avenida de Europa. The selection of books is woefully limited, but there are numerous daily newspapers on offer in English, German, Dutch, French, Italian and even Spanish. If you don't find your favourite journal here, not to worry, we haven't come here to improve our minds. We are here to veg in the shade and admire the female of the species from the safe confines of our favourite Sports Section.

So as not to be a sexist slug, for those of you who love to check out the male of the species, don't worry, you can do that in Benidorm, as well. All you have to do is walk down the beach and away from the *Biblioplaya* until you come to the *Rincon* ('corner') at the northern end of Playa de Levante where the beach ends. Here you will find a 'cable' water-ski area, a floating platform bedecked with well-oiled, young lads (built like brick shit-houses) and a pitch of sand where a lot of football is played by the future of FC Barcelona. Benidorm, you will soon find out, has something for everyone.

* * *

Late one night, I ventured into the most dangerous area of Benidorm. Yes, scarier than a bad book, I penetrated the outskirts of package-holiday hell.

And here's what I saw: I saw frightfully vulgar establishments, I saw minefields of rubbish piled high on the pavement and I saw drugged out, misguided touts (who had been in town for a week already and were calling themselves 'locals'). The night air was hot and dry so I walked deeper into the quarter and was met by a rancid package-holiday smell, sort of a mix of candy floss, sizzling day-old bacon and expired deodorants. To escape the offending stench I crossed the street and came upon a Country & Western saloon that reeked of stinky toilets and stale beer. Here, stale folk were line dancing and a Geordie dressed up as a buckaroo was plunking on the guitar and singing 'Achy Breaky Heart'.

It broke my heart to hear him sing it.

Deeper and deeper I ventured and I happened upon a naughty little venue advertising two 'bosom-and-bottom' sisters who did a lesbian act, a club offering a Michael Jackson impersonator (oh, wow) and a Dolly Parton impersonator (oh, wow, wow), another club featuring Sticky Vicky (a beast on the experienced side of sixty, who dances naked and shoots ping pong balls out of an area not usually associated with ping pong), then suddenly I saw a wave of people who looked as if they had forgotten to dress in front of a mirror and this is when I knew that I had arrived. I had finally reached the eye of the hurricane, that infamous and tatty and well-littered area known as the 'Square' (cue: dramatic music and loud screams).

The Square is really not a square at all but a pedestrian zone located on Avenida de Mallorca between the streets of Gerona and Ibiza, more or less. Don't try to find this area by following the street signs as pissheads have ripped them all down. If you feel that you just have to spend some time in this depraved wasteland, but can't seem to locate it, just go up to any lager lout who looks as if he's between mistakes in his life and ask him how to get there.

It's not just the down-market clubs and sticky pubs and greasy restaurants that make this area what it is, and it's certainly not the atmosphere here (because there is no atmosphere here), rather it is the herds and flocks and gaggles who set the height of the crossbar.

It is rock-bottom humanity's perfect storm.

Anyway, enough said, I don't want to offend any connoisseurs of lower-class entertainment and bacchanal sleaze, but I would like to leave you with this last thought: The Square is the only area of Benidorm where I saw a police presence. I went up to the policemen (as that is now what I do) and asked them how they kept control of wave after wave of drunken, raging yobbos when things got seriously out of control. 'We shoot our guns up in the air,' answered one matter-of-factly. (I later asked Sylvia about this method of crowd control and she verified it.)

* * *

Mateo had a date one night, so after I had finished wrestling with my Spanish homework (*¿Dónde está el baño?*), I thought I would have a peek at Spain's prime-time TV fayre. I flipped on the telly and right there before my eyes was none other than *Who Wants To Be A Millionaire*. Well, was I ever the lucky one. The show was in Spanish, of course, and featured an exceedingly charming compère (sort of a Latin Martin Clunes). Great fun. And perfect for improving the language as everything is repeated a thousand times. I can't order a beer in Spanish yet, but I now know how to say: 'Is that your final answer?'

Spanish TV has an unusual approach regarding commercial advertisement, at least during the early morning and the late evening, and all hours in between. Here are some of the wondrous low-lights: I saw a commercial for a doll. It was a boy doll, in fact, and it had an anatomically correct penis (circumcised, thank you very much), genitals *and* the doll actually peed! What will they think up next? A doll with messy nappies? Or how about a doll that is cute and cuddly when you first buy it, but two years later it starts to get really terrible tantrums?

The evening news has to get a mention on account of the, get ready, Hollywood-esque sound effects. You heard right. When a tragic news story was read, hilariously moody background music was played over the video clip. Where I grew up hard news was not meant to be jocular. It was almost as if you were watching a really old (and really bad) black and white movie at one of those grand old movie houses where the organ player sat up front by the screen. Imagine watching news footage regarding the mysterious circumstances surrounding a swimmer who has gone missing while the soundtrack from *Jaws* plinked away in the background, or a story about a horrible car crash with a bit of *Starsky and Hutch* over, or late-breaking news about a mauling at the zoo put to a few bars of *The Jungle Book*?

* * *

Mateo mentioned that he had had a particularly fruitful day at the beach behind the, ah, water-ski platform and wished to celebrate his good fortune and creativity by treating himself to dinner. And asked if I would be so kind as to join him. I said I was game for anything as long as it involved alcohol but not running from the restaurant without paying as we had done -- to my horror -- the previous time out. Mateo assured me that he would be on his best behaviour and that we would dine in fine style and exit gracefully.

'How hungry are you, Jon?'

'I could eat the arse-end out of a cow.'

Mateo appreciated my hale devotion to food and smiled. 'Don't know if I can promise you that,' he said, 'but I'll take you to a street where they'll serve just about anything else.'

We threw on long trousers so we wouldn't be taken for *Girufos* and jumped in the lift. I prayed to the lift gods to let it glide all the way to the lobby without interference, but it screeched to a stop on the 19th floor. Mateo and I exchanged looks. The door slid open and standing there were, you got it, the two female Russian steroid-abusers. Mateo and I faltered backwards and the hairy beasts entered. If this interlude had been on the news on Spanish TV, we would have heard the nails-on-blackboard soundtrack from the shower scene in *Psycho*.

The two of us studied the two of them in a silence bred of mutual disrespect. 'Want to bolt on the 18th?' I whispered.

'No. After today's events I'm feeling particularly frisky,' Mateo whispered back. 'Let's make it just as uncomfortable for them as they always make it for us.'

'What do you have in mind?'

'I was thinking silent rude-noise, but I've come up with something even worse.'

I shot Mateo a look.

Mateo pushed the button to close the door, then said: 'I'm going to flirt with them.' And flirt with them he did, indeed. Both women were so taken aback they gasped deeply at the same time and I didn't think there would be enough oxygen to go around to reach the lower floors. As we approached the eighth, one of the shot-putters (the one with the braided armpit hair) apparently couldn't take it any longer and reached out and jabbed *número ocho*. The lift ground to a stop, the door silently yielded and the thunder-thighs fled into darkness.

I looked at Mateo.

'Bet they're walking down. Let's wait in the lobby and see.' And sure enough a few moments later we were in the lobby and we heard disturbed Slavonic sounds echoing down through the stairwell. Mateo and I gave each other a feigned look of fright and laughed so hard we had to run out the front door.

* * *

If you are famished, but don't have a clue where to go, let me be your guide and point you in the direction of the street Mateo took me to for dinner. The street is only one-block long but it has 23 long-and-skinny restaurants to choose from. They don't serve arse-end-of-cow, but they will most certainly have many other delights. 'Euro Street' as Mateo likes to call it is located on Gerona near Avenida del Doctor Orts LLorca (such names), and the cuisine is Euro, indeed: two Belgian restaurants, five Spanish, two British, seven Italian, four Dutch, one Turkish and a Chinese.

Did you add them up to see if they came to 23? I thought you might.

We ended up in an air-conditioned restaurant called Café de Kroon. How can you go wrong at an eatery where Belgian beer is served? I had a lovely meal of a mystery entrée called *Frikandel*, and I wish I could tell you what it was, but I don't know myself. I had a peep at the English side of the menu to quell any worries and to see what it was called. In English it was called *Frikandel*.

The night was gloriously warm with a gentle, gardenia breeze (I just love nights like these), so after dinner Mateo took me some circuitous route deep into the *Casco Antiguo* where we clambered up a long steep hill and all the way to the end of the *Plaça del Castell*. This plaza rests upon a rocky promontory and here you will find an immensely beautiful view. Directly in front of you, and lit at night by floodlights, is a plume of water rising magically from the sea to dizzying heights as if squirted from some great passing whale. To your left is a breathtaking vista of high-rise and twinkly Playa de Levante, and it surely must be one of the finest vistas in all of coastal Spain, or so I assume, as it's featured throughout the Thomson brochure. To your right is Playa de Poniente. This panorama is quite a sight and not to be missed (especially with the sun setting behind Europe's tallest hotel).

Just below this plaza is the lively artists' quarter and here we lingered at a little café, drank sangria and people watched. From our position we could enjoy all the talented artists moodily scratching out awful caricatures, or hunched over easels colouring startlingly realistic portraits, or even spray painting with seriously toxic aerosols creating celestial moonscapes as they depleted the ozone levels.

Later, we waded through a surging sea of happy humanity and a young *chica* with a T-shirt, which read: *aqui, se habla vino tinto* ('red wine spoken here') and came upon the church of Our Lady of Some Place or Another. Here a big wedding was underway and I fear it may have been the lonely young girl 'in need of gratification... searching for a *chico*'.

Then Mateo took me to pub just down the hill. 'I don't think you will have ever seen the likes of this.'

A sign out front said it was the Golden Last Public House. There were also these inscriptions: Honour All Men, Love the Brethren, and Derry Somme Boyne, and Fields of Ulster, and A Loyalist is For Life, Not Just For Xmas -- Old Town, Benidorm...Scarborough, Yorkshire...ALL WELCOME. (Well, am I ever glad they included that ALL WELCOME bit because up till then I was just a wee bit uncertain.)

We slipped silently and cautiously inside its stuffy, floodlit confines and saw walls decorated with Ulster Volunteer Force flags, balaclavas, regalia from paramilitary groups, Glasgow Rangers' jerseys and prominent leaders of the six counties.

'It's a shrine to bigotry and violence,' Mateo whispered.

'Your English is too good,' I hissed back.

We exhumed a couple of pints from a young woman of diminished cognizance and took a seat. Music pounded out on dusty speakers. Music different from anything I had ever heard growing up. The only way I can describe it to you is to say it would be what I think 'Protestant Rap' would sound like.

I considered having yet another pint, but I kept thinking that at any moment somebody was going to toss a bomb into the establishment. In fact, I had just voiced those very thoughts to Mateo when there was a great deafening explosion. Mateo and I shot outside and into the street and that's when we heard all the applause and laughter. The wedding party was exiting the church just up the street and all the bachelors had lit a string of impressively loud fire crackers. And no, we did not return to the Loyalist pub to finish our beers, and yes, we did return to our flat to change our underwear.

* * *

Benidorm has a bit of a reputation for hosting more fiestas than any other town in Spain -- but you won't know this if you sequester yourself in the Square, will you? You see, these fiestas take place deep in the Old Town, and usually there will be a parade -- an improbably long parade -- with locals dressed up as Moors in flowing garments and Christians in not-so-flowing chain-mail. Even the horses in the parade dress up. You know how in the real world the horses are traditionally placed discreetly at the back of a parade for obvious reasons? Well, that tradition is not practiced here. In Benidorm the great beasts are spaced evenly throughout so all costumed participants have an equal opportunity to march through steaming great piles of horse manure.

These fiesta parades are lively affairs and the whole town turns out to line the route and applaud and wave and sometimes scrape their shoes on the kerb. And there's much to see: high school marching bands (playing curious dirges), pretty girls, handsome fellas, elaborate flags, ribbons and banners. It's all good fun and great pageantry.

Late in the parade I was applauding the tuba player and

laughing as he marched by because he held proudly the mighty tuba with one hand and a diminishing piece of pizza with the other. Yes, I was laughing and applauding and really enjoying myself here in Benidorm of all places when I realised that someone across the street was looking at me. This person was laughing and applauding like all the other folk from Bendiorm, only difference was this person wasn't from Benidorm, rather Hove, actually.

When there was a break in the marching bands (and the mighty shitting steeds) I slalomed my way across the street and over to Kinkie's side. Kinkie was wearing shorts and a tight, white T-shirt, which read: 'People Tell Me I Have No Taste ... But I Like You'.

'What are you doing here?' I asked.

'Same as you. Enjoying the warm evening. Enjoying the parade. Enjoying the fiesta.'

'You alone?'

'Not anymore.'

I looked behind, then realised Kinkie was talking about me. Self-consciously and shyly I moved my foot back and forth in an 'ah, shucks' kind of manner and realised that I had a generous dollop of green horse shit on the toe of my right Puma.

Kinkie and I watched the rest of the parade and we laughed and applauded and cheered all the participants and the night turned hot and sultry and sensual and all kinds of delicious heady aromas were wafting through the Old Town's narrow streets. When the parade was over (which took almost as long as that last sentence to finish), I invited Kinkie for a coffee.

'Thanks anyway,' she said. 'I think it's too late for coffee.'

'But ... but ... but ...' I stammered, having a certain flair for appropriate responses in these sort of life-or-death situations.

'But some wine would be quite nice right now,' Kinkie said, rescuing me.

With one eye on Kinkie and one eye on where we were stepping, we slipped off deeper and deeper into the romantic warren that is the *Casco Antiguo* and eventually unearthed a little hole-in-the-wall of a bodega. I ordered some robust, full-bodied, cheap Spanish wine and when the waiter brought the carafe and asked: 'Is this all you want?' I said, in Spanish: 'Yes -- and that is my final answer,' and we all had a laugh about that.

The hole-in-the-wall was on the Poniente Beach side of the *Casco Antiguo* and we could see the ocean and smell the salt in the air and the feeling was one of being lost well back in time, or perhaps that was the cheap Spanish wine. Anyway, nothing seemed to matter and for some reason Kinkie listened with rapt attention to all my stories and laughed at all my jokes, and when Kinkie was able to get a word in edgewise, I, too, listened and laughed. We reminisced about how travelling had changed each of our lives and made us a better person and gave us the insight to respect and enjoy other cultures and peoples different from ourselves. And we even reminisced about language school and marvelled over the fact that I hadn't been expelled and just simply enjoyed the warm evening and the company of another who doesn't shy away from a little adventure. Simply said, the evening was perfect and there was nothing else on earth that I could think of that I really needed or wanted at that time to make the evening even more pleasurable.

'So, do you like Benidorm?' Kinkie asked.

Well, it's a good question, isn't it? When I was in Los Cristianos, I didn't know if I liked it or didn't like it, but with Benidorm it was different. So do I like Bendiorm? The answer is an unequivocal yes/no. You see, the town is on the way back up. There are parts of Benidorm I like very much, indeed, but there are also scabby areas that I hope I never see again. So with all this in mind, I would like you to remember: You are not allowed to trash Benidorm unless you have actually been there.

So that's it. Thanks for reading my book and getting this far (or are you at the bookshop having a little illicit peek?).

Oh, what's that?

Could you speak up just a bit, please?

You want to know about what?

Kinkie?

Well, okay, then. I wasn't going to tell anyone what happened, but I guess I can make an exception, just this once. After all, we've been through a lot together.

Here's what transpired: Somewhere near the end of the evening Kinkie looked at me with bedroom eyes and said: 'Let's go.'

Being inordinately sensitive to the female of the species, I said: 'Where? For chocolate?'

'Your place.'

Well, a raging current of joy and sexual electricity coursed through my body. Mateo was up in the foothills in the village of Finestrat visiting his dear old mother -- and there was a full moon.

And just like that we were in the lift, climbing slowly to the twenty-second floor. My mind raced with frightful possibilities that would prevent me from reaching climatic nirvana with Kinkie: The Russian tag team would get on at the 19th and want to borrow a 50-kilo sack of sugar; the Russian tag team would get on at the 19th and want to borrow two cucumbers, unsliced; the Russian tag team would get on at the 19th and want to borrow Kinkie!

The lift glided by the 19th and three floors later yesss! shunted to a gentle hump-me stop. Kinkie and I exchanged looks loaded with kinky subtext. The little button said 22. The door opened. I led Kinkie into the darkened hallway. 'The wine has put me into just the right mood,' Kinkie whispered oh so deep in my ear.

And the wine had put me into a mood of sorts, as well. It must have been a good ten minutes later when I realised that I had been endeavouring to put the key into the doorbell button.

Back in full control of my faculties, I inserted the key into the door, turned the knob, and as the door swung open, shouted 'HOLY SHIT!' Sitting on the couch watching bad Spanish TV was Mateo. And he was drinking straight from a bottle of cheap Spanish wine.

'Thought you were going to Finestrat,' I said in a high-pitched disembodied voice.

'Car broke down,' he slurred. 'Never should've bought a fucking Lada. Want some wine you two? Let's party!'

Well, the three of us sat there like the Budweiser frogs on a log watching, yes, Spanish TV's answer to *Candid Camera*, and with Mateo back in the picture I feared I would never get a chance to *chinga* a girl from Hove, actually. I looked at my watch. It had expired from sexual frustration. An ugly creeping fear was enveloping my mind. I was sitting here with an intelligent, cultured, bilingual, libidinous lady -- an inviting bed was only a matter of crawling distance away -- yet I was caught on some horribly cruel hamster wheel, running round and round, going nowhere.

But my fears were soon quashed, Mateo only needed to swill one more glass of wine and then as if by divine cheap-provincial intervention, a switch was flicked and his head rolled forward and presto, his chin was resting happily on his chest. He was fast asleep. Opportunity was finally knocking at the door and the door it was knocking at was the gate to the Benidorm version of the Garden of Eden.

I glanced over at Kinkie and realised with mounting joy that she was shamelessly on the same wavelength.

I took Kinkie's hand and silently led her out onto the darkened balcony. We stopped in front of the sliding glass door that led to my bedroom, our temple of passion where we would be spending our first night together -- where intimacy was going to be our means of communication (not whistle language). We peered off at the Mediterranean far below, then looked at the pulsing, surging lights of Benidorm by night. The sounds of the city: honking cars, wailing sirens, screeching mopeds metamorphosed into the sounds of the jungle. And the wild carnal sounds made the beast in each of us come alive and all we could do in the steamy heat was stand there panting like leopards, pulsing with enough sexual energy to power the Republic of San Marino for a week.

The moonlight filtered through the balcony and splashed a pool of light in the shape of a badly drawn heart on the bedroom floor. We stepped through the open doorway to my bedroom and stood in the pool of moonlight. We were indeed in the Garden of Eden. I turned and looked at Kinkie. She turned and looked at me. I put my arms around the small of her back. She put her arms around my neck. I pulled her hips into mine -- and she let out the most bloodcurdling scream I have ever heard in my life.

'Over there!' she shrieked.

Mateo? No. Crawling across the wall above the bed was a large frightening creature with orange rusty spots.

'Put him outside! Put him outside!' Kinkie danced in place.

Sensing the mood was fragile, I gently dropped-kick the little bugger out onto the balcony. But I knew it would do no good. It was so hot in the room we had to leave the sliding glass door open to try to catch a breath of sea breeze. Kinkie spent a few minutes looking under the bed then finally relaxed -- completely. Seductively she removed all her clothes, climbed on top of the bed and just lay there, invitingly.

And it was about the time I was removing all my clothes that I saw the Tokay Gecko crawling back into the bedroom. But what could I do? What would *you* have done? One has not learned much in life, but one has learned don't put sex (or lawyers) on hold. Was I to postpone foreplay until all the animals of the jungle were done carousing for the night? Dilemma: If I put the creature back out and shut the doors, we would suffocate. If I put him back out and left the doors open, he would find his way back in again. I had to make an executive decision. I decided to let Son of Godzilla roam around. What could possibly happen?

Gently I lay down on the bed next to Kinkie. There was so much electricity in the air it was as if an electrical storm was taking place right there between us. We just lay there listening to each other breathing and let me tell you, with the simulated jungle sounds and the fragrant Spanish blossoms and the heat of the night and our imaginations, it was complete ecstasy.

And we hadn't even begun yet.

As I patiently waited for nature to plan my first move, nature decided to do something else instead. To be more specific, it was gravity. And the timing was just awful, you see, at the precise moment Kinkie couldn't take the sexual tension anymore and she cooed: 'Touch me. Do whatever you want to me,' a Tokay Gecko with rusty orange spots and a wrestler's build fell from the ceiling where it had been strolling -- and landed right between Kinkie's subtropical thighs.

* * *

WHAT NOBODY WILL TELL YOU:

Tokay Geckos are known for being among the most aggressive reptiles in the pet trade. The little blighters have powerful jaws and they will bite. You do not want to piss off a Tokay Gecko by drop-kicking one.

* * *

On account of so many 'loyalists' now hiding in Benidorm and environs, the area has been nicknames the Costa Balaclava.

CHAPTER 22 - The Rock of Gibraltar: Time has come to say *hasta la vista* to Europe

The next morning was fresh and clear. The way it is after a big storm blows through (or your date blows out the front door, screaming).

To rid gecko-induced cobwebs, I took a stroll along the beach promenade and then cut into the Old Town and sought refuge in the Café Brasil. I sat in the same seat I always sat in. It was a good place to wring my hands.

I had suggested to Kinkie's answer phone that we meet for coffee. I really wanted to see her again. I consulted my watch. Kinkie was late.

I looked around. Businessmen in sartorial splendour were scurrying in, throwing down quick shots of espresso and hurrying back out; students were sipping colas, pouring through books and flirting; tourists were scarfing hundreds of milligrams of cholesterol in the form of rich creamy pastries and reading the newspapers of their respective countries (I counted eight different newspapers from seven different countries: England, Belgium, Holland, Germany, Russia!, Italy and Spain).

223

I ordered a *con leche* and watched with great interest as the little lady behind the counter pushed enough buttons and turned enough dials on the espresso machine to fly a 747. I heard the hiss of the steamed milk, saw the delicate blend of the foam and my favourite *camerera* brought out my *con leche*. She placed the cup in front of me, gave me a big smile and then hurried off to charm seven other nationalities.

I took a sip and let the caffeine work its magic. I cast my mind back to the subtropical disaster of the previous evening. I reflected on Kinkie's little interlude with the Tokay Gecko. Tokay Geckos have little suction cups on their feet. They can hang upside down from a ceiling all day long if they feel like it. That gecko had dropped down on purpose.

I heard laughter.

A young couple at a neighbouring table were trying to decipher a map. They were Spanish and seemed very much in love. They saw me staring and smiled. To my surprise, they both got up and came over to me. Asked me in Spanish if I knew where the 'Hotel Alone' on Avenida Marina was. I said, indeed, I did. Then, you know what? I was actually able to give them directions -- in their mother tongue. They thanked me profusely and then went back to their table. The Hotel *Alone*? They must have been on their honeymoon.

Still no Kinkie. I guess she wasn't coming. Would there ever be anybody out there for me?

I sipped some more of my *con leche*, then reflected about life on the roller coaster of travelling: One day might be a full-fledged nightmare, but then some little event would transpire the next day that would bring a modicum of joy.

I peeked over at the young couple radiantly in love. I cased the café with my eyes again. Everyone seemed to have someone to share his or her life or pastries or newspaper with.

And then for no known reason I decided to head back to the UK.

But that meant culture shock.

I always suffered from culture shock when I left countries with funny languages behind and entered the English-speaking world. Don't ask me why. Then, suddenly, a twenty-five-watt light bulb flickered in my head. Instead of waiting until I came down with culture shock why not immunize myself against it before I went back. That's why I decided to pay a visit to Gibraltar. It would be the perfect place to acclimate. Budweiser and Pringles and Cadbury's and Trebor and Safeway and Bhs would do for me what the decompression chamber does for the diver.

I wouldn't get the bends.

Mateo offered to drive me to Gibraltar. He said he wanted to test-drive his Lada after wrestling it back from his mechanic. The Lada drove like a grand touring Mercedes and Mateo chirped: 'You should get yourself a Lada, Jon, I wouldn't drive anything else.'

* * *

It was late in the afternoon by the time Mateo stopped the car on the Spanish side of the border and we stared silently across the frontier at the Rock of Gibraltar. Gibraltar really is something to behold with its dorsal-fin eminence rising to over 1,400 feet. It's impressive and it's spine-tingling.

'What do you see in front of you?' Mateo asked, pointing just beyond the guards standing at the frontier checkpoint.

'I see a runway.'

'Very observant, Juanito,' he said. 'You show your passport here at the border, and then you have to walk across the Gibraltar Airport runway to get to the town centre.'

'You've got to be kidding.'

'Ah, but I'm not. There was nowhere else for them to build a runway.'

'What if I'm about to cross the runway and a plane appears on the horizon?'

'I would suggest you make a run for it.'

I laughed then Mateo fell silent for a moment as we watched a small GB Airways commuter aircraft bank over the Bay of Gibraltar and set down with a puff of smoke from its tyres. We continued to watch as the plane taxied off the active and over to a man waving two orange flashlights by the small terminal.

I turned to Mateo: 'Never been this close to a runway, even when I was at the airport, and here, technically, we're watching all this while standing in a different country.'

'Gibraltar is weird like that,' Mateo said.

Then, I said: 'You're a Spaniard. Do you want it back?'

'I may be Spanish, but I'm not the Spanish government -- thank God -- let the Gibraltarians enjoy their "island".'

Then: 'Guess I'd better get going,' I said.

'Come back,' Mateo said. 'You will always have a home with me. You are always welcome, *amigo*.'

And on that he gave me a big hug and I headed toward the border crossing. I reached into my rucksack, pulled out my passport, showed it to the sour guards at the gate, then walked out onto a skinny runway and into the English-speaking world.

My plan was to spend the night in Gibraltar, then fly to Gatwick the next day.

Halfway across the runway, I stopped and looked back. Mateo was still standing there on the Spanish side of the border, one arm raised in the air. So this was it. This was the end. It was just hitting me.

I decided to splurge, so I spent the night at the famous, colonial Rock Hotel ('standards of service and guest care from that bygone, more genteel era'). From my window I could actually see the Rif Mountains of Morocco off to my left (this was a glorious sight, seeing Africa just over there!), and the Spanish mainland off to my right.

There was a rogue fog bank hanging over the Rock the next morning (apparently this is quite common) and it was surprisingly chilly, so I threw on a sweater and took a stroll around downtown Gibraltar. This is, indeed, a decidedly unusual part of the world. I passed by a group of uniformed, kilted school girls, all looking very dark-haired and dark-skinned and decidedly Spanish, but they were speaking English. I overheard a taxicab driver, who looked as uniformly British as anyone could, speaking rich Spanish. There were kitted bobbies standing on the corner and red wooden English telephone boxes and zebra crossings and fish & chip shops and tearooms and a Marks & Sparks and English pubs, but the locals didn't drive on the left, they drove on the right. Everything looked English (at least the parts that didn't look Moroccan), but much of it sounded Spanish.

I left the high street behind and ambled around the corner to Bell Books on Bell Lane. Bell Books is a wonderful little bookshop and it is a great place to buy a book to read on the flight back to England.

I entered the bookstore and immediately found just what I was looking for. Then I went to the cashier, but was stopped in my tracks. A heated discussion was taking place at the till.

I listened with rapt attention as the proprietor switched from fluent Spanish to flawless English. He was negotiating a big publishing deal with a local writer.

The writer, an elderly Gibraltarian, wanted to sell the proprietor 10 copies of his latest book. The proprietor wanted just eight -- on consignment.

The author prattled doggedly on, presenting his case. When that failed -- for no known reason -- he turned to me.

And that's when the elderly scribe noticed that I was buying a copy of *Driving Over Lemons*, the heartwarming tale of a young couple who emigrate from civilized England to backwater Spain.

'That author lives just across the border in Andalucia,' the scribe said. 'His books are selling like hot cakes.'

I just smiled back.

My newfound friend returned to the delicate art of negotiation.

I glanced at my watch, not out of frustration but out of sincere interest. I had been waiting 15 minutes. Gibraltar may be a British territory, but it had a decidedly Spanish approach to book selling.

Finally, I politely interrupted the proprietor: 'If you buy the books, how much will you charge?'

'Four pounds each.'

'Gibraltar pounds?'

'Gibraltar pounds or pounds sterling.'

'I'll take five books,' I said.

The proprietor was thrilled.

The author was delirious.

I had him autograph all five copies. Then I said: 'Now *your* books are selling like hot cakes!'

Someone laughed and I looked over to see a young lady with bright green eyes smiling at me.

I smiled back then departed the bookshop and turned right down Bell Lane. These books would make great gifts for friends back in the UK.

Pretty pleased with myself, I walked over to the cafés in Casemates Square, sat in the sun and ordered an Americano. My coffee arrived and I sipped its rich flavour and then reached into my bag from the bookstore. And then had a good laugh, you see, that's when I realised the books I had just purchased bore the riveting title: *Roman Artifacts in Gibraltar.*

And they were in Spanish.

A highly technical Spanish that would make your eyes bleed.

I heard a familiar laugh. Sitting at the table across from me was the young lady with the green eyes.

'Felt sorry for him,' came an English accent.

'Felt sorry for whom?'

She held up one of the books.

And we both had a good laugh together. I asked if it would be okay if I joined her. She said yes, and then we commiserated and laughed about buying the books.

'Do you speak Spanish?' she asked.

'I'm trying. I love languages.'

'Me, too.'

'Excuse me?'

'I, too, love languages,' she said and those green eyes twinkled back.

'What's your name?'

'Gabrielle. What's yours?'

'Jon.' And then I spelled it in Spanish, 'Hota-Oh-Enay-seen-Aatche.'

'Jon without an "H",' Gabrielle said.

And then I found out we were on the same flight to Gatwick, and we sat together, and even though it was a short flight Gabrielle snoozed a bit, her head just touching my shoulder -- and then I did something I've never done before on an airplane, I, too, fell asleep.

* * *

WHAT NOBODY WILL TELL YOU:

I married Gabrielle. We moved to Glasgow. And I've never been happier in my life.

And then we went on holiday to Key West, Florida, where they never get hurricanes.

If you've enjoyed *NAKED EUROPE*, check out *KEY WEST* available as a paperback and as an eBook on Amazon, your favourite online book store, or high street retailer: (ISBN # 978-0-9856398-0-8)

For those of you lusting for grittier fayre, *DEATH BY GLASGOW*, a crime/thriller set in the means streets of Glasgow, Scotland, will be hitting the bookshelves soon.

www.JonBreakfield.com

25786736R00143

Printed in Poland
by Amazon Fulfillment
Poland Sp. z o.o., Wrocław